The Canadian Private Pilot Answer Guide

7th Ed. (updated)

For PPL Study & Exam Preparation

Published by Aviation Publishers Co. Ltd.

About this Publication

CHRIS HOBBS, author of this latest edition of *The Canadian Private Pilot Answer Guide*, is a mathematician by training and a software engineer by profession. He learned to fly gliders in Wales before moving to Canada where he continued his flying activities in the realm of powered aircraft. Chris was one of the first in Canada to hold a Recreational Pilot Permit from which he soon upgraded to a Private Pilot Licence. He now holds a Commercial Pilot Licence, and carries both instrument and instructor ratings. Chris has extensive experience in the teaching of PPL, CPL, and IFR groundschools, a background that has lead him to authoring acclaimed material written to enhance groundschool instruction, such as his CPL textbook entitled *Flying Beyond*. Chris is also the author of titles in the field of mathematics and software design. He flies actively from his home base at Rockcliffe Airport in Ottawa, Ontario, Canada.

Resources for this Publication

The resources listed below should be used as primary reference materials for the questions contained in this publication:

- *From The Ground Up*
- *Canadian Aviation Regulations*
- *Aeronautical Information Manual*
- *Flight Training Manual*
- *Canada Flight Supplement*
- *AWARE Aviation Weather*

The Canadian Private Pilot Answer Guide is also available on-line to purchasers of this publication. To access the dedicated site for the material, please go to the following website address:

www.avpubonline.com

Follow the instructions on your computer to register for the site.

Your unique Access Code to gain admission to the site is listed below. Questions pertaining to the material contained in this publication and on-line may be directed to the editor at:

tutor@avpubonline.com

Questions regarding technical matters pertaining to the site may be addressed to:

support@avpubonline.com

We hope you enjoy using the avpubonline site.

Your Access Code is

WNHR-F6E6-DK39-V478

The Canadian Private Pilot Answer Guide

7th Edition

ISBN 978-0-9919221-1-6

This comprehensive question and answer book, also available in an on-line format, is developed for those preparing to write the examination for the Canadian Private Pilot Licence. Its content reflects the material and style of the questions found in Transport Canada's examinations. The knowledge gained from use of this study guide is intended to provide readers, in the most thorough of ways, with all the required information necessary to meet the written standards to qualify for a Private Pilot Licence.

Published by:

Aviation Publishers Co. Ltd.
P.O. Box 1361, Station B
Ottawa, Ontario
Canada, K1P 5R4
Email: info@aviationpublishers.com
Web: www.aviationpublishers.com

Printed by:

Gilmore Printing Services Inc.
110 Herzberg Road
Ottawa, Ontario
Canada, K2K 3B7
Web: www.gilmoreprinting.com

Cover Design by Don Wong

Mooney M20R Ovation Cover Photo by Paul Bowen

Cirrus SR22 Drawings Courtesy of Cirrus Aircraft

ACKNOWLEDGMENTS

Many people helped in the development of this latest edition of this title. Particular thanks go to Alison Hobbs and Angelina Gomes for their valuable proof-reading, and to Francis Papai, Michel Lemay and Simon Berry for their diligent roles in extensively reviewing content.

Also from Aviation Publishers Co. Ltd.:

- *From the Ground Up*
- *From the Ground Up Workbook*
- *Flying Beyond: The Canadian Commercial Pilot Textbook*
- *Instrument Procedures Manual*
- *Unmanned: Textbook for UAS Studies*
- *Canadian Commercial Pilot Answer Guide*
- *Flight Test Notes*

Table of Contents

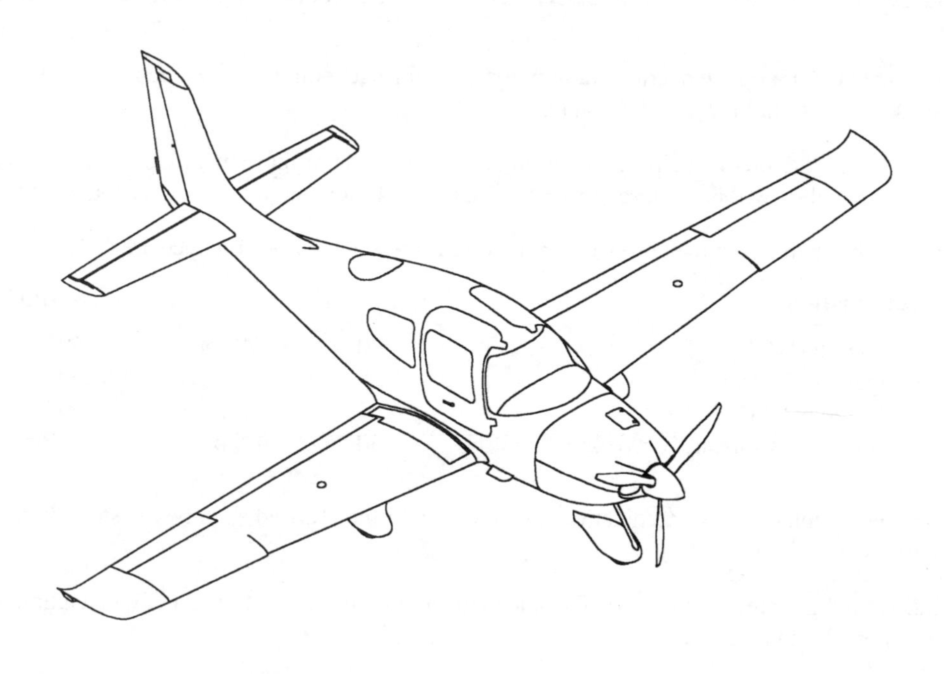

Summary

Study and Reference Guide for Written Examinations for the Private Pilot Licence (Aeroplane)

This page is a summary of relevant points contained within Transport Canada's Study and Reference Guide for the Private Pilot Licence Aeroplane (TP 12880).

Examination Prerequisites
Examination prerequisites are set out in CAR 401.13(1). Prior to taking a written examination, applicants for a flight crew permit, licence or rating must meet the guidelines described with respect to: (1) medical fitness, (2) identification requirements, (3) instructor recommendation requirements, and (4) experience requirements.

Examinations must be completed during the 24-month period immediately preceding the date of the application for the permit, licence or rating.

Knowledge Requirements
Applicants for the Private Pilot Licence in the Aeroplane Category in Canada shall demonstrate their knowledge by writing the respective Transport Canada multiple choice examination for the licence being sought, on the mandatory subject areas listed below.

Examination	Questions	Time Limit	Pass Mark
Private Pilot – Aeroplane (PPAER)	100	3 hours	60%

An overall pass mark of 60% is required on the respective written examinations, and candidates must also achieve a 60% mark in each of the four mandatory subjects. These mandatory subjects are:

1. Air Law (Air Law and Procedures; TSB; Air Traffic Services and Procedures)
2. Navigation (Navigation and Radio Aids)
3. Meteorology (Meteorology and Meteorological Services Available to Pilots)
4. Aeronautics and General Knowledge (Airframes, Engines, Systems; Theory of Flight; Flight Instruments; Flight Operations; Human Factors)

Applicants who obtain less than 60% on the overall examination will, for licencing purposes, be required to rewrite the complete paper. The rewrite provisions are found in CAR 400.04(1).

Applicants who obtain 60% or more on the main examination but who fail one or more mandatory subject areas will be assessed a partial pass. During one sitting, they will be required to write supplementary examinations for each subject failed.

Details on the mandatory subject area supplementary examination for the Private Pilot Licence are as follows:

Examination	Questions	Time Limit	Pass Mark
Air Law (PALAW)	20	1 hour	60%
Navigation (PNAV)	20	2 hours	60%
Meteorology (PAMET)	30	1.5 hours	60%
Aeronautics – General Knowledge (PAGEN)	30	1.5 hours	60%

When writing more than one supplementary examination, the maximum time allowed shall be the sum of the times indicated for each examination, not to exceed 3 hours.

For additional information on flight crew licensing in Canada, contact your Transport Canada Civil Aviation Services regional office or access the Transport Canada website at `http://www.tc.gc.ca`.

Introduction

The Private Pilot Written Examination

Transport Canada publishes a document, TP 12880, (a summary of which appears on page 4), which lists the subjects on which questions may be asked in the Private Pilot written examination. TP 12880 is freely available from the Transport Canada web site and you should have a copy—it not only lists the topics you need to know, but also provides hints at what will appear on the examination. Keep a copy of TP 12880 beside you throughout your ground school and ensure that your instructors cover every topic and specifically address those that are indicated in TP 12880 as likely to appear on the examination.

Using this Book

This answer guide follows TP 12880 closely. Its chapter and section headings are taken directly from it and questions are included on all topics flagged by Transport Canada as being particular targets in the written examination.

This book is written for examination preparation. Answering the questions herein successfully ensures that you are ready to take the Transport Canada examination. It is not meant to *teach* you material—that is the role of *From the Ground Up*, which should be used as your primary source to acquire the overall theoretical knowledge necessary to earn your Private Pilot Licence.

The PSTAR questions are another source of useful information before taking the written examination. You may have taken the PSTAR examination some time ago, but some PSTAR-type questions are almost certain to appear on the Private Pilot examination.

As you explore the questions in this book, make notes of those areas where you are frequently making mistakes or are unclear on the theory that forms the basis for the question. Then research those topics with your instructor and repeat the questions on those topics. The index at the back of this book will help you find relevant questions on subjects where you feel you still need review.

Examination Technique

Everyone who has been subjected to multiple-choice examinations knows that 80% of doing well in them is achieved by understanding the material, and 20% by knowing how to handle the questions. Here are a few tips and techniques.

A major factor in obtaining that extra 20% is attitude. Some students go into the examination room as though they were sheep going to slaughter. The flight tests and examinations that you take *en route* to your pilot's licence are opportunities for you to demonstrate how much you know and how skilled you are. Many pilots fly for their whole career without being able to demonstrate their superior skills and knowledge except in the simulator and examination room. Simulator sessions with failing engines, deteriorating weather and other problems are the opportunity for a competent pilot to demonstrate his or her abilities. Think of the written examination in the same way. Take it to demonstrate to yourself, your instructor and anyone else whose respect you find important, that you have mastered the material needed to become a pilot.

Secondly, know your strengths and weaknesses. There are students who have trouble remembering arbitrary facts: for example, whether the definition of "mist" (see question 279 below) is a surface-based layer where the visibility is less than 1 km or less than 1 statute mile. These are the sort of facts that you either know or you don't. While some students struggle to remember these facts, others seem to learn them effortlessly, but have problems with computation and deductive reasoning.

One way to handle a weakness with memory recall is to write, on a piece of paper, a list of facts that you have difficulty remembering. Review the list the night before the examination and again just before going into the examination room. Then destroy the list because it obviously cannot be taken in. As soon as you are in the examination room, write down as many of the facts as you can remember on a piece of scrap paper. This takes a couple of minutes but can be invaluable later during the examination.

Another preparation for the examination is reading around the subject. Do not limit your reading to textbooks: read the flying magazines, incident reports and any books on the subject of aviation. You will be surprised how much knowledge (and, in particular, vocabulary) you will pick up without conscious effort. This is especially important for the topic most likely to make you a safe pilot: Human Factors. Human Factors are effectively impossible to test with multiple-choice questions, but it is not your knowledge of the definition of "mist" that will keep you safe in the air—it's your understanding of your own human aspects of flying.

Once settled into the examination, consider the following:

1. Read the questions at a talking speed, otherwise key words such as "not" may be missed: see question 268.
2. Each correctly answered question gains you 1 point—you get the same reward from correctly answering a question that takes 5 seconds as one that takes 5 minutes. Leave the 5 minute calculations until you have finished the quick and easy questions. Then you know how much time remains for the more time-consuming ones.
3. Pace yourself. You have 3 hours to answer 100 questions. To allow a little time for review at the end, you should have answered 40 questions by the end of the first hour and 80 by the end of the second. If you are using the technique outlined in point 9 below, then you should have 50 questions complete by the end of the first hour and all 100 completed by the end of the second hour. If you find yourself falling behind, remember point 2 above and complete the questions that you can answer quickly.
4. Remember that, if you get 98% on three of the four topics and 59% on the fourth, you will obtain only a partial pass and will have to rewrite the topic you failed. By getting 61% on each of the four topics, you will pass. Do not spend too much time perfecting some topics at the cost of not completing others.
5. Ensure that you use all of the resources available in the examination room. For example, consider question 356. It is not, superficially, a question about GFAs but it can be answered easily by considering the GFA provided in the examination material (e.g., figure B.8 on page 95). Sometimes, one question will give you a hint about the answer to another one.
6. If you do encounter a question where the answer seems immediately intuitive to you, then your first thought is probably correct. Unless you remember something specific later, don't change your answer.
7. It is not always necessary to do the calculations: work back from the answers where possible. If, for example, you are calculating the heading needed to fly a track of 090° with a wind from the north, then it's clear—whatever the wind and aircraft speeds, the answer is going to be somewhat less than 090°. If the possible answers are 090°, 085°, 095° and 060° then you don't need to do any work. If there are two sensible answers and you are running short of time, then guess the more likely one.
8. Use an approved electronic aviation calculator rather than an E6B to save time in the examination. Whether you use an electronic calculator or an E6B, ensure that you are *very* familiar with its use: the examination room is no time to be learning the key strokes or use of the E6B slider.
9. If you have time, attempt every question twice. The first time through write the answers on a piece of scrap paper. At the end, return to the beginning and do the questions again. If you get the same answers, enter them onto the computer. Otherwise, investigate why the answers differ. You can typically gain an extra two or three percent by using this technique.
10. If you have no idea as to the answer to a question, then at least exclude impossible answers before making a guess. For example, in question 250 on page 31, if you have any understanding of isobars, the answer about magnetic variation is clearly wrong. Even the fact that the question appears in the meteorology section is probably enough to alert you to that. If you have to guess, only guess amongst the answers that could reasonably be correct.
11. If you run out of time, complete a random answer for all the questions you did not reach—on average, 25% of them will be right.

A Note on Angles

Latitudes and longitudes are angles and there are many ways to represent these. The latitude of 45° 13' 12"N, for example, may be written in that form, or as 45.22°N, N45 13 12, or 45° 13.2'N. You must be prepared on charts, in the Canada Flight Supplement and in flight planning applications to meet all of these formats. For that reason, all four formats are used in questions in this book.

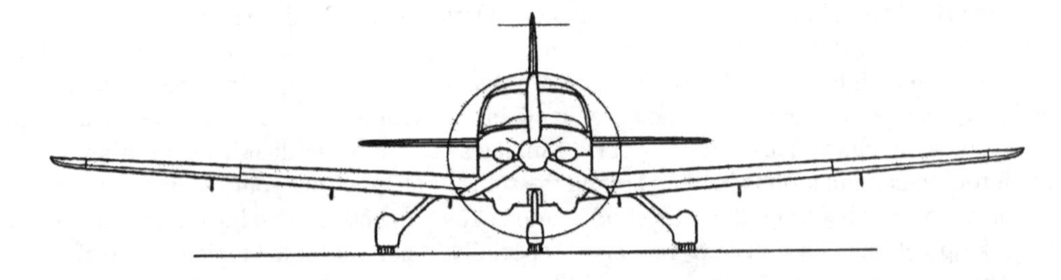

Chapter 1

Air Law

Contents

1.1 Aircraft Marking and Registration

Question 1: The certificate of registration of an aircraft must

1. always be carried on the aircraft when flying in Canada.
2. not be carried on an aircraft as it will be needed during an accident investigation should the aircraft crash.
3. be carried on board the aircraft for all flights where a landing is to be made at an aerodrome other than the point of departure.
4. be carried on the aircraft for flights of more than 25 nautical miles from the point of departure.

Question 2: Which type(s) of registration would be appropriate for an aircraft used for flight training purposes under a flight training unit operator certificate?

1. A commercial or a flight training registration.
2. A commercial or, if the aircraft is not used for sight-seeing purposes, a private registration.
3. A private registration.
4. A commercial registration.

1.2 Aerodromes

Question 3: When closing an aerodrome permanently, the operator

1. must notify the managers of all other aerodromes within 25 NM within 3 working days.
2. must disconnect runway lighting.
3. must notify Transport Canada within 3 working days.
4. must immediately remove all of the wind direction indicators installed at the aerodrome.

Question 4: Taxiways used for night operations must be marked with fixed ______ lights or retro-reflective markers ______.

1. blue; at the edges of the taxiway
2. blue; along the centre of the taxiway
3. yellow; at the edges of the taxiway
4. green; at the edges of the taxiway

Question 5: Any unserviceable portion of the movement area of an aerodrome used at night must be marked with ________ lights or retro-reflective markers.

1. green
2. red
3. white
4. blue

1.3 Airports

Question 6: Consider the sign shown in figure B.3 on page 93 (white letters on a red background). This sign indicates

1. the distance that an aircraft must hold short of the runway during the day (150 ft) and at night (330 ft).
2. that runway 15/33 is out of operation.
3. the position of the hold line for runway 15/33.
4. the slope of the glide path on the current runway.

Question 7: You are taxiing at a controlled airport and see the markings shown in figure B.4 on page 94. These indicate that

1. you are approaching a runway and should not cross the solid lines without a clearance.
2. there is a disused or inactive runway ahead of you which you may cross without further clearance.
3. there is a runway used only jet traffic ahead of you. You may cross it but it is not available for takeoff or landing by piston-engined aircraft.
4. you have just crossed a runway and should clear beyond the dashed lines as quickly as possible.

Question 8: When part of a taxiway is closed, this is indicated by

1. a yellow cross (each leg of which is 9 metres long) placed in the centre of the taxiway.
2. two white crosses (each leg of which is 4.5 metres long) placed to the left and right of the taxiway centre-line.
3. a white cross (each leg of which is 9 metres long) placed in the centre of the taxiway.
4. a STOP sign, no less than 3 metres from the ground and illuminated at night, to the left of taxiway, at the beginning of the closed section.

Question 9: An airport is an aerodrome

1. with a paved runway at least 75 ft wide and 3,000 ft long.
2. within a built-up area.
3. with commercial airline traffic.
4. for which the Minister has issued airport certificate.

1.4 Permits, Licences and Ratings

Question 10: A pilot underwent a class 3 medical examination on her 38th birthday. She can use the resulting medical certificate to validate her Private Pilot Licence for

1. 5 years.
2. 2 years.
3. 1 year.
4. 4 years.

Question 11: A pilot last flew as pilot-in-command two weeks ago when he completed six takeoffs and landings. To fly a day VFR trip with a passenger he must also

1. have successfully completed a recurrent training programme within the last 24 months.
2. have passed a Transport Canada written examination within the last 5 years.
3. have flown with a passenger or flight instructor within the last 24 months.
4. have acquired at least 50 hours of flight time within the last 24 months.

Question 12: A pilot has just been awarded a Private Pilot Licence, her flight test having been flown in a Cessna 172. Her licence does not authorise her to

1. act as pilot-in-command of a light twin-engined aircraft.
2. act as pilot-in-command of a Piper Cherokee 180.
3. act as pilot-in-command of an ultra-light.
4. receive reimbursement for acting as pilot-in-command of a rented Cessna 172 for a charity event.

Question 13: A student is training for a Private Pilot Licence, has successfully soloed and has a student pilot permit, but not a recreational pilot permit. When may he act as pilot-in-command with a passenger on board?

1. Never.
2. If the flight is within 25 nautical miles of the departure airport.
3. During a flight test where the passenger is the examiner.
4. When signed out by an instructor.

1.5 Medical Requirements

Question 14: A pilot is pregnant. She is allowed to operate as pilot-in-command of an aircraft until the

1. 30th week of pregnancy.
2. onset of labour.
3. beginning of the second trimester.
4. date on which the baby is due.

Question 15: No one is allowed to act as a crew member of an aircraft having consumed alcohol within the last ----- hours or -------.

1. 8 hours; while under the influence of alcohol
2. 8 hours; having a blood alcohol level over 0.08%
3. 10 hours; having a blood alcohol level over 0.10%
4. 6 hours; while under the influence of alcohol

1.6 Airspace Structure & Classification

Question 16: An irregularly shaped area on a map labelled "CYA 600(S)(T) TO BELOW 4000 OCSL DAYLIGHT BY NOTAM (CZUL)" indicates an area of

1. class F airspace from 600 ft ASL to 3,999 ft ASL.
2. class A airspace from the ground to 4,000 ft, associated with the CZUL airport.
3. class F airspace occasionally used for training and gliding.
4. class F restricted airspace.

Question 17: To fly into the airspace in question 16, when it was active, you

1. would have to be flying a Canadian military aircraft.
2. could simply fly in but should exercise caution.
3. would need to establish two-way radio communications with a controller.
4. would need to alert the owner of the airspace to your intentions.

Question 18: VFR flight

1. requires a special VFR clearance to enter class C airspace.
2. is not permitted in class C airspace.
3. requires a flight visibility of at least 6 statute miles and no clouds below 5,000 ft AGL in class C airspace.
4. requires a clearance to enter class C airspace.

Question 19: Consider the town of Northbrook on the map enclosed with this book. It lies about 73 NM WSW of Ottawa International Airport at approximately 44° 44'N, 77° 10'W at 900 ft ASL. The classes of airspace over Northbrook at 1,000 ft, 5,000 ft, 14,000 ft, 17,000 ft and 23,000 ft ASL are

1. G, G, G, G, A.
2. G, E, B, B, A.
3. G, G, B, B, A.
4. E, E, E, B, A.

Question 20: VFR flight

1. requires two-radio communication between the pilot and controller before entering class D airspace.
2. is not permitted in class D airspace.
3. requires a clearance before entering class D airspace.
4. requires a special VFR clearance to enter class D airspace.

Question 21: To fly into class F restricted airspace, a pilot must

1. obtain the permission of the user agency as defined in the Designated Airspace Handbook.
2. exercise caution, although no permission is required.
3. establish two-way radio communications with the operating authority defined in the Designated Airspace Handbook.
4. obtain a clearance from the ATC unit defined in the Designated Airspace Handbook as the operating authority.

Question 22: Consider the portion of VNC chart enclosed with this book. The ring of radius 45 NM around Ottawa International Airport indicates

1. that a working mode C transponder is required to fly above 6,500 ft AGL.
2. class D airspace upwards from 6,500 ft.
3. that a working mode C transponder is required to fly above 6,500 ft ASL.
4. controlled airspace for commercial aircraft landing at Ottawa International.

Question 23: Consider the town of Kaladar on the map enclosed with this book. It lies a few miles south of Northbrook (see question 19) at 900 ft ASL. The classes of airspace over Kaladar at 1,000 ft, 5,000 ft, 14,000 ft, 17,000 ft and 23,000 ft are

1. G, G, B, B, A.
2. G, G, G, G, A.
3. E, E, E, B, A.
4. G, E, B, B, A.

Question 24: Controlled airspace is airspace

1. from which VFR aircraft are excluded.
2. for which a VFR pilot needs clearance to enter.
3. within which a controller may issue a clearance or instruction.
4. above 18,000 ft ASL.

1.7 Operating and Flight Rules

Question 25: Consider the CFS entry for Fort Cushing given in figure B.11 on page 98. A pilot is approaching Fort Cushing from the south-west for landing on runway 25. When about 4 NM from the field, he hears another aircraft reporting 2 miles north of Fort Cushing also inbound for landing. The pilot may join the circuit by

1. crossing the aerodrome from the south at 1,000 ft AGL.
2. crossing the aerodrome from the north at 1,000 ft AGL.
3. flying straight in to a left downwind at 1,000 ft AGL.
4. crossing the aerodrome from the north or entering straight in to a right downwind at 1,000 ft AGL.

Question 26: Consider the CFS entry for Bear Lake Lookout given in figure B.10 on page 97. When flying directly over Bear Lake Lookout without the intention of landing, an aircraft must be no lower than

1. 3,322 ft ASL.
2. 2,000 ft ASL.
3. 3,322 ft AGL.
4. 2,322 ft ASL.

Question 27: The minimum visibility required for aerobatic flight is

1. an horizontal distance equivalent to the cloud height.
2. 5 miles.
3. 3 miles.
4. 1 km.

Question 28: A widow approaches a private pilot and asks him to scatter the ashes of her late husband over the centre of his favourite lake (this was his last wish). Is the pilot permitted to do this from his light aircraft?

1. Yes, as long as it does not endanger anyone on the ground.
2. No, dropping items from an aircraft in flight is not permitted.
3. No, carrying human remains in a light aircraft is not permitted.
4. Not unless she installs a special chute to carry the ashes well away from the control surfaces of the aircraft.

Question 29: Two aircraft are approaching an aerodrome for the purposes of landing. Priority is given to the

1. first aircraft to make a radio call.
2. faster of the aircraft.
3. heavier of the aircraft.
4. aircraft at the lower altitude.

Question 30: In the altimeter setting region, before departing from an aerodrome where an altimeter setting is provided, a pilot should set her altimeter to

1. display the elevation of the aerodrome.
2. the local altimeter setting.
3. the station pressure.
4. 29.92 inches of mercury.

Question 31: A pilot needs to start the engine of his aircraft by swinging the propeller. Which of the following is not a permitted way of securing the aircraft while he starts the engine?

1. He ensures that he is in a position where, as soon as the engine fires, he can get directly into the pilot's seat.
2. He asks his wife, who is familiar with the aircraft but who is not a pilot, to sit in the pilot's seat and apply the brakes.
3. He secures a rope around the tail wheel and ties this to a nearby strong tree.
4. He places chocks under the main wheels.

Question 32: When flying over the centre of downtown Vancouver, the minimum altitude at which the pilot must fly if she is not approaching an aerodrome to land is ______ ft above ______ and able to glide clear of the city in case of an engine failure.

1. 1,000; the highest obstacle within 1 statute mile
2. 1,000; the highest obstacle within 2,000 ft
3. 2,000; the highest obstacle within 2,000 ft
4. 1,000; ground level

Question 33: A pilot intends to take a passenger while performing aerobatics. She has logged a total of 50 hours of aerobatic flight. Additionally she must have

1. carried out at least 6 landings in the preceding six months.
2. flown at least one hour of aerobatics in the preceding six months.
3. at least 200 hours total experience in the type of aircraft she will be using.
4. flown at least 5 hours in the preceding six months.

Question 34: Which of the following statements is true?

1. Aerodromes in the standard pressure region always have a sea-level pressure of 29.92 inches of mercury.
2. When flying in cruise flight in the standard pressure region the altimeter should be set to 29.92 inches of mercury.
3. When taking off from an aerodrome in the standard pressure region the altimeter should be set to 29.92 inches of mercury.
4. When flying in cruise flight in the altimeter setting region the altimeter should be set to 29.92 inches of mercury.

Question 35: What would be appropriate altitudes for a VFR flight on a heading of 355°M and a track of 002°M in the southern domestic airspace?

1. 4,500 ft ASL, 6,500 ft ASL, 8,500 ft ASL.
2. 4,500 ft AGL, 6,500 ft AGL, 8,500 ft AGL.
3. 3,500 ft AGL, 5,500 ft AGL, 7,500 ft AGL, 9,500 ft AGL.
4. 3,500 ft ASL, 5,500 ft ASL, 7,500 ft ASL, 9500 ft ASL.

Question 36: When landing at an aerodrome in a Mandatory Frequency (MF) Zone, a pilot must

1. report being on final approach on the mandatory frequency.
2. obtain a landing clearance from the ground controller.
3. cross the aerodrome at least 1,000 ft above circuit height.
4. fly a complete circuit including downwind and base legs.

Question 37: When taking a passenger flying in a Piper Cherokee, the safety briefing does not need to include

1. whether smoking is allowed on the flight.
2. the approximate duration of the flight.
3. the location and use of the ELT.
4. the location of the First Aid kit.

Question 38: The ADIZ is the

1. Aircraft Direct Impact Zone around large Canadian cities.
2. Air Defence Identification Zone around all Canadian borders.
3. Automated Direct Information Zone, a service provided by Flight Service Stations within a specific area.
4. Air Defence Identification Zone situated around the marine borders of Canada.

Question 39: While flying VFR in class D airspace you have a radio failure. You should

1. squawk 7500 and leave the class D as quickly as possible.
2. use the VOR receiver in the aircraft to communicate with ATC through any close-by VOR.
3. squawk 7600 and leave the class D as quickly as possible.
4. fly left-hand triangles with each leg taking 1 minute.

Question 40: A private pilot intends to fly his Cessna 172 to an island in the mouth of the St Lawrence River and he estimates that he will be out of gliding range of land for 13 minutes. He

1. must ensure that he and each of his passengers is wearing a life preserver, individual flotation device or personal flotation device while the aircraft is out of gliding range of land.
2. need take no special precautions unless the period outside gliding range of land exceeds 30 minutes.
3. need take no special precautions unless the aircraft will be more than 50 nautical miles from land.
4. must ensure that he and each of his passengers has a life preserver, individual flotation device or personal flotation device on board the aircraft.

Question 41: The amount of fuel that must be on board a propeller-driven aircraft making a night VFR flight must be no less than the fuel required to reach the destination and then fly for

1. an additional 45 minutes at cruise speed.
2. an additional 45 minutes at best endurance speed.
3. an additional 30 minutes at cruise speed.
4. an additional 30 minutes at best range speed.

Question 42: A flight plan must be filed for all VFR flights

1. that are international.
2. of more than 25 nautical miles from the departure aerodrome.
3. when all or part of the flight takes place at night.
4. of more than 25 statute miles from the departure aerodrome.

Question 43: When two aircraft are approaching each other approximately head-on and there is a risk of collision, then

1. both pilots shall turn left.
2. the pilot on the more westerly heading shall climb, the other descend.
3. both pilots shall turn right.
4. the pilot on the more westerly heading shall turn right, the other left.

Question 44: The pilot of an aircraft must give way to

1. any aircraft in an emergency situation.
2. an aircraft overtaking him.
3. an aircraft at a lower altitude.
4. a commercial jet.

Question 45: A pilot on a VFR flight plan may fly without visual reference to the ground

1. when the flight is in uncontrolled airspace.
2. if qualified to fly VFR over-the-top and the flight is taking place in instrument meteorological conditions.
3. if the period of flight without reference to the ground lasts no longer than 10 minutes by day or 5 minutes by night.
4. if qualified to fly VFR over-the-top and in the weather conditions specified for VFR over-the-top flight.

Question 46: A pilot with neither an instrument rating nor a VFR Over-the-Top rating is allowed to fly VFR above clouds if

1. the clouds cover no more than 50% of the ground in uncontrolled or 30% of the ground in controlled airspace.
2. there is no further layer of cloud above the aircraft.
3. there are sufficient gaps in the clouds to allow the pilot to operate with reference to the ground.
4. the clouds are at least 3,000 ft below the cruise altitude.

Question 47: What action could a pilot take when flying VFR to an aerodrome with a class E control zone when the visibility is reported to be $1\frac{1}{2}$ mile and the lowest cloud is at 5,000 ft AGL?

1. No special action—simply fly in.
2. Request a VFR Over-the-Top clearance.
3. Request a special VFR clearance.
4. Remain clear of the control zone—VFR flight requires 3 miles visibility in controlled airspace.

1.8 Aircraft Requirements

Question 48: A functional landing light is required on an aircraft in night VFR flight when

1. flying in controlled airspace.
2. travelling more than 25 NM from the departure aerodrome.
3. passengers are carried.
4. a landing is to be made on an unlit runway.

Question 49: A pilot is taking two parachutists aloft. The parachutists are required to wear a restraint system

1. until immediately before the jump.
2. when the aircraft is taxiing for takeoff.
3. at all times until the parachute drop run commences.
4. during the climb after takeoff.

Question 50: A pilot is flying an unpressurised aircraft at 12,500 ft ASL. The flight at that altitude is planned to last 45 minutes. What special conditions does the pilot need to take into account regarding oxygen?

1. She must use supplemental oxygen for the whole of the flight at 12,500 ft.
2. She must use supplemental oxygen for the last 15 minutes of the flight at 12,500 ft.
3. She must not use supplemental oxygen because it can cause the "bends" at such a high altitude.
4. She does not need supplemental oxygen as long as she remains below 13,000 ft.

Question 51: It is not necessary to have the journey log on board an aircraft during a flight if

1. the distance from the departure to the destination aerodrome is less than 25 nautical miles.
2. the absence of the journey log is placarded in such a manner that the placard can be seen by all crew members.
3. the aircraft is on a training flight with a flight instructor on board.
4. the aircraft will not land and shut down at any aerodrome other than the departure point.

Question 52: Which of the following maintenance tasks may not be carried out by a pilot on a small, privately operated aircraft without the approval or supervision of a certified mechanic?

1. Cleaning and changing of an oil filter.
2. Removal and replacement of the heading indicator.
3. Cleaning and replacement of spark plugs.
4. Adjustment of the alternator drive belt tension.

Question 53: A pilot has placed the Pilot Operating Handbook for her Cessna 172 in a water-proof bag in the baggage compartment. Is this sufficient?

1. Yes, it is sufficient that the POH be on board the aircraft.
2. Yes, as long as the POH is for the precise model of the aircraft being flown.
3. No, the POH must be within reach when the pilot is seated at the controls.
4. No, the POH must not be placed in a sealed container.

Question 54: Which of the following instruments is not required for a day VFR flight in uncontrolled airspace?

1. An altimeter adjustable for barometric pressure.
2. An airspeed indicator.
3. An oil pressure indicator for each engine employing an oil pressure system.
4. A magnetic compass or a magnetic direction indicator.

1.9 Transportation Safety Board

Question 55: When an aviation accident occurs, it must be reported to the Transportation Safety Board of Canada

1. before the next annual inspection of the aircraft (for privately-registered aircraft), or next required maintenance (for commercially-registered aircraft), by completing the form published in the Aeronautical Information Manual.
2. within 10 working days by completing the form published in the Aeronautical Information Manual.
3. within one calendar week of the accident by completing the form on the TSB website.
4. as soon as possible and by the quickest means of communication.

Question 56: Following an aircraft accident, it is not permitted to displace, move or interfere with the aircraft to

1. prevent destruction by fire.
2. extricate a person.
3. remove flight data and cockpit voice recorders.
4. avoid danger to a person on the ground.

1.10 Air Traffic Services and Procedures

Question 57: While you are radar-identified in VFR flight, the controller calls opposite direction traffic at your 12 o'clock at 5 miles. You look but cannot see the oncoming traffic and are concerned about the risk of collision. One ATC service you could usefully request is

1. IFR separation.
2. flight following.
3. flight advisory.
4. conflict resolution.

Question 58: Which of the following needs to be read back to the controller when you are on a VFR flight-plan?

1. A landing clearance.
2. An instruction, when taxiing, to hold short of a runway.
3. A takeoff clearance.
4. An assigned transponder code.

Question 59: You have been radar identified. When you are handed from one controller to another, you should provide the new controller on first contact with

1. your full call-sign and altitude.
2. your full call-sign and location.
3. your full call-sign, type of aircraft and destination.
4. your full call-sign, location and the phrase "with you".

Question 60: Which of the following statements regarding an ATC instruction or clearance is false?

1. A pilot who does not understand an instruction from ATC should request a clarification.
2. An ATC clearance is required to enter class C airspace.
3. A pilot must always comply with an ATC instruction, even if it will result in an unsafe situation.
4. ATC may not issue an instruction or clearance to an aircraft in uncontrolled airspace.

Question 61: You are flying a track of 120°M with a heading of 110°M. ATC reports traffic for you at your "12 o'clock position". The traffic is

1. directly ahead of you as you look out of the front window.
2. slightly to your left.
3. directly behind you.
4. slightly to your right.

Question 62: A pilot is landing at an airport where *Land and Hold Short Operations* (LAHSO) are in use and is given the clearance: "Alfa, Bravo, Charlie cleared to land runway 25, hold short of runway 32". The pilot is not confident that she can land without over-running runway 32. She should

1. go into slow flight.
2. say that she is unable to comply with the clearance.
3. extend the circuit to give herself a longer final approach.
4. do her best to stop before the intersection with runway 32.

Question 63: You are departing a controlled airport and have contacted ground control for a taxi clearance. You get no response on the radio and then you see a flashing green light aimed at you from the control tower. This means that you

1. are cleared to taxi and take off.
2. should contact tower on its alternative frequency.
3. should remain in position.
4. are cleared to taxi.

Chapter 2

Flight Operations

Contents

2.1 General

Question 64: 145 nautical miles is roughly

1. 145 statute miles.
2. 126 statute miles.
3. 290 statute miles.
4. 167 statute miles.

Question 65: Obstacles of up to 150 metres in height (AGL) must be marked with

1. a steady white light and flashing red beacon.
2. a steady red light and flashing red beacons.
3. a flashing blue light.
4. rotating yellow lights.

Question 66: When taxiing a Cessna 172 with the wind blowing from over the pilot's left shoulder, the controls should be held so that the elevator

1. is down and the left aileron is up.
2. is up and the left aileron is up.
3. is up and the left aileron is down.
4. is down and the left aileron is down.

Question 67: Consider the CFS entry for Fort Cushing in figure B.11 on page 98. On which VNC does Fort Cushing appear?

1. E-15.
2. CYET.
3. AIR 5014.
4. ADJ.

Question 68: Consider the CFS entry for Bear Lake Lookout in figure B.10 on page 97. How much landing distance is available on runway 22?

1. 250 ft.
2. 2,200 ft.
3. 4,100 ft.
4. 3,850 ft.

Question 69: The number at the southern end of runway 19 is

1. 01.
2. 91.
3. 18.
4. 10.

Question 70: You are asked by the pilot of another aircraft to provide her with a radio check. The signal strength is fair but her speech is only understandable with difficulty. The response you should give is

1. strength 3, readability 4.
2. strength 4, readability 2.
3. strength 4, readability 4.
4. strength 3, readability 3.

Question 71: When flying at night, a pilot sees the lights of another aircraft ahead of her. There is a red light to the right and green light to the left. This indicates that the other aircraft is

1. flying away from her.
2. declaring an emergency.
3. intercepting her.
4. flying towards her.

Question 72: What is the correct phonetic pronunciation of the call-sign FPTN?

1. FOCKS trot, pah PAH, TAN go, no VEM bar.
2. focks TROT, PAPA, tan GO, no VEM bar.
3. focks TROT, pah PAH, TAN go, no vem BAR.
4. FOCKS trat, PAPA, tan GO, no VEM bar.

Question 73: Consider the CFS entry for Bear Lake Lookout in figure B.10. When approaching for landing on runway 04, you see three red and one white lights in a line to the left of the runway. This indicates that you are

1. much too high.
2. much too low.
3. slightly too low.
4. slightly too high.

Question 74: Runways in the ______ domestic airspace are numbered in accordance with their alignment with ______ north.

1. southern; local
2. northern; true
3. northern; magnetic
4. southern; true

Question 75: The main wheel tires on Joe's aircraft are inflated to 25 lbs/square inch. What is the minimum speed at which hydroplaning could occur in wet conditions if the wheels are not locked?

1. 25 knots.
2. 45 knots.
3. 50 knots.
4. 9 knots.

Question 76: Wheelbarrowing is most likely to occur during landing

1. when the aircraft touches down on the main wheels before the nose wheel.
2. when too much weight is placed on the nose-wheel.
3. when the nose is held too high.
4. when a tail-dragger aircraft touches down on its tail wheel before the main wheels.

Question 77: A side slip differs from a forward slip because

1. in a side slip, the pilot cross-controls with ailerons in one direction and rudder in the other.
2. a pilot entering a side slip maintains track.
3. a pilot entering a side slip maintains heading.
4. in a side slip the airspeed indicator is inaccurate.

Question 78: An aircraft is on final approach at an aerodrome with a VASI and is descending at 400 ft per minute on a 3° glide slope. The headwind into which it is flying reduces in speed. To maintain the 3° glide slope with the same airspeed, the pilot will need to

1. increase his rate of descent.
2. maintain the 400 ft per minute descent.
3. reduce the rate of descent.
4. enter a side slip.

Question 79: To which of the following transmissions from ATC might *"ROGER"* be an appropriate response if you were flying VFR in a Cessna 172?

1. Alfa, Bravo, Charlie, you will be number 3 for landing behind an Airbus on 5 miles final.
2. Alfa, Bravo, Charlie, turn left 20 degrees for traffic.
3. Alfa, Bravo, Charlie, say again your last transmission.
4. Alfa, Bravo, Charlie, are you a Cessna 172?

Question 80: When flying into a controlled airport, the sequence of radio frequencies likely to be used is

1. terminal, tower, ATIS, ground.
2. terminal, ATIS, tower, ground.
3. ATIS, tower, terminal, ground.
4. ATIS, terminal, tower, ground.

Question 81: At 15°C, a US gallon of AVGAS weighs approximately

1. 7.38 lbs.
2. 7.20 lbs.
3. 6.01 lbs.
4. 1.59 lbs.

Question 82: The number at the western end of runway 28L is

1. 10R.
2. 46R.
3. 10L.
4. 28R.

Question 83: Consider the CFS entry for Bear Lake Lookout in figure B.10 on page 97. When landing on runway 04, a pilot could expect to see a

1. PAPI suitable for aircraft with eye-to-wheel height up to 10 ft.
2. PAPI suitable for aircraft with eye-to-wheel height up to 45 ft.
3. two-bar VASI.
4. three-bar VASI.

Question 84: When flying on a special VFR clearance, responsibility for ensuring that the aircraft does not fly into terrain lies with the

1. pilot-in-command and the air traffic controller jointly.
2. flight services staff at the FSS within the control zone.
3. pilot-in-command.
4. air traffic controller who issued the clearance.

Question 85: 1 knot is a speed of

1. one statute mile per hour.
2. one nautical mile per hour at the equator, decreasing towards to poles.
3. 100 ft per minute.
4. one minute of latitude per hour.

Question 86: When in level flight at 120 knots at 6,000 ft, an aircraft burns 8.5 US gallons of fuel per hour. In 3 hours of such flying it will consume

1. 32.2 litres.
2. 96.5 litres.
3. 25.5 litres.
4. 95.3 litres.

Question 87: You are flying with another aircraft towards a distant aerodrome in the Southern Domestic Airspace. A suitable radio frequency for you to use to exchange information about times of arrival, current position and other similar information during the flight would be

1. 121.5 MHz.
2. 126.7 MHz.
3. 122.75 MHz.
4. 114.6 MHz.

Question 88: You are flying at 6,500 ft indicated when ATC asks you to report your altitude. The correct response would be

1. six point five.
2. sixty five hundred.
3. six and a half.
4. six thousand five hundred.

2.2 Use of Performance Charts

For questions 89 to 93 use of the CFS entry for Fort Cushing given in figure B.11 on page 98 and the takeoff and landing performance charts given in figures B.1 (page 93) and B.2 (page 93). The current altimeter setting in Fort Cushing is 30.60 inches of mercury, the temperature is 15°C and the winds are from 280°M at 21 knots.

Question 89: The runway ground roll required to take off at Fort Cushing in a Cessna 172M loaded to 2300 lbs is

1. 1,038 ft.
2. 955 ft.
3. 925 ft.
4. 830 ft.

Question 90: The distance required to clear a 50 foot obstacle when taking off from Fort Cushing in a Cessna 172M loaded to 2300 lbs is

1. 1,686 ft.
2. 1,591 ft.
3. 1,466 ft.
4. 955 ft.

Question 91: A broken down truck is blocking the threshold of runway 07 at Fort Cushing and takeoff will have to be made from runway 07 (away from the truck). What ground roll distance is required for a Cessna 172M loaded to 2300 lbs?

1. 955 ft.
2. Take-off from runway 07 is not permitted.
3. 1,038 ft.
4. The distance cannot be determined.

Question 92: Immediately after takeoff from runway 25 at Fort Cushing (the truck was removed), you find that you have left your wallet behind and need to return and land. The ground roll and distance to clear a 50 foot obstacle on approach are

1. 448 ft and 1,256 ft.
2. 650 ft and 1,256 ft.
3. 448 ft and 1,054 ft.
4. 650 ft and 1,528 ft.

Question 93: You take off from Fort Cushing and climb to your planned cruising altitude of 6,500 ft indicated, where the temperature is forecast to be 3°C. You decide to use a power setting of 2500 rpm. Using figure B.6 on page 94, the airspeeds you should achieve are

1. 110 knots true, 101 knots calibrated.
2. 101 knots true, 101 knots calibrated.
3. 101 knots true, 110 knots calibrated.
4. 110 knots true, 110 knots calibrated.

Question 94: While in cruise as described in question 93, if you lean the mixture correctly you could expect a fuel burn of

1. just under 7.2 gallons per hour.
2. 7.9 gallons per hour.
3. just over 7.2 gallons per hour.
4. exactly 7.2 gallons per hour.

Question 95: The maximum speed at which it is safe to extend or retract the landing gear on a retractable gear aircraft is known as

1. V_H.
2. V_a.
3. V_{lo}.
4. V_w.

Question 96: You intend to take off from runway 12 at an airport where the wind is reported to be from 150°M at 23 knots. The approximate head and crosswind components you will meet are

1. 18 knots headwind, 14 knots crosswind from the right.
2. 20 knots headwind, 12 knots crosswind from the left.
3. 20 knots headwind, 12 knots crosswind from the right.
4. 12 knots headwind, 20 knots crosswind from the right.

Question 97: You are taking off on a runway with a 1.5% upslope. The runway is 3,000 ft long but, for the purposes of calculating takeoff distance, you should assume its length to be

1. 2,550 ft.
2. 2,900 ft.
3. 3,000 ft.
4. 3,450 ft.

Question 98: You are approaching a major airport to land and are told that the CRFI is 0.6. This indicates that the runway

1. is slippery because of a layer of water, snow or ice.
2. is bare and dry.
3. is 60% covered in snow or ice.
4. is slippery from a contaminant other than a layer of water.

2.3 Aircraft Performance

Question 99: V_a is the speed above which

1. hydroplaning can occur when landing on a water-covered runway.
2. full and abrupt nose-up deflection of the controls cannot damage the airframe.
3. the load factor of the aircraft cannot be exceeded by making full control movements.
4. full and abrupt nose-up deflection of the controls can damage the airframe.

Question 100: An aircraft is most likely to exceed its V_{NE} during a

1. stall.
2. spin.
3. spiral dive.
4. steep turn.

Question 101: Slow flight is flight

1. below the normal cruise speed.
2. between the stall speed and the best endurance speed.
3. below the stall speed.
4. when the angle of attack is greater than $14°$.

Question 102: The major difference between a spiral dive and a spin is that

1. in a spiral dive recovery is impossible after the first turn, whereas in a spin recovery can be achieved after several turns.
2. in a spin the airspeed increases rapidly.
3. in a spiral dive the aircraft is stalled, in a spin it is not.
4. in a spin the aircraft is stalled, in a spiral dive it is not.

Question 103: Which of the following statements is true?

1. V_x is the speed at which height is gained as quickly as possible.
2. V_y is the speed at which height is gained as quickly as possible.
3. V_x is normally greater than V_y.
4. V_y is the climb speed that should be used if there is an obstacle at the departure end of the runway.

Question 104: When an aircraft is flown close to the ground, ground effect is caused by

1. an increase in power of a piston-engined aircraft.
2. a decrease in drag.
3. a "cushion" of air below the aircraft's wings.
4. increased wing-tip vortices.

Question 105: Which of the following statements is correct?

1. best range speed is normally higher than best endurance speed.
2. a pilot should normally cruise at best range speed.
3. best endurance speed is normally higher than best range speed.
4. stall speed is normally higher than best endurance speed.

Question 106: At a pressure altitude of 1,000 ft, an aircraft stalls in level flight at 55 KIAS. At a pressure altitude of 9,000 ft it will stall at

1. 52 KIAS.
2. 55 KIAS at a true airspeed less than 55 knots.
3. 63 KIAS.
4. 55 KIAS at a true airspeed greater than 55 knots.

Question 107: An aircraft will stall only

1. when its speed drops below a certain value.
2. when its nose is well above the horizon.
3. at pressure altitudes above 3,000 ft.
4. if its angle of attack exceeds a certain value.

Question 108: To remain in the air for as long as possible on a single tank of fuel, a pilot should fly at

1. the best endurance speed.
2. cruise speed.
3. the best range speed.
4. the stall speed.

Question 109: The primary hazard associated with ice on the wing of an aircraft is that it

1. disturbs the flow of air over the wing, decreasing the lift.
2. increases the risk of electrical fires from landing and navigation lights.
3. makes the air flow faster over the wing, increasing the lift and making the aircraft unstable.
4. increases the weight of the aircraft, making it more difficult for it to climb.

Question 110: Aircraft A and B each fly a $360°$ rate one turn. Aircraft A is flying at 100 knots and aircraft B at 150 knots. Which of the following statements is true?

1. Aircraft A's bank angle is greater than aircraft B's.
2. Aircraft B will complete the turn more quickly than aircraft A.
3. Aircraft B's radius of turn is greater than aircraft A's.
4. Aircraft A will complete the turn more quickly than aircraft B.

Question 111: The handbook for an aircraft states that the aircraft's service ceiling is 13,000 ft. This means that

1. the aircraft's best rate of climb at a density altitude of 13,000 ft is 100 ft per minute.
2. the aircraft cannot maintain level flight above a density altitude of 13,000 ft.
3. supplemental oxygen must be used for flights above 13,000 ft ASL.
4. the aircraft's best rate of climb at an altitude of 13,000 ft ASL is 100 ft per minute.

Question 112: An aerodrome has a low density altitude. For a light aircraft with a carburetted engine the takeoff distance will be ______ than normal and the climb rate after takeoff will be ______ than normal.

1. longer; lower
2. shorter; lower
3. shorter; higher
4. longer; higher

2.4 Weight and Balance

Question 113: Consider figure B.26 on page 103. This shows three weights balanced on a see-saw; the plank itself is very light. The pivot is

1. 75 inches to the right of A
2. 145 inches to the right of B
3. 75 inches to the left of B
4. 20 inches to the left of C

Question 114: Consider the weight and balance chart for an experimental aircraft in figure B.24 on page 102. The datum position for this aircraft is the

1. firewall at the rear of the engine.
2. pilot's seat.
3. baggage compartment.
4. tip of the spinner.

Question 115: When an aircraft is loaded in such a way that its centre of gravity lies within the utility category, then

1. the aircraft is not permitted to take off.
2. aerobatic flight is prohibited.
3. aerobatic flight as specified in the Pilot Operating Handbook is permitted.
4. fuel needs to be removed to move the centre of gravity into the normal category.

Question 116: You are to fly the aircraft whose weight and balance chart is given in figure B.24. You weigh 180 lbs, your front-seat passenger 220 lbs, your rear-seat passenger 180 lbs and you will be carrying 30 lbs of baggage in the baggage compartment. The tanks are full with 38 US gallons of avgas. Under these conditions, where will the aircraft's Centre of Gravity lie?

1. 51.8 inches from the firewall.
2. 51.8 inches in front of the datum.
3. at the datum.
4. 51.8 inches behind the datum.

Question 117: Under the conditions described in question 116, you fly for 2 hours 43 minutes burning 8.5 US gallons per hour of fuel. During the flight, the aircraft's centre of gravity will move

1. 0.3 inches towards the rear of the aircraft.
2. 0.3 inches towards the front of the aircraft.
3. 0.2 inches towards the front of the aircraft.
4. 0.2 inches towards the rear of the aircraft.

Question 118: On most light aircraft, the effect of loading an aircraft so that its Centre of Gravity is further towards the rear than permitted by the Pilot Operating Handbook would be to

1. increase the wing loading.
2. increase the stall speed.
3. decrease the stall speed.
4. make it easier to recover from a stall.

2.5 Wake Turbulence

Question 119: Wake turbulence behind a heavy aircraft is most dangerous when there is a

1. strong, gusty wind.
2. wind shear a few thousand feet above the runway.
3. strong, non-turbulent wind.
4. light, non-turbulent wind.

Question 120: Wake turbulence is primarily caused by

1. wing-tip vortices.
2. jet blast.
3. breaking the sound barrier.
4. the rotation of air by the propeller.

Question 121: You are landing in a light aircraft behind a heavy aircraft. The best way of avoiding the wake turbulence is to

1. follow the heavy aircraft as closely as possible to reduce the chances of the wing-tip vortices forming before you arrive.
2. remain above the heavy aircraft's glide path and land beyond the point where it landed.
3. remain below the heavy aircraft's glide path and land before the point where it landed.
4. fly as close to the heavy aircraft's glide path as possible, remaining just below it.

2.6 Search and Rescue

Question 122: The terms *Mayday* and *Pan Pan* mean respectively

1. urgency and emergency.
2. emergency and urgency.
3. emergency and end of emergency.
4. fuel shortage and other emergency.

Question 123: The transponder codes associated with radio failure, hijack and emergency are respectively

1. 1200, 1400 and 1000.
2. 7600, 7500 and 7700.
3. 7500, 7600 and 7700.
4. 9600, 9700 and 9800.

Question 124: You are forced by deteriorating weather to land in a field and do not need immediate assistance. You have no way of closing your flight plan (no cellular telephone coverage). You should

1. not activate your ELT.
2. activate your ELT at the estimated time of arrival on your flight plan.
3. activate your ELT immediately on landing.
4. activate your ELT one hour after the estimated time of arrival on your flight plan.

2.7 Critical Surface Contamination

Question 125: "Cold Soaking" occurs when an aircraft

1. has been flying at a high altitude for an extended period and then descends into warmer air to land.
2. has its fuel tanks filled from an underground storage container that has been allowed to cool.
3. passes through the de-icing process at an airport before takeoff.
4. has been flying at a low altitude for an extended period and then ascends rapidly into cooler air, causing the fuel in the wings to cool rapidly.

Question 126: The "clean aircraft concept" states that all critical surfaces of an aircraft must be clean of surface contamination. The critical surfaces of an aircraft are the wings, control surfaces, rotors and ___________. In the case of an aircraft with rear mounted engines, the upper surface of the fuselage is also a critical surface.

1. stabilising surfaces but not propellers
2. propellers and stabilising surfaces including horizontal stabilisers and vertical stabilizers
3. any surface over which the air is designed to pass while the aircraft is in flight
4. the entire fuselage

Chapter 3

Airframe, Engines and Systems

Contents

3.1 Airframes

Question 127: Polymer-based and fibre-reïnforced composite materials are used in many light aircraft and airliners rather than duralumin. One advantage of using composites is that

1. composite materials provide better protection against lightning strikes in the air.
2. composite materials are easier to form into intricate shapes than metals.
3. composite structures are easier to repair.
4. the failure mechanisms of composite materials are better understood than those of metals.

Question 128: The primary difference between a monocoque and truss-type fuselage is that

1. the skin of a monocoque fuselage is load-bearing.
2. a truss-type fuselage is lighter for a given strength.
3. a monocoque fuselage is normally covered with a fabric skin.
4. the skin of a truss-type fuselage is load-bearing.

3.2 Landing Gear, Brakes and Flaps

Question 129: When landing in a crosswind, tail-dragger aircraft are more susceptible to ground-looping than tricycle gear aircraft because their cente of gravity

1. lies in front of the main wheels.
2. is lower (closer to the ground).
3. is higher (further from the ground).
4. lies behind the main wheels.

Question 130: Extending flaps on an aircraft

1. does not affect its stall speed.
2. reduces its stall speed.
3. increases its stall speed.
4. makes it impossible to calculate its stall speed.

Question 131: Extending flaps does not alter a wing's

1. span.
2. coefficient of lift.
3. camber.
4. chord.

Question 132: It is not a function of an aircraft's landing gear to

1. accelerate the aircraft to takeoff speed.
2. absorb the shock of landing.
3. support the aircraft's weight when it is parked on the ramp.
4. provide braking and steering on the ground.

3.3 Engines

Question 133: A manifold pressure gauge measures the pressure

1. at the peak of compression of a cylinder, and thereby gives a measure of the health of the engine.
2. at the intake manifold of a cylinder, and thereby gives a measure of the power of the engine.
3. at the exhaust manifold of a cylinder, and thereby gives a measure of the power of the engine.
4. during the exhaust stroke of a cylinder, and thereby gives a measure of whether the fuel/air mixture is being completely burned.

Question 134: The purpose of an aircraft's magnetos is to

1. create the electrical spark to ignite the fuel/air mixture even in the absence of a battery.
2. ensure that the battery remains charged.
3. produce the electrical power to drive the radios and navigation instruments.
4. ensure that the circuitry producing the spark for the engine remains grounded at all times.

Question 135: The strokes of a four-stroke engine, in order, are

1. exhaust, compression, induction and power.
2. power, exhaust, compression and induction.
3. exhaust, induction, compression and power.
4. induction, compression, exhaust and power.

Question 136: The primary purpose of turbo-charging an aircraft engine is

1. to reduce the amount of fuel in the fuel/air mixture at high altitude.
2. to reduce the power provided by the engine.
3. to improve the engine's performance at low altitude.
4. to increase the amount of air in the fuel/air mixture at high altitude.

Question 137: The reason why many piston-engined aircraft have two magnetos is that

1. having two spark plugs in each cylinder reduces the chances of having carburetor icing.
2. having two magnetos allows a better burning of the fuel/air mixture in the cylinder.
3. it allows half of the cylinders to be operated from one magneto and the other half from the other.
4. having two magnetos provides redundancy, so that if one fails the engine can continue operating.

Question 138: A mixture control allows a pilot to

1. reduce the possibility of carburetor icing.
2. reduce engine power in cruise.
3. pass the air in the fuel/air mixture over a heated surface (normally the exhaust stack).
4. change the amount of fuel in the fuel/air mixture.

Question 139: A pilot flies a piston-engined aircraft with dual ignition. During her magneto checks before flight, she switches to the left magneto position and finds that there is no drop in engine speed. This is most probably an indication that

1. the grounding wire has become disconnected from the right magneto.
2. everything is OK with the ignition system.
3. the grounding wire has become disconnected from the left magneto.
4. the left magneto has failed.

3.4 Carburation

Question 140: Applying carburetor heat

1. has no effect on the fuel/air mixture.
2. removes all air from the fuel/air mixture.
3. makes the fuel/air mixture richer.
4. makes the fuel/air mixture leaner.

Question 141: A pilot takes off in an aircraft which has a carbureted engine with manual mixture control. When he reaches 5,000 ft ASL he applies mixture leaning and notices that the exhaust gas temperature

1. remains constant until the correct mixture is reached and then drops.
2. remains constant until the correct mixture is reached and then rises.
3. initially rises and then drops.
4. initially drops and then rises.

Question 142: In an aircraft with a fixed-pitch propeller and a conventional carburetor, the most likely first indication of carburetor icing would be the

1. exhaust gas temperature rising.
2. tachometer showing a reduced value.
3. tachometer showing an increased value.
4. exhaust gas temperature dropping.

Question 143: Applying carburetor heat can encourage the formation of carburetor ice when

1. the outside air temperature is very high.
2. the outside air is very cold.
3. there is significant moisture in the air.
4. the aircraft is flying above 5,000 ft pressure altitude.

Question 144: When no carburetor icing is present, applying carburetor heat during a run-up causes a slight ______ in power because the mixture becomes ______.

1. increase; richer
2. drop; richer
3. drop; leaner
4. increase; leaner

Question 145: Carburetor icing causes a loss of power because it

1. restricts the flow of fuel to the engine.
2. restricts the flow of the fuel/air mixture to the engine.
3. cools the fuel/air mixture and thereby makes it burn at a colder temperature.
4. reduces the temperature of the spark.

Question 146: The purpose of a carburetor is to

1. mix air with vapourised fuel.
2. mix air with water vapour.
3. change the speed at which fuel/air mixture is passed to the cylinder.
4. reduce the temperature of the fuel/air mixture.

3.5 Fuel Injection

Question 147: Alternate air is often provided on fuel-injected engines to provide a source of

1. air accelerated through a venturi system.
2. static air.
3. air at high pressure.
4. warm air.

Question 148: One characteristic of fuel-injected piston engines is that they

1. have fuel inserted directly into the intake manifold or cylinder.
2. normally work with a gravity-fed fuel system.
3. cannot suffer from induction ice.
4. suffer more from carburetor icing than other piston engines.

3.6 Electrical System

Question 149: The immediate effect of an alternator failure in a light aircraft would be to cause

1. a complete failure of all electrical equipment.
2. the turn co-ordinator to fail.
3. a drain on the battery.
4. the engine to stop.

Question 150: One advantage of a generator over an alternator in an aircraft is that

1. a generator is normally lighter than an alternator of the same power.
2. a generator can operate even without a battery in the aircraft.
3. a generator provides a more stable output voltage at low revolution speeds.
4. a generator is normally smaller than an alternator of the same power.

Question 151: Many light aircraft have an "avionics master" switch in their electrical systems which is switched off during engine start. This is to

1. ensure that the regulator that converts the 12V or 24V aircraft electrical supply to 5V for the electronics is disconnected.
2. isolate the avionics from the starter motor so that the high voltage generated by the starter motor does not damage the avionics.
3. reduce the power drain on the alternator or generator to provide more power for starting the engine.
4. isolate the avionics from the aircraft's electrical system to avoid damage to the electronics.

Question 152: The primary difference between a circuit breaker and a fuse is that

1. a circuit breaker acts a lot faster than a fuse.
2. a circuit breaker acts by a wire heating and melting, and thereby breaking the circuit.
3. a circuit breaker can carry more electrical current than a fuse before tripping.
4. a circuit breaker can be reset, whereas a fuse has to be replaced after it has tripped.

Question 153: Unless otherwise instructed in the Pilot Operating Handbook, what action would you take if a circuit breaker tripped while you were in cruise flight?

1. Reset it once; if it trips again do not reset it.
2. Continue to reset it until it remains set, holding it in if necessary.
3. Remove it and replace it with a serviceable one.
4. No action.

3.7 Lubricating Systems and Oils

Question 154: The engine in a particular aircraft uses 20W-50 oil. The letter W stands for _______, 20 indicates its viscosity in ______ conditions and 50 its viscosity in ______ conditions.

1. weight; hot; cold
2. winter; hot; cold
3. weight; cold; hot
4. winter; cold; hot

Question 155: When the running in period finishes, the mineral oil should be

1. drained and replaced with fresh mineral oil.
2. used until the first annual inspection following the running in period and then be replaced with synthetic oil.
3. topped up with synthetic oil as required so that, over time, the mineral oil is replaced.
4. flushed from the system before synthetic oil is added.

Question 156: Mineral rather than a synthetic oil is used in a new engine during the running in period because

1. it is better at preventing wear.
2. it is less viscous.
3. it is less expensive.
4. it is less good at preventing wear.

Question 157: A wet-sump lubrication system differs from a dry-sump system in that it

1. stores the oil in a tank separate from the engine itself.
2. stores the oil in the sump of the engine rather than in a separate tank.
3. can provide more oil to the engine and is therefore more suitable for large engines.
4. is more suitable for use in aerobatic aircraft.

Question 158: While in cruise flight the oil pressure indication drops to zero while the oil temperature indication remains normal. This is most likely caused by

1. a loss of electrical power.
2. a failure in the oil pressure indication circuit.
3. a failure in the oil circulation pump.
4. a loss of oil from the engine.

Question 159: Oil dilution in an aircraft engine is a method of

1. reducing the viscosity of cold oil.
2. increasing the viscosity of cold oil.
3. increasing the time between oil changes.
4. reducing the cost of oil.

Question 160: Which of the following is not a function of oil in a reciprocating engine during cruise flight?

1. Cooling.
2. Cleaning.
3. Lubrication.
4. Warming.

3.8 Fuel Systems and Fuels

Question 161: When fuelling an aircraft from a fuel truck, the truck and aircraft are electrically bonded

1. to ensure that there is no temperature difference between them.
2. to provide a baseline for the measurement of the amount of fuel pumped.
3. to ensure that there is no static-electrical charge between them.
4. to ensure that any spark that occurs during the fuelling is drawn away from the aircraft.

Question 162: 100LL AVGAS is coloured

1. blue.
2. green.
3. clear.
4. red.

Question 163: Detonation is the burning of the fuel/air mixture

1. after the spark plug has fired when mixture that the flame front has not reached spontaneously starts to burn.
2. when the pilot has flown at a high power setting with the mixture too rich.
3. before the spark plug has fired when the mixture starts to burn because of a hot spot in the cylinder.
4. when the pilot has used fuel with too high an octane rating.

Question 164: MOGAS is not as suitable for use in piston-engined aircraft as AVGAS because

1. it has a higher octane rating than AVGAS.
2. it is more volatile than AVGAS.
3. it has a lower freezing point than AVGAS.
4. it contains more lead than AVGAS (particularly more than 100 low lead).

Question 165: The higher the octane rating of a fuel, the greater is

1. its resistance to auto-ignition.
2. its ability to pour in cold weather.
3. the speed at which it burns.
4. its energy content.

3.9 Other Aircraft Systems

Question 166: Pilots of unpressurised aircraft are recommended to use supplemental oxygen at lower altitudes at night because

1. the density altitude at a particular flight level is higher at night.
2. the retina of the eye is particularly sensitive to lack of oxygen, reducing night vision.
3. there is less oxygen in the atmosphere at night, caused by the ionisation of the upper atmosphere after sunset.
4. lack of oxygen can cause hypothermia more readily at night.

Question 167: You are performing a run-up in a Cessna 172 and notice that the vacuum pressure which normally is about 6 inches of mercury is reading $6\frac{1}{2}$ inches, but that neither of the vacuum-driven instruments is operational. One cause of this problem might be

1. a failed vacuum pump.
2. blockage of the static system.
3. a blocked vacuum filter.
4. toppling of the gyroscopes in the instruments.

Chapter 4

Flight Instruments

Contents

4.1 Pitot Static System

Question 168: In an unpressurised aircraft, if the pilot suspects that the static port has become blocked then she should

1. open the alternate static port.
2. turn on carburetor heat.
3. not use the attitude indicator.
4. turn on pitot heat.

Question 169: If the pitot tube were to become blocked, then this might affect

1. only the ASI.
2. the Heading Indicator and Attitude Indicator.
3. the ASI, Altimeter and VSI.
4. the Altimeter and VSI.

Question 170: If the static port were to become blocked, then this might affect

1. the Heading Indicator and Attitude Indicator.
2. the Altimeter and VSI.
3. the ASI, Altimeter and VSI.
4. only the ASI.

Question 171: The static port on a pressurised aircraft is best mounted

1. outside the aircraft in such a way that air is not forced into it as the aircraft flies.
2. within the cockpit, close to the pitot-static instruments.
3. on the wing facing directly into the air flow, as far from the fuselage as possible.
4. inside the passenger cabin.

4.2 Airspeed Indicator

Question 172: The pitot tube on an aircraft blocks while it is in a 500 ft per minute climb at 120 knots. What effect will this have on the ASI?

1. It will have no effect as the ASI is not connected to the pitot tube, only to the static port.
2. The ASI will continue to record 120 knots.
3. The ASI will indicate an increasing air speed.
4. The ASI will indicate a decreasing air speed.

Question 173: The static port on an aircraft blocks while it is in a 500 ft per minute climb at 120 knots. What effect will this have on the ASI?

1. The ASI will indicate an increasing air speed.
2. The ASI will indicate a decreasing air speed.
3. It will have no effect as the ASI is not connected to the pitot tube, only to the static port.
4. The ASI will continue to record 120 knots.

Question 174: Which of the following are not marked on the face of a traditional ASI in a twin-engined aircraft?

1. Minimum airspeed at which the aircraft can be controlled with the critical engine inoperative.
2. The speeds at which flaps may be deployed.
3. V_{NE}.
4. Manoeuvring speed.

Question 175: To determine CAS from IAS use

1. the Pilot Operating Handbook for the aircraft.
2. the rule of thumb that says CAS = IAS + half flight level.
3. an E6B.
4. a CX-2 or equivalent calculator.

Question 176: A pilot is flying at a pressure altitude of 8,000 ft where the temperature is 4°C. Her ASI indicates an airspeed of 104 knots. Assuming that the CAS is the same as the IAS, her true airspeed is

1. 118 knots.
2. 95 knots.
3. 112 knots.
4. 104 knots.

4.3 Vertical Speed Indicator

Question 177: The static port on an aircraft blocks while climbing at 300 ft per minute. What effect will this have on the VSI?

1. The VSI will indicate that the aircraft is flying level.
2. The VSI will indicate a descent.
3. The VSI will freeze at the value it had before the blockage.
4. It will have no effect.

Question 178: The basic principle of a conventional VSI is

1. firing a beam of radio energy downwards from the bottom of the fuselage and using the Doppler effect to measure how fast the aircraft's altitude is changing.
2. integrating the altitude information being transmitted by the aircraft's transponder.
3. a microprocessor integrating the changes in the altimeter reading over periods of 5 and 10 seconds and displays the resulting value.
4. making a measurement of the rate at which air passes into or out of a container through a controlled leak.

Question 179: The pitot tube on an aircraft blocks while it is in a climb at a constant speed of 100 knots. What effect will this have on the VSI?

1. The VSI will indicate that the aircraft is flying level.
2. The VSI will freeze at the value it had before the blockage.
3. It will have no effect.
4. The VSI will indicate a descent.

4.4 Altimeter/Encoding Altimeter

Question 180: An aircraft is climbing at 400 ft per minute at 100 knots when the static port blocks. How will this affect the altimeter?

1. It will not affect it at all.
2. It will cause it to remain at the altitude the aircraft was at when the blockage occurred.
3. It will cause it to show a slowly decreasing altitude.
4. It will cause it to read 0 (i.e., sea-level).

Question 181: A pilot correctly sets his altimeter and takes off from an aerodrome and climbs several thousand feet. Which of the following conditions might cause his altimeter to over-read (i.e., display an altitude higher than he actually is)?

1. A very humid day.
2. A very cold day.
3. A very hot day.
4. A day with limited visibility.

Question 182: A blind encoding altimeter is an

1. encoded feed from a conventional altimeter used to provide input to the transponder.
2. altimeter that is only accurate when set to the local atmospheric pressure.
3. altimeter that broadcasts an encoded version of the aircraft's altitude.
4. altimeter without a display that feeds a coded version of the aircraft's altitude to the transponder and GPS.

Question 183: Consider the barometric altimeter shown in figure B.13 on page 99. If the pressure setting were adjusted to 30.10 inches of mercury, then

1. a higher altitude would be displayed.
2. the displayed altitude would be unchanged.
3. a lower altitude would be displayed.
4. the local pressure altitude would be displayed.

Question 184: An aircraft is climbing at 400 ft per minute at 100 knots when the pitot tube blocks. How will this affect the altimeter?

1. It will cause it to read 0 (i.e., sea-level).
2. It will not affect it at all.
3. It will cause it to show a slowly decreasing altitude.
4. It will cause it to remain at the passing altitude when the blockage occurred.

Question 185: The basic principle of operation of a barometric altimeter is that it measures the

1. rate at which the atmospheric pressure at the static port is changing.
2. atmospheric pressure at the static port.
3. difference between the atmospheric pressure at the static port and the pitot tube.
4. time that radio waves take to return when bounced off the ground.

4.5 Magnetic Compass

Question 186: A pilot is flying at 3,000 ft ASL on an easterly heading in southern Canada when he applies carburetor heat. This causes his aircraft to decelerate, causing the magnetic compass to

1. register a climb.
2. incorrectly register a turn towards the north.
3. incorrectly register a turn towards the south.
4. tumble.

Question 187: Magnetic dip is greatest at

1. a latitude of 45° north or south.
2. the true north and south poles.
3. the equator.
4. the magnetic north and south poles.

Question 188: The compass in an aircraft must be swung

1. at least once per year and whenever an event such as a lightning strike on the aircraft occurs.
2. only after an event such as a lightning strike.
3. whenever there is an error of more than $\pm 10^\circ$ on any heading.
4. at least at every second annual inspection and whenever an event such as a lightning strike on the aircraft occurs.

Question 189: A pilot is flying at 3,000 ft on a westerly heading when he starts a rate one turn to the north. Initially, his magnetic compass will

1. lead the turn.
2. remain indicating west.
3. lag behind the turn.
4. correctly register the turn.

4.6 Gyroscope

Question 190: Which devices in a light aircraft typically contain a gyroscope?

1. Attitude indicator, VOR receiver and turn co-ordinator.
2. Heading indicator, encoding altimeter and turn co-ordinator.
3. Encoding altimeter, transponder and strikefinder.
4. Turn and bank indicator, heading indicator and attitude indicator.

Question 191: The fundamental law that makes a gyroscope useful in flight instruments is that when it is rotating

1. it will move at right-angles to any force applied to it.
2. the indentations on its rim induce a low pressure around it.
3. it automatically aligns with the earth's magnetic field and thereby detects any movement of the aircraft.
4. the difference in phases of a beam of light sent around the disk can be used to detect movement of the aircraft.

4.7 Heading Indicator

Question 192: The gyroscope in a heading indicator of a light aircraft is most commonly rotated by

1. a stream of air from the vacuum system.
2. a geared drive from the engine.
3. a stream of air from the aircraft's movement.
4. an electric motor.

Question 193: The axis of the gyroscope within a heading indicator is mounted

1. upwards at about 35° to the horizontal.
2. vertically.
3. horizontally along the longitudinal axis of the aircraft.
4. horizontally along the lateral axis of the aircraft.

Question 194: One limitation of many heading indicators is that they

1. will "tumble" if the aircraft banks or pitches too steeply.
2. are a trend instrument and can only be used to detect trends in heading changes.
3. lag significantly on turns towards the east.
4. only work at one particular latitude.

Question 195: Which of the following statements about precession in a heading indicator is not correct?

1. Precession is seen as a slow drifting of the displayed heading, even if the aircraft's heading remains constant.
2. The rotation of the earth is the major cause of precession.
3. Friction in the bearings is the major cause of precession.
4. Precession is greater at 70°N than at 30°N.

4.8 Attitude Indicator

Question 196: Consider the attitude indicator in figure B.14 on page 99. The aircraft is

1. banking right with the nose pitched up.
2. in level flight banking to the right.
3. in level flight banking to the left.
4. banking left with the nose pitched down.

Question 197: The aircraft containing the attitude indicator in figure B.14 on page 99 is banking at approximately

1. 18°.
2. 20°.
3. 13°.
4. 8°.

Question 198: When an aircraft accelerates, the attitude indicator displays

1. a pitch-up attitude.
2. a turn to the right.
3. a pitch-down attitude.
4. a turn to the left.

Question 199: A pilot is circling around a point on the ground while maintaining altitude. After some minutes, the attitude indicator will display

1. the aircraft as being in straight and level flight.
2. the aircraft as being at a greater bank angle than it is.
3. the aircraft as descending.
4. the aircraft as climbing.

Question 200: The vacuum system is used in many attitude indicators to

1. suspend the mechanism.
2. turn the gyroscope.
3. turn an electrical generator.
4. provide a baseline from which attitude is measured.

Question 201: The axis of the rotating gyroscope within an attitude indicator is mounted

1. vertically.
2. upwards at about 35° to the longitudinal axis of the aircraft.
3. horizontally along the lateral axis of the aircraft.
4. horizontally along the longitudinal axis of the aircraft.

4.9 Turn Co-ordinator

Question 202: A pilot is making a rate one turn to the right and has applied too much right rudder for a co-ordinated turn. The slip ball in the turn co-ordinator will be

1. to the right.
2. oscillating between right and left.
3. to the left.
4. in the centre.

Question 203: The axis of a rotating gyroscope within a turn co-ordinator indicator is mounted

1. horizontally along the lateral axis of the aircraft.
2. vertically.
3. horizontally along the longitudinal axis of the aircraft.
4. upwards at 30° to the longitudinal axis of the aircraft.

Question 204: The important difference between a turn co-ordinator and a turn and bank indicator is that a turn co-ordinator

1. only registers roll (around the aircraft's longitudinal axis).
2. only registers turn (around the aircraft's vertical axis).
3. registers roll (around the aircraft's longitudinal axis) as well as turn (around the aircraft's vertical axis).
4. only displays turn when it is accompanied by a change in pitch.

Question 205: The attitude indicator of an aircraft appears as shown in figure B.14 on page 99. Assuming that all instruments are working properly, which of the items shown in figure B.15 will the turn and bank indicator in the aircraft most resemble?

1. Indicator A if in a slip to the right.
2. Indicator B if in a co-ordinated turn.
3. Indicator A if in a co-ordinated turn.
4. Indicator B if in a slip to the right.

4.10 Instrument Flying

Question 206: If a VFR pilot accidently enters cloud, the primary instrument to monitor is the

1. attitude indicator.
2. turn co-ordinator.
3. heading indicator.
4. GPS receiver.

Question 207: When flying in IMC in a light aircraft with a traditional set of instruments (no glass cockpit) the pilot finds that the heading indicator is indicating a rapid turn to the right, the attitude indicator is indicating a bank to the left, the compass is indicating no change of direction and the turn co-ordinator is indicating wings-level. What is the most likely cause of this?

1. A vacuum failure.
2. A blockage of the pitot tube.
3. An electrical failure.
4. A blockage of the static port.

Question 208: A VFR pilot has inadvertently entered cloud and notices that her airspeed is increasing rapidly and the attitude indicator shows a steep, descending turn to the left. The most probable explanation is that she

1. has entered a spiral dive.
2. is in straight and level flight.
3. is about to stall.
4. has entered a spin.

Question 209: A pilot has entered a spiral dive while in cloud and, seeing the airspeed increasing rapidly, has instinctively pulled the nose of the aircraft up. The most likely result of this action is that the

1. spiral will become tighter.
2. spiral dive will convert into a spin.
3. aircraft will stall.
4. spiral dive will stop and the aircraft will recover to straight and level flight.

Question 210: If a VFR-only pilot accidently enters cloud, the most important first action is to

1. turn on the pitot heat.
2. note the aircraft's heading.
3. slow the aircraft down.
4. squawk 7700.

Chapter 5

Theory of Flight

Contents

5.1 Principles of Flight

Question 211: The wing of an aircraft in flight forces air downwards and this generates lift, forcing the aircraft upwards. This is an example of

1. the principle of special relativity.
2. Bernoulli's principle.
3. Newton's third law of motion.
4. Pythagoras' theorem.

Question 212: Newton's third law of motion says

1. heat travels from a warmer to a cooler body.
2. when a fluid passes through a constriction, its temperature and pressure increase.
3. when a fluid (such as air) passes through a constriction, its temperature and pressure drop and its speed increases.
4. if a body A applies a force to a body B, then body A experiences an equal and opposite force.

5.2 Forces Acting on an Aeroplane

Question 213: In level flight a particular aircraft stalls at 65 knots. The aircraft is banked and has a load factor of 1.3. Its stall speed in this condition is approximately

1. 85 knots.
2. 50 knots.
3. 74 knots.
4. 57 knots.

Question 214: In cruise flight, the lift to drag ratio of a _______ is much higher than that of a _________.

1. Boeing 747, competition glider
2. Cessna 152, competition glider
3. Cessna 172, Boeing 747
4. competition glider (sailplane), Cessna 152

Question 215: Two aircraft are identical in construction but one is loaded more heavily than the other. The heavier load will

1. affect both the parasitic and induced drag equally.
2. will not affect the drag.
3. affect the parasitic drag more than the induced drag.
4. affect the induced drag more than the parasitic drag.

Question 216: Induced drag is greatest

1. for an aircraft flying quickly with flaps down.
2. for an aircraft flying slowly with flaps down.
3. for an aircraft in clean configuration (flaps and wheels up) at cruise speed.
4. for an aircraft flying slowly in clean configuration.

Question 217: Which of the following statements about drag is true?

1. Parasitic drag reduces as airspeed increases.
2. Induced drag reduces as airspeed increases.
3. Cleaning bugs off the leading edge of the wings will reduce induced drag.
4. Parasitic drag is the major cause of drag at low speeds.

Question 218: An aircraft is in level flight at a constant speed of 100 knots and the pilot adjusts the controls so that the aircraft's weight is equal to its lift and its drag is equal to its thrust. The aircraft will

1. continue in level flight at 100 knots.
2. accelerate.
3. slow down and start to descend.
4. stall.

Question 219: An aircraft is flying in straight and level flight at 110 knots with a gross weight of 2234 lbs force. Its engine is providing a thrust of 600 lbs force. In this condition the drag is

1. 600 lbs and the lift 2234 lbs.
2. less than 600 lbs and the lift is greater than 2234 lbs.
3. less than 600 lbs and the lift is 2234 lbs.
4. 600 lbs and the lift is greater than 2234 lbs.

Question 220: The forces acting on a powered aircraft in flight are

1. lift, drag, weight and gravity.
2. thrust, power, weight and drag.
3. thrust, lift, drag and weight.
4. thrust, lift, weight and power.

Question 221: An aircraft has a weight of 2300 lbs and is in a 60° banked turn while holding altitude. The lift being generated is

1. 2,300 lbs.
2. 1,150 lbs.
3. 4,600 lbs.
4. 2,000 lbs.

Question 222: An aircraft is in a rate one turn to the right flying at a constant speed of 150 knots and maintaining an altitude of 10,500 ft ASL. Under these circumstances

1. there is no net force acting on the aircraft—the forces are in equilibrium.
2. there is a net force acting to the left.
3. there is a net force acting to the right.
4. the thrust is greater than the drag.

5.3 Aerofoils

Question 223: The angle of incidence of a Cessna 172 can be changed by

1. raising the aircraft's nose.
2. lowering the flaps.
3. adjusting the vertical trim.
4. banking at angles greater than 45°.

Question 224: The centre of pressure of a wing is the point

1. at which, in side view, the whole of the lift of the wing can be assumed to act.
2. on the lower surface of the wing where the incident air flow creates the most pressure.
3. at which the whole of the weight of the aircraft can be assumed to act.
4. 25% of the chord backwards from the leading edge.

Question 225: Wing-tip vortices from an aircraft's wing can be reduced by having a wing with

1. a small camber.
2. a large camber.
3. a small aspect ratio.
4. a large aspect ratio.

Question 226: An aircraft is in slow cruise at 60 knots. If its speed were to increase to 120 knots, the lift generated by the wings would

1. increase by 50%.
2. increase by a factor of 4.
3. double.
4. increase by 41%.

Question 227: Which of the following statements is correct?

1. The same angle of attack of an aircraft wing can be achieved at widely different speeds.
2. A particular angle of attack of an aircraft wing can only be achieved at one particular airspeed.
3. The angle of attack of an aircraft wing depends only on the airspeed of the aircraft—the slower the aircraft, the higher the angle of attack.
4. The angle of attack of an aircraft wing depends only on the ground speed of the aircraft—the faster the aircraft, the higher the angle of attack.

5.4 Propellers

Question 228: An aircraft with a constant-speed propeller is cruising at 130 knots. The pilot climbs by pulling back on the controls without adjusting any engine controls. The pitch of the propeller will

1. become finer.
2. remain the same.
3. become coarser.
4. adjust automatically to keep the airspeed constant.

Question 229: "Feathering" a propeller means

1. setting its pitch angle to 90°.
2. disconnecting it from the engine to allow it to "windmill."
3. setting it to its fully fine position.
4. setting its pitch angle to 0°.

Question 230: In general, fixed-pitch propeller blades are aerofoils

1. that have constant angle of attack along their length.
2. that are unaffected by a build up of ice.
3. that are washed in.
4. that are washed out.

Question 231: A fixed-pitch propeller is most effective at

1. low airspeeds.
2. high airspeeds.
3. low groundspeeds.
4. high groundspeeds.

5.5 Design of the Wing

Question 232: Which of the following statements regarding wash-out of a wing is correct?

1. Wash out of a wing is designed to make the root of the wing stall before the tip.
2. Wash out of a wing is designed to make the tip of the wing stall before the root.
3. On a washed out wing, the angle of incidence is constant along the wing from root to tip.
4. On a washed out wing, the angle of attack at the root of the wing is smaller than the angle of attack at the tip.

Question 233: The aspect ratio of a wing can be calculated by

1. dividing the square of the wing span by the area of the wing.
2. dividing the area of the wing by the wing span.
3. multiplying the square of the wing span by the area of the wing.
4. dividing the square of the mean chord of the wing by the area of the wing.

Question 234: Vortex generators are fitted to the upper surface of some wings to

1. increase the camber of the wing at low speed.
2. prevent air flowing over the top of the wing from moving towards the wing-tip.
3. break up the smooth airflow across the top of the wing.
4. ensure that the root of the wing stalls before the tip, creating a more controlled stall.

Question 235: When an aircraft approaches and reaches the stall in level flight, the centre of pressure

1. remains fixed at approximately 25% of the way back from the leading edge.
2. moves rearward as the angle of attack increases and then moves rapidly forward when the stall occurs.
3. moves forward until it reaches the aircraft's centre of gravity and then moves rapidly rearward.
4. moves forward until the stall is reached and then rapidly rearward.

5.6 Stability

Question 236: Balancing a pencil on its non-pointed end is an example of

1. unstable equilibrium.
2. neutral equilibrium.
3. graphitic equilibrium.
4. stable equilibrium.

Question 237: Which of the following contribute to lateral stability in an aircraft?

1. Anhedral, high wing and wash-out.
2. Dihedral, low wing and sweep back.
3. Wash out, high wing and large aspect ratio.
4. Dihedral, high wing and sweep back.

Question 238: The axis of an aircraft that runs from the front to the back is known as the _______ axis and stability around that axis is known as _______ stability.

1. longitudinal; longitudinal
2. lateral; roll
3. vertical; yaw
4. longitudinal; lateral

Question 239: Longitudinal stability of an aircraft refers to the restoration of

1. the direction of flight after an in-flight disturbance.
2. the wings-level attitude after an in-flight disturbance.
3. the angle of incidence of the wing after an in-flight disturbance.
4. the angle of attack of the wing after an in-flight disturbance.

5.7 Flight Controls

Question 240: The purposes of a horizontal tail on an aircraft include

1. allowing the pilot to adjust the attitude of the aircraft around the longitudinal axis.
2. increasing the longitudinal stability of the aircraft.
3. reducing the wing loading of the aircraft.
4. adding to the lift produced by the wing.

Question 241: When the stick or control column is moved to the right, then

1. both ailerons go up.
2. the left aileron goes up and the right one down.
3. the right aileron goes up and the left one down.
4. both ailerons go down.

Question 242: With differential ailerons, the angle of the up-going aileron to the wing chord is ________ the angle of the down-going aileron and the purpose of this is to ________ the drag on the wing with the up-going aileron.

1. greater than; increase
2. less than; decrease
3. greater than; decrease
4. less than; increase

Question 243: An elevator control horn is

1. characterised by having part of the elevator move above the stabiliser when the elevator moves downwards.
2. designed to increase the negative lift of the horizontal tail at high speeds.
3. a venturi system used to provide vacuum on aircraft without an engine-driven vacuum pump.
4. provided to warn people of the aircraft's approach during taxiing.

Question 244: When the elevator trim control is set to full "nose-up", then the trim tab is

1. in line with the rudder.
2. neutral.
3. fully down.
4. fully up.

Chapter 6

Meteorology: General

Contents

6.1 The Earth's Atmosphere

Question 245: Most light aircraft flight takes place in the

1. mesosphere.
2. troposphere.
3. tropopause.
4. stratosphere.

Question 246: Within the tropopause, the environmental lapse rate

1. changes in a manner dependent on the season.
2. changes from positive to neutral or negative.
3. changes to the saturated adiabatic lapse rate.
4. changes to the dry adiabatic lapse rate.

Question 247: Within the troposphere

1. temperature increases and pressure decreases with height.
2. temperature decreases and pressure increases with height.
3. both temperature and pressure decrease with height.
4. both temperature and pressure increase with height.

Question 248: Within the troposphere, a package of rising air will typically

1. contract and warm.
2. expand and cool.
3. contract and cool.
4. expand and warm.

Question 249: The primary constituents of the earth's atmosphere are

1. nitrogen and oxygen.
2. methane and oxygen.
3. carbon dioxide and argon.
4. oxygen and water vapour.

6.2 Atmospheric Pressure

Question 250: Isobars on a weather map join points having the same

1. station pressure.
2. sea-level pressure.
3. magnetic variation.
4. altitude.

Question 251: Atmospheric pressure is recorded on meteorological reports and forecasts in

1. millibars.
2. hectoPascals.
3. inches of mercury.
4. all of the above.

Question 252: Two weather recording stations are very close to each other. Station A is at 8,000 ft ASL on a mountainside, station B is at 1,000 ASL in a nearby valley. Which of the following statements is true?

1. The station pressure at A and B will be the same but the sea-level pressure at A will be lower than that at B.
2. The station pressure at A and B will be the same but the sea-level pressure at A will be higher than that at B.
3. The sea-level pressure at A and B will be the same but the station pressure at A will be higher than that at B.
4. The sea-level pressure at A and B will be the same but the station pressure at A will be lower than that at B.

6.3 Meteorological Aspects of Altimetry

Question 253: Consider the METARs for Bear Lake Lookout in figure B.17 on page 100 and its entry in the CFS in figure B.10 on page 97. At 1600Z, a pilot on the ground at Bear Lake Lookout adjusts his altimeter to a 29.92 inches of mercury. It then reads

1. 1,322 ft.
2. sea-level.
3. 893 ft.
4. 1,751 ft.

Question 254: Consider the METARs for Bear Lake Lookout in figure B.17 and its entry in the CFS in figure B.10. What was the density altitude at the aerodrome at 1600Z?

1. 1,751 ft.
2. 2,966 ft.
3. 1,322 ft.
4. Sea-level.

Question 255: A higher than normal density altitude at the aerodrome from which you are departing might lead to

1. a shorter takeoff roll than normal.
2. a longer than normal takeoff roll.
3. greater power from your reciprocating engine.
4. significantly reduced visibility.

Question 256: A pilot departs from an aerodrome where he correctly set his altimeter to 29.58" Hg and flies to Bear Lake Lookout (see CFS entry in figure B.10), landing at 1600Z without adjusting his altimeter. Considering the METAR for Bear Lake Lookout in figure B.17, once on the ground at Bear Lake Lookout, his altimeter will read

1. 1,434 ft.
2. 1,538 ft.
3. 1,210 ft.
4. 1,322 ft.

6.4 Temperature

Question 257: The upper atmosphere is closer to the sun than the lower atmosphere yet within the troposphere, temperature generally decreases with height. This is because

1. of the emission of volcanic ash and other hot debris from the earth.
2. the atmosphere is mainly heated from below by the earth.
3. of global warming.
4. of the presence of the tropopause.

Question 258: A Canadian pilot visiting the USA has been told by someone using the Fahrenheit scale that the local temperature is 10 degrees and that it will increase by 10 degrees by the next day. The temperature is ______ and the increase is expected to be ______.

1. $-12°$C; 6 Celsius degrees
2. $6°$C; -12 Celsius degrees
3. $-12°$C; -12 Celsius degrees
4. $6°$C; 6 Celsius degrees

Question 259: What sort of visibility normally accompanies a prolonged inversion?

1. Visibility is unaffected by the inversion.
2. Visibility is good both above and below the inversion layer.
3. Visibility below the inversion layer is poor, visibility above relatively better.
4. Visibility above the inversion layer is poor, visibility below it relatively better.

Question 260: Which of the following conditions is likely to lead to a temperature inversion?

1. A cloud-covered night in summer following a hot day.
2. A cloud-covered day in winter with strong winds.
3. A clear night with light winds following a hot day.
4. A clear afternoon on a hot summer's day.

Question 261: A temperature inversion is

1. an error in the reading of the temperature published in a METAR, requiring a correction METAR with the designation CCA to be issued.
2. the condition where temperature remains unchanged from the surface to the tropopause.
3. the condition where temperature decreases with altitude.
4. the condition where temperature remains constant or increases with altitude.

Question 262: In the international standard atmosphere, the temperature in the troposphere decreases at approximately ______ °C per 1000 ft.

1. 3
2. 1.2
3. 1.7
4. 2

6.5 Moisture

For questions 263 and 264 consider the following two METARs issued at the same time for airports both situated at 1000 feet ASL.

```
METAR CYXA 120000Z 18007KT 15SM FEW070
FEW240 20/18 A2988 RMK AC1CI1 SLP117=
METAR CYXB 120000Z 15003KT 15SM FEW050
FEW120 FEW240 20/12 A2988 RMK CU1AC1CI1
SLP117=
```

Question 263: Which of the following statements is false?

1. The relative humidity is greater at CYXA than at CYXB.
2. If the temperature at both stations were to drop, then fog would occur first at A.
3. An athlete would find it more uncomfortable to run at CYXA than at CYXB.
4. The relative humidity at B is approximately 90%.

Question 264: Which of the following statements is true?

1. The pressure altitude is greater at CYXA than at CYXB.
2. The sea-level pressure at CYXA is 911.7 hectoPascals.
3. The lowest cloud at CYXA is at 7000 ASL.
4. The density altitude is greater at CYXA than at CYXB.

Question 265: The processes of water vapour becoming liquid water and water vapour becoming frost are known respectively as

1. evaporation and sublimation.
2. evaporation and deposition.
3. condensation and sublimation.
4. condensation and deposition.

Question 266: The saturated adiabatic lapse rate is

1. the rate at which the atmospheric pressure drops with altitude on a day when the relative humidity is 100%.
2. the altitude to which a parcel of air at sea-level must be raised before its moisture condenses.
3. the rate at which the temperature of a parcel of saturated air decreases as it rises through the atmosphere.
4. the rate at which the temperature of the atmosphere decreases with height on a day when the relative humidity is 100%.

Question 267: The dew point of a parcel of air is

1. the temperature to which it must be cooled to become stable.
2. the pressure to which it must be raised to become saturated.
3. the temperature above which it must be warmed to become non-saturated.
4. the temperature to which it must be warmed to become saturated.

6.6 Stability and Instability

Question 268: Which of the following is not likely to cause lifting in an unstable air mass?

1. The formation of stratus cloud.
2. A wind blowing onto the side of a hill.
3. Localised heating of the ground.
4. A rapidly-moving cold front.

Question 269: What types of cloud are normally associated with unstable air?

1. Cumulus clouds.
2. Cirrus clouds.
3. Layered clouds.
4. Stratus clouds.

Question 270: Which of the following conditions is most likely to lead to unstable air?

1. A temperature inversion.
2. A high environmental lapse rate.
3. A low environmental lapse rate.
4. A high saturated adiabatic lapse rate.

Question 271: What term is used to describe an air mass that continues to rise once that rise has started?

1. Unstable.
2. Stable.
3. Inversion.
4. Neutral.

6.7 Clouds

Question 272: The term "nimbus" means

1. thunder.
2. dark.
3. mid-level.
4. rain bearing.

Question 273: Contrails behind high-flying jet aircraft are a form of

1. altocumulus clouds.
2. cumulus fractus clouds.
3. nimbostratus clouds.
4. cirrostratus clouds.

Question 274: What type of cloud is associated with drizzle?

1. Stratus.
2. Cirrus.
3. Cumulonimbus.
4. Cumulus.

Question 275: A continuous layer of milky-looking, high cloud which is so thin that it is almost transparent is likely to be

1. altocumulus.
2. nimbostratus.
3. cirrostratus.
4. cumulonimbus.

Question 276: Cumulonimbus clouds are associated with

1. temperature inversions.
2. thunderstorms.
3. steady, light rain.
4. dry, settled weather.

Question 277: The term "virga" is used to describe precipitation

1. that is too light to appear on weather radar.
2. that evaporates before it reaches the ground.
3. that is a mixture of snow and ice pellets.
4. that falls from cirrus clouds.

Question 278: Cirrus clouds are composed of

1. small water droplets.
2. dust particles.
3. ice crystals.
4. super-cooled water droplets.

6.8 Surface-Based Layers

Question 279: A surface layer is called mist rather than fog when

1. the horizontal visibility is greater than 1 statute mile.
2. the depth of the layer is no greater than 1,000 ft.
3. the horizontal visibility is greater than 1 km.
4. the layer has persisted for no more than 1 hour in the southern domestic airspace, or 2 hours in the northern domestic airspace.

Question 280: Fog is

1. cumulus cloud at ground level.
2. altostratus cloud at ground level.
3. stratus cloud at ground level.
4. cirrus cloud at ground level.

Question 281: Fog is most likely to form when

1. the dew point and temperature are very widely separated.
2. the dew point and temperature are close together.
3. the dew point is greater than the temperature.
4. the dew point is much lower than the temperature.

Question 282: Fog that forms when warm, moist air is blown over a cooler surface is called

1. steam fog.
2. upslope fog.
3. radiation fog.
4. advection fog.

6.9 Turbulence

Question 283: Turbulence caused by air being warmed by a surface feature and rising through the atmosphere is known as

1. mechanical turbulence.
2. convective turbulence.
3. advective turbulence.
4. clear air turbulence.

Question 284: What degree of turbulence would normally be encountered when flying under an overcast of stratus cloud?

1. Severe.
2. Moderate.
3. Little or none.
4. Light.

Question 285: Which of the following is not a term used when reporting turbulence?

1. Moderate chop.
2. Severe turbulence.
3. Light turbulence.
4. Extensive turbulence.

Question 286: An aircraft is on final approach to a runway when a wind shear causes the headwind to become a strong tailwind. Unless corrective action is taken, this may cause the aircraft to

1. land a long way down the runway.
2. pitch nose-up.
3. rise above the glide path.
4. sink below the optimal glide path.

Question 287: A significant change in the speed or direction of the wind over a short distance is known as

1. wind vector.
2. wind shear.
3. wind correction.
4. backing.

6.10 Wind

Question 288: Generally, in the northern hemisphere, winds blow from areas of ______ to areas of ______ and deflect to the ______.

1. low pressure; high pressure; right
2. low pressure; high pressure; left
3. high pressure; low pressure; left
4. high pressure; low pressure; right

Question 289: An hour ago, the wind was reported as 32006KT and now it is reported as 30012KT. In the past hour the wind has

1. backed and strengthened.
2. veered and weakened.
3. veered and strengthened.
4. backed and weakened.

Question 290: Kingston airport lies close to the north shore of Lake Ontario and its main runway is 01/19. When there are no larger weather systems (e.g., areas of low pressure) close by, which runway would you expect to be in use in mid-afternoon in summer and why?

1. Runway 01, because of the off-shore breeze.
2. Runway 19, because of the off-shore breeze.
3. Runway 19, because of the on-shore breeze.
4. Runway 01, because of the on-shore breeze.

Question 291: During a climb from sea-level to 500 ft, you would expect the winds to

1. back and reduce in strength.
2. back and increase in strength.
3. veer and reduce in strength.
4. veer and increase in strength.

Question 292: On a surface analysis chart, the isobars being particularly close together in an area implies that the pressure gradient is

1. steep in that area and winds will be strong.
2. shallow in that area and winds will be weak.
3. shallow in that area and winds will be strong.
4. steep in that area and winds will be weak.

Question 293: Winds above 3,000 ft AGL tend to blow

1. at right angles to the isobars and clockwise around a low pressure.
2. parallel to the isobars and clockwise around a low pressure.
3. parallel to the isobars and counter-clockwise around a low pressure.
4. at right angles to the isobars and counter-clockwise around a low pressure.

6.11 Air Masses

Question 294: The term "continental" is used to describe an air mass which is

1. moist.
2. dry.
3. warm.
4. cold.

Question 295: The Continental Arctic air mass is

1. warm and wet.
2. warm and dry.
3. cold and dry.
4. cold and wet.

Question 296: In the winter the arctic front

1. does not move.
2. moves north.
3. converges with the polar front.
4. moves south.

Question 297: The polar front lies to the south of

1. the tropical air mass.
2. the polar air mass.
3. the Ferrel cell.
4. the arctic air mass.

6.12 Fronts

Question 298: It is summer and a pilot is about 50 miles in front of a cold front (i.e., in the warmer air) that is approaching at 15 knots. The warmer air mass is moist and unstable. What type of weather might she experience over the next few hours?

1. Cirrus clouds becoming altostratus and then stratus with rain.
2. Cumulus clouds, thunderstorms.
3. Nimbostratus with heavy rain until the front passes.
4. Stratus clouds developing into thunderstorms.

Question 299: A pilot is flying in the cooler air mass towards a warm front and is experiencing light ice pellets mixed with snow. What precipitation is probably occurring above him?

1. Freezing rain.
2. Hail.
3. Clear icing.
4. Snow.

Question 300: A pilot is flying a track of 330°M in Canada and passes through a cold front from the warmer air side to the cooler air side. To maintain his track he will need to

1. adjust his heading to the right.
2. reset his heading indicator from his GPS reading.
3. adjust his heading to the left.
4. continue on the same heading.

Question 301: A TROWAL occurs when

1. a cold front catches up with a warm front.
2. cold and warm fronts meet head on.
3. a warm front catches up with a cold front.
4. a low pressure area initially forms.

Question 302: When a body of warmer air moves north and overrides a body of cooler air, this is known as

1. a cold front.
2. a warm front.
3. a combined front.
4. an occluded front.

Question 303: A body of warmer air is moving north and overriding a body of cooler air. The front on a weather chart indicates the position

1. at the ground where the warmer and cooler air masses meet.
2. of the leading edge of the warmer air, typically 150 to 200 miles ahead of the boundary of the warmer air on the ground.
3. of the top of the cooler air mass being overridden.
4. of the maximum cloud thickness associated with the front.

6.13 Aircraft Icing

Question 304: During flight, ice is likely to form first on

1. light coloured parts of the airframe.
2. blunt objects such as wing struts.
3. sharp objects such as antennæ.
4. dark coloured parts of the airframe.

Question 305: Freezing rain is most likely to be associated with

1. an approaching warm front.
2. an approaching cold front.
3. very low temperatures (below −20°C).
4. moist, unstable air.

Question 306: When flying through freezing rain, what type of icing is likely to form on the aircraft?

1. Moderate to severe clear icing.
2. Light to moderate rime icing.
3. Rime icing if the temperature is below −20°C, otherwise clear icing.
4. Moderate to severe rime icing.

6.14 Thunderstorms

Question 307: What type of cloud is associated with a thunderstorm?

1. Cumulostratus (abbreviated to CS).
2. Cirrus (abbreviated to CI).
3. Cumulonimbus (abbreviated to CN).
4. Cumulonimbus (abbreviated to CB).

Question 308: A squall line is a line

1. drawn on a GFA to indicate the boundary between two different weather systems.
2. of severe thunderstorms, often associated with a cold front.
3. of light drizzle associated with the edge of a band of stratus cloud.
4. along which the jet stream is flowing.

Question 309: The most severe threat to aircraft taking off or landing when a thunderstorm is in the vicinity

1. is the increased possibility of clear icing.
2. is a sudden reduction in visibility.
3. is the increased possibility of rime icing.
4. are sudden changes in the wind direction.

Question 310: Weather radar detects _______ whereas sferics devices (e.g., Strikefinders, Stormscopes) detect _______.

1. clouds; lightning
2. precipitation; thunder
3. lightning; precipitation
4. precipitation; lightning

Question 311: Which of the following conditions are conducive to the creation of thunderstorms?

1. A moist, unstable air mass with an approaching cold front.
2. A low environmental lapse rate with an approaching cold front.
3. A moist, stable air mass with an approaching cold front.
4. An inversion at the surface with an approaching warm front.

Question 312: A pulse thunderstorm is

1. an isolated thunderstorm, usually weak and short-lasting.
2. an intense thunderstorm, caused by a strong wind-shear aloft.
3. a section of a squall line.
4. an intense thunderstorm, caused by a weak wind-shear aloft.

Chapter 7

Meteorology: Information Sources

Contents

7.1 Meteorological Services

Question 313: A METAR is a weather ________, a TAF is a weather ________ and a GFA is a weather ________.

1. forecast; report; report
2. report; forecast; report
3. forecast; forecast; forecast
4. report; forecast; forecast

Question 314: Which of the following information would not be contained within the ATIS of an aerodrome?

1. The station pressure at the aerodrome.
2. The identification of the runway(s) in use.
3. The surface wind speed and direction.
4. Details of local navigation devices that are out of service.

Question 315: How does a Flight Service Station (FSS) differ from a Flight Information Centre (FIC)?

1. Personnel at an FIC can provide DF steers to lost pilots.
2. There are many FICs, typically based at medium-sized airports, but only nine FSSs.
3. Personnel at an FSS may read weather information to a pilot but not interpret it.
4. The closest FSS can be contacted by dialling 1-866-WX-BRIEF or 1-866-GO-METEO on a telephone.

Question 316: A pilot with a Private Pilot Licence is intending to fly from Trois-Rivieres, QC, to Rutland, Vermont. The total distance is 170 NM and the anticipated air time is 1 hour 30 minutes. Which of the following statements is true?

1. The pilot must obtain a weather briefing from a flight service specialist because the flight is international; self-briefing is not adequate.
2. The pilot must obtain a weather briefing from a flight service specialist because the flight will take longer than 1 hour; self-briefing is not adequate.
3. The pilot must obtain a weather briefing from a flight service specialist because the flight is over 100 NM; self-briefing is not adequate.
4. The pilot does not need to obtain a weather briefing from a flight service specialist, self-briefing is adequate.

7.2 Aviation Weather Reports

Question 317: METARs are usually issued every

1. 8 hours (starting at 0600Z).
2. hour on the local time hour and when significant changes to the weather occur.
3. 6 hours (starting at 0000Z).
4. hour on the Zulu (UTC) hour and when significant changes to the weather occur.

Question 318: Consider the SIGMET given in figure B.19 on page 100. Why was this SIGMET issued?

1. Because all thunderstorms result in a SIGMET being issued.
2. It is a routine SIGMET, and these are always issued at 0000Z, 0600Z, 1200Z and 1800Z.
3. Because a meteorological event has occurred that may affect the safety of aircraft operations.
4. Because the phenomenon reported is happening within 50 nautical miles of an major airport (having a class C control zone).

Question 319: Consider the SIGMET given in figure B.19 on page 100. What does the SIGMET indicate?

1. A line of thunderstorms that has been observed from overhead the CYMW airport to overhead the CYTA airport and which is moving eastwards at 15 knots.
2. A line of thunderstorms that is predicted to occur between 2325Z and 0325Z.
3. A line of thunderstorms that is predicted to occur between 1623Z and 1703Z on the 25th of the month.
4. A line of thunderstorms that has been observed and which is moving eastwards at 15 knots.

Question 320: For questions 320 to 322, refer to the following METARs, both issued at the same time on the same day:

```
METAR CYTZ 130200Z AUTO 25002KT 9SM CLR
22/19 A3005 RMK SLP175=
METAR CYTR 130200Z 00000KT 15SM SKC
20/19 A3004 RMK SLP172=
```

The sea-level pressure at CYTZ is

1. 175 inches of mercury.
2. 175 millibars.
3. 917.2 millibars.
4. 1017.5 millibars.

Question 321: What do the METARs report about the cloud cover at 0200Z at CYTZ and CYTR?

1. There are no clouds at CYTR and no clouds below 12,000 ft ASL at CYTZ.
2. There are no clouds at CYTR and no clouds below 12,000 ft AGL at CYTZ.
3. There are no clouds at CYTZ and no clouds below 12,000 ft AGL at CYTR.
4. There is no cloud at either CYTZ or CYTR.

Question 322: At 0200Z, which airport had the higher relative humidity?

1. CYTR.
2. There is insufficient information in a METAR to determine relative humidity.
3. The relative humidity was the same at both airports.
4. CYTZ.

Question 323: An aerodrome is reported to be CAVOK. This means that there is no cloud above the aerodrome

1. lower than 5,000 ft AGL.
2. lower than 10,000 ft ASL.
3. lower than 1,000 ft AGL.
4. at all.

Question 324: For questions 324 to 327, consider the following PIREP.

```
UACN10 CYXU 151221 YZ
UA /OV YVV 180002 /TM 1220 /FL025 /TP C182
/TA 20 /WV 240006 /RM VSBY 4SM HZ
```

The observation was made at a

1. pressure altitude of 25,000 ft.
2. density altitude of 2,500 ft.
3. pressure altitude of 2,500 ft.
4. density altitude of 25,000 ft.

Question 325: The observation was taken at

1. 1221Z on the 15th of the month.
2. 1220Z on the 15th of the month.
3. 1512Z on the 21st of the month.
4. 12:21 local time on the 15th of the month.

Question 326: The observation was made

1. 18 miles from the YVV VOR.
2. overhead the YVV VOR.
3. 2 miles north of the YVV VOR.
4. 2 miles south of the YVV VOR.

Question 327: The wind speed and direction recorded in PIREP are

1. from the south at 2 knots.
2. towards the south at 2 knots.
3. from the north-east at 6 knots.
4. from the south-west at 6 knots.

Question 328: You are approaching Rocky Mountain House (CYRM) and notice in its CFS entry under COMM

```
LWIS (Pvt): 122.55
```

This means that by tuning your

1. VHF radio to 122.55 MHz, you can receive a spoken message describing the wind conditions, temperature, dew point and altimeter setting at CYRM.
2. VHF radio to 122.55 MHz, you can contact a weather observer who will read the latest METAR to you.
3. ADF to 122.55 kHz, you can receive a spoken message describing the wind conditions, temperature, dew point and altimeter setting at CYRM instead of the Morse Code identity.
4. VHF radio to 122.55 MHz, you can receive a spoken message describing the wind conditions, temperature, dew point, density altitude, visibility and altimeter setting at CYRM.

Question 329: The weather radar reports provided by Environment Canada are created by measuring

1. the strength and delay of echoes of radio waves reflected from precipitation.
2. the strength and delay of echoes of radio waves reflected from clouds.
3. the attenuation of transponder responses from aircraft flying in a particular area.
4. the rainfall or snowfall in a particular area over a period of 1 hour (in the southern domestic airspace), or 30 minutes (in the northern domestic airspace).

Question 330: Consider the following weather report.

```
SPECI CYKF 280038Z AUTO 22002KT 9SM
BKN012 13/12 A2956=
```

The term SPECI indicates that this is a

1. weather report specific to one aerodrome issued at the request of a pilot.
2. report generated specifically for the purposes of reporting a ceiling below the IFR minimum altitude.
3. report generated by an automated station rather than a human observer.
4. special weather report issued other than in the normal hourly sequence.

Question 331: Consider the following METAR.

```
METAR CYMX 140000Z 22002KT 25SM FEW045
FEW240 24/18 A3008 RMK SC1CI1 SLP187=
```

The types of cloud observed at CYMX at 0000Z were

1. cirrus above strato-cumulus.
2. cirro-stratus and lenticular.
3. stratified ceiling and cumulo-interruptus.
4. strato-cumulus above cirrus.

Question 332: Refer to the METAR in figure B.18 on page 100. At 2100Z, the sea-level pressure at CYOW was

1. 29.72 inches of mercury.
2. higher than 29.72 inches of mercury.
3. 1007.0 millibars.
4. lower than 29.72 inches of mercury.

Question 333: Refer to the METAR in figure B.18 on page 100. The winds at CYOW at 2200Z were blowing at

1. 24 knots from 330°T and gusting to 29 knots.
2. 24 knots from 330°M and gusting to 29 knots.
3. 24 knots to 330°T and gusting to 29 knots.
4. 24 knots to 330°M and gusting to 29 knots.

Question 334: In a METAR the term *MIFG* means

1. drifting smoke.
2. shallow fog.
3. moderate intensity fog.
4. patches of fog.

Question 335: Consider the following METAR

```
METAR CYSN 151108Z CCA 00000KT 6SM BCFG
FEW070 20/19 A3012 RMK AC2 SLP199=
```

If the observer found at 1115Z that she had made an error in this METAR and issued a correction, then the correction would be

1. indicated by the date and time being set to 151115Z.
2. indicated by the inclusion of the term CORR.
3. indicated by the inclusion of a CCB term.
4. indicated by the inclusion of the term AMD.

7.3 Aviation Forecasts

Question 336: The validity times on the next set of GFAs to be issued after that shown in figure B.8 on page 95 are

1. 1200Z and 0000Z on the 23rd August and 1200Z on the 24th of August.
2. 1200Z on the 23rd August and 0000Z and 1200Z on the 24th of August.
3. 1800Z, 0000Z and 0600Z on the 23rd August.
4. 1800Z on the 23rd August and 0000Z and 0600Z on the 24th of August.

Question 337: In the GFA in figure B.8 on page 95, the dashed line running southeastward in the top left-hand corner indicates

1. a warm front emanating from an area of low pressure off the north-west corner of the GFA.
2. a TROWAL emanating from an area of high pressure off the north-west corner of the GFA.
3. a TROWAL emanating from an area of low pressure off the north-west corner of the GFA.
4. a cold front emanating from an area of low pressure off the north-west corner of the GFA.

Question 338: On the GFA in figure B.9 on page 96 the area marked H to the east of James Bay (to the right of the picture)

1. indicates an area of high pressure (075 hectoPascals) moving north-eastwards at 10 miles per hour.
2. indicates the position where the icing level is highest within an area bounded by 5° lines of latitude and longitude.
3. indicates an area of high pressure (1020 millibars) moving north-eastwards at 10 knots.
4. indicates an area with a high probability of icing.

Question 339: On the GFA in figure B.9, the line marked [075] that passes just south of the H to the east of James Bay (at the two o'clock position) connects points where the

1. freezing level is forecast to be at 7,500 ft ASL.
2. atmospheric pressure is forecast to be 907.5 millibars.
3. 850 millibar pressure level is forecast to be at 7,500 ft ASL.
4. 850 millibar pressure level is forecast to be at 7,500 ft AGL.

Question 340: The large H towards the north east corner of the GFA in figure B.8 on page 95 represents a high pressure area with a

1. station pressure of 102.0 cm of mercury.
2. sea-level pressure of 102.0 cm of mercury.
3. sea-level pressure of 1020 mbars.
4. station pressure of 1020 hectoPascals.

Question 341: The IFR outlook in figure B.8 on page 95 indicates that IFR conditions will prevail between 00Z and 12Z

1. to the west of Hudson Bay due to low ceilings and visibility.
2. in the onshore flow from Hudson Bay due to low ceilings and visibility.
3. in the onshore flow from Hudson Bay due to thunderstorms and mist.
4. over Hudson Bay due to reduced ceilings and visibility.

Question 342: Refer to the TAF for CYYZ given in figure B.21 on page 100. The TAF was issued at ______ and is valid for ______.

1. 2211Z on 30th of the month; 6 hours
2. 1130Z on 22nd of the month; 6 hours
3. 1130Z on 22nd of the month; 30 hours
4. 1130Z on 22nd of the month; 6 hours

Question 343: Refer to the TAF for CYYZ in figure B.21 on page 100. What is the earliest that a ceiling is forecast to exist at CYYZ?

1. 1400Z on the 22nd of the month.
2. 1200Z on the 23rd of the month.
3. 2000Z on the 22nd of the month.
4. 1400Z on the 23rd of the month.

Question 344: Refer to the TAF for CYYZ given in figure B.21 on page 100. What is the earliest time for which the possibility of thunderstorms is forecast for CYYZ?

1. 1400Z on the 22nd of the month.
2. 1400Z on the 23rd of the month.
3. 2100Z on the 22nd of the month.
4. 2000Z on the 22nd of the month.

Question 345: Refer to the TAF for CYYZ given in figure B.21 on page 100. The local time zone time at CYYZ is UTC - 5 hours. You are thinking of departing CYYZ at 07:00 local time on the 23rd of the month. At that time winds from ________ and a broken layer of cloud at ________ can be expected.

1. 330°M at 7 knots; 2,000 ft ASL
2. 330°T at 7 knots; 4,000 ft ASL
3. 330°T at 7 knots; 2,000 ft AGL
4. 330°M at 7 knots; 2,000 ft AGL

Question 346: Refer to the TAF for CYYZ given in figure B.21 on page 100. The local time zone time at CYYZ is UTC - 5 hours. The next forecast will be issued at or before

1. 17:15 local time on the 23rd of the month.
2. 10:00 local time on the 22nd of the month.
3. 20:00 local time on the 22nd of the month.
4. 15:00 local time on the 22nd of the month.

Question 347: Refer to the TAF for CYYZ, an airport in the southern domestic airspace, given in figure B.21 on page 100. How is the wind forecast to change between 1200Z and 1500Z on the 23rd of the month?

1. It will veer and decrease in strength.
2. It will back and decrease in strength.
3. It will back and increase in strength.
4. It will veer and increase in strength.

Question 348: On the GFA in figure B.9, what type of the turbulence is anticipated within the shaded area to the east of Hudson Bay in the 12 o'clock position?

1. No turbulence below 300 ft AGL.
2. Moderate from a low-level jet stream up to 300 ft AGL.
3. Moderate mechanical turbulence from the surface to 3,000 ft AGL.
4. Severe mechanical turbulence from the surface to 3,000 ft ASL.

Question 349: In the GFA shown in figure B.8, the weather forecast for the area around the western shore of James Bay and southern Hudson's Bay (the 10 o'clock position in the figure) is

1. broken cloud from 6,000 to 16,000 ft ASL with isolated altocumulus castellanus based at 20,000 ft ASL.
2. broken cloud from 6,000 to 16,000 ft AGL with isolated altocumulus castellanus reaching to 20,000 ft ASL.
3. broken cloud from 600 to 1,600 ft ASL with isolated altocumulus castellanus based at 20,000 ft ASL.
4. broken cloud from 6,000 to 16,000 ft ASL with isolated altocumulus castellanus reaching to 20,000 ft ASL.

Question 350: Consider the upper winds forecast for Jasper, Alberta given in figure B.7 on page 94. What is the approximate forecast freezing level over Jasper at 0000Z on the 24th of the month?

1. Just below 9,000 ft AGL.
2. The upper winds forecast does not state a freezing level.
3. 6,000 ft ASL.
4. Just below 9,000 ft ASL.

Question 351: Consider the upper winds forecast for Jasper, Alberta given in figure B.7 on page 94. The forecast wind at 6,000 ft ASL at 1800Z on the 23rd of the month is

1. 99 knots from true north (000°T).
2. light and variable.
3. 6 knots from true north (000°T).
4. 99 knots from magnetic north (000°M).

Question 352: Consider the upper winds forecast for Jasper, Alberta given in figure B.7 on page 94. The forecast lapse rate between 6000 and 12,000 ft ASL at 0000Z on the 24th of the month

1. cannot be determined without knowing the humidity of the air.
2. is the same as the standard lapse rate.
3. is less than the standard lapse rate.
4. is greater than the standard lapse rate.

Question 353: Consider the upper winds forecast for Jasper, Alberta given in figure B.7 on page 94. No values are given in the 3,000 ft column because

1. winds are expected to be light and variable at 3,000 ft.
2. the synoptic conditions did not allow the forecaster to produce a prediction for 3,000 ft.
3. Jasper is higher than 1,500 ft ASL.
4. the temperature is forecast to be above +10°C.

7.4 Weather Maps and Prognostic Charts

Question 354: The term QS placed close to a Low Pressure on a surface analysis chart means

1. Qualified Surface.
2. Quasi-Stationary.
3. Quadratic Sieve.
4. Qualified Subsidence.

Question 355: A line on a weather map with semi-circles spread along it indicates the position of a

1. TROWAL.
2. cold front.
3. trough of low pressure.
4. warm front.

Question 356: The three symbols in figure B.16 on page 99, from left to right, are used on weather charts to represent

1. ice pellets, thunderstorm and severe icing.
2. freezing rain, thunderstorm and ice pellets.
3. severe turbulence, thunderstorm and fog.
4. freezing drizzle, thunderstorm and ice pellets.

Question 357: On an upper air chart (e.g., 850 mb chart), lines join points having the same

1. temperature (in °C).
2. height (in decametres).
3. visibility (in statute miles).
4. pressure (in millibars).

Question 358: Surface analysis charts are issued

1. four times per day at 0400Z and then every 6 hours.
2. four times per day at 0000Z and then every 6 hours.
3. eight times per day at 0000Z and then every 3 hours.
4. six times per day at 0000Z and then every 4 hours.

Chapter 8

Navigation

Contents

8.1 Definitions

Question 359: The difference between a *rhumb line* and a *great circle* is that

1. a rhumb line is the shortest distance between two points.
2. a great circle is a straight line on a map with cylindrical projection.
3. an aircraft flying along a great circle changes track continuously.
4. a rhumb line is the quickest way to fly between two points.

Question 360: The *prime meridian* is

1. the line of longitude that passes through Greenwich in London, UK.
2. another name for the international date line.
3. the point on the earth's surface where the sun is directly overhead.
4. the line of latitude that passes through Greenwich in London, UK.

Question 361: The *equator* is

1. parallel to the international date line.
2. the circle of latitude passing through Greenwich.
3. a line of longitude.
4. a great circle.

Question 362: A track of 135° is towards the

1. south-east.
2. south-west.
3. north-west.
4. north-east.

Question 363: An aircraft is flying on a track of 095°M and the wind is reported to be 130°M at 20 knots. Under these circumstances the aircraft's groundspeed will be _______ than its airspeed and its heading will be more ______ than its track.

1. greater; southerly
2. less; southerly
3. less; northerly
4. greater; northerly

Question 364: Latitude and longitude are measured in degrees, minutes and seconds. There are _____ minutes in a degree and _____ seconds in a minute.

1. 60; 60
2. 10; 10
3. 60; 10
4. 10; 60

8.2 Maps and Charts

Question 365: Which of the common aviation maps are not Lambert conformal conical projections?

1. HI charts.
2. VTAs.
3. LO charts.
4. VNCs.

Question 366: 10 cm on a VNC represents ______ on the ground.

1. 5 nautical miles
2. 50 km
3. 25 km
4. 100 km

Question 367: The great circle between point A and point B is

1. a circle on the surface of the earth passing through A, B and the north pole.
2. a line of latitude passing through either A or B.
3. a circle centred on A passing through B.
4. a circle with its centre at the centre of the earth passing through A and B.

Question 368: A nautical mile is the distance of one

1. minute of longitude.
2. minute of latitude.
3. degree of latitude.
4. degree of longitude.

Question 369: The projection of a VNC is

1. Lambert cylindrical equal-area.
2. transverse Mercator.
3. dymaxion.
4. Lambert conformal conical.

Question 370: To determine whether a VNC is current or out-of-date it is best to check the

1. issue date on the cover and add 6 months.
2. latest version available at the pilot supply store.
3. expiry date on the cover.
4. Nav Canada web site.

Question 371: The Lambert conformal conical projection is used for many aviation charts because

1. a straight line on such a chart is exactly a great circle on the ground.
2. a straight line on such a chart is close to being a great circle on the ground.
3. when flying along a straight line drawn on such a chart, an aircraft will maintain a constant heading.
4. this projection preserves area.

Question 372: Consider the section of a VNC provided with this book. What is shown on the map at N44 56 45, W75 56 29?

1. Smith Falls aerodrome.
2. Massena aerodrome.
3. Morrisburg aerodrome.
4. Smiths Falls NDB.

Question 373: Consider the section of a VNC provided with this book. What is shown on the map at N44 21 53, W79 18 00?

1. Orillia Aerodrome.
2. Georgina Island.
3. Four Mile Lake.
4. Lindsay Aerodrome.

Question 374: Consider the section of a VNC provided with this book. About 7 NM to the west of Kingston aerodrome (44.23° N 76.60° W) on the north shore of Lake Ontario there is a circle passing close to the town of Bath. This circle indicates

1. a class D terminal control area.
2. class F restricted airspace.
3. class F advisory airspace.
4. a control zone.

Question 375: Consider the section of a VNC provided with this book. On the southern shore of Rice Lake (44° 07' N 78° 14' W), there is a circle enclosing a cross entitled Gore's Landing. This indicates a

1. target used by military aircraft for bombing practice.
2. helicopter landing pad.
3. disused aerodrome.
4. float plane base.

Question 376: Consider the section of a VNC provided with this book. About 18 NM to the north-west of Kingston aerodrome (N44 13 31 W76 35 49), there is a lake labelled as Camden Lake. You are flying directly over the centre of this lake and want to make a position report. Which of the following is your current position?

1. N44 26, W76 52.
2. N45 26, W77 08.
3. N44 26, W77 08.
4. N44 56, W76 52.

Question 377: Consider the section of a VNC provided with this book. There is a dashed line running approximately North/South close to the eastern edge of Lake Ontario, labelled 13°W. This is an ------ line indicating that, at points along the line, --------.

1. isogonal; true north lies 13° west of magnetic north
2. agonic; magnetic north lies 13° west of true north.
3. isogonal; magnetic north lies 13° west of true north
4. agonic; true north lies 13° west of magnetic north

Question 378: Consider the section of a VNC provided with this book. At the Simcoe navigation device (N44 14 W79 10), there are two symbols: a hexagon and a square. These indicate respectively that the device is

1. a VOR and an NDB.
2. an NDB.
3. a VOR and a DME.
4. a DME and a VOR.

Question 379: Using the section of a VNC provided with this book, consider the information given for Kingston airport (44° 14' N 76° 36' W): *305* [*L*] *50M 122.5*. This means that Kingston airport

1. has a Mandatory Frequency of 305 kHz.
2. is 122.5 ft ASL.
3. has a runway between 4,950 and 5,050 ft in length.
4. has a runway between 4,970 and 5,069 ft in length.

Question 380: Using the section of VNC enclosed with this book, consider V300-308, the airway that runs south-westward from the Ottawa VORTAC (YOW: 45.45°N 75.90°W) to the Coehill DME/VOR (VIE: 44.67°N 77.88°W). The track of this airway out of the Ottawa VOR is 256°, and the track out of Coehill is 072°. Although these are reciprocal tracks along the airway, they do not differ by 180° because

1. a straight line on a VNC does not represent a constant track.
2. the VOR radials are not always aligned perfectly accurately.
3. the magnetic variations of the two locations are different.
4. all of the above.

Question 381: Consult the section of VNC enclosed with this book, How far is it from Kingston aerodrome (N44 13 31 W76 35 39) to Toronto City Centre aerodrome (N43 37 39 W79 23 46)?

1. 138.4 nautical miles.
2. 145.2 statute miles.
3. 126.2 statute miles.
4. 145.2 nautical miles.

Question 382: Consult the section of VNC supplied with this book. A reasonable approximation of the track from Kingston aerodrome (N44 13 31 W76 35 39) to Toronto City Centre aerodrome (N43 37 39 W79 23 46) is

1. 085° Magnetic.
2. 265° True.
3. 265° Magnetic.
4. 085° True.

Question 383: About 5 NM to the north-west of Kingston aerodrome (N44 13 31 W76 35 39) on the section of VNC supplied with this book, there is a tower labelled "763 (300)". This means that the

1. tower is 763 ft tall.
2. top of the tower is 763 ft AGL.
3. height of the ground at the base of the tower is 463 ft ASL.
4. height of the ground at the base of the tower is 463 ft AGL.

Question 384: The dashed line of radius 5 NM around the Kingston aerodrome (44° 13' 31" N 76° 35' 49" W) on the section of VNC supplied with this book indicates

1. the extent of a class E control zone.
2. the area from which boats with masts over 32 ft ASL are excluded.
3. that parachuting activity takes place at Kingston.
4. the extent of a class D control zone.

Question 385: Which of the following is not (part of) a great circle?

1. The Greenwich meridian.
2. The arctic circle.
3. The 76°W line of longitude.
4. The equator.

8.3 Time and Longitude

Question 386: Although the boundaries of time zones are irregular, each zone is, on average, ______ of longitude wide.

1. 1°
2. 15°
3. 30°
4. 10°

Question 387: Consider the entry from the CFS for Bear Lake Lookout in figure B.10 on page 97. In mid summer the local (clock or time zone) time at 1300Z would be

1. 9 o'clock in the evening.
2. 1 o'clock in the afternoon.
3. 9 o'clock in the morning.
4. 7 o'clock in the morning.

8.4 Pilot Navigation

Question 388: For questions 388 to 397 refer the VNC provided. How far is it from the Peterborough aerodrome (N44 13 48 W78 21 48) to Plevna/Land O'Lakes (N44 54 58 W76 56 09) and what is the track between these two aerodromes?

1. 84.7 nautical miles, 055° true.
2. 73.6 nautical miles, 055° true.
3. 84.7 nautical miles, 055° magnetic.
4. 73.6 nautical miles, 055° magnetic.

Question 389: What is the minimum visibility required to depart from the Peterborough aerodrome on a VFR flight plan?

1. 1 statute mile.
2. 2 statute miles.
3. 5 statute miles.
4. 3 statute miles.

Question 390: You pass over the Peterborough aerodrome at 1230Z on your way to Plevna/Land O'Lakes. At 1242Z, you pass Norwood aerodrome. What is your groundspeed and at what time do you expect to be over Plevna?

1. 85 knots, 1322Z.
2. 85 knots, 1412Z.
3. 85 mph, 1322Z.
4. 42 knots, 1403Z.

Question 391: You pass over the Peterborough aerodrome on your way to Plevna/Land O'Lakes. At the altitude you are flying, you find you need to maintain a heading of 075°M to fly the track of 067°M. The weather ahead of you is deteriorating and you decide to turn around and return to Peterborough. What would be a reasonable heading to adopt initially?

1. 239°M.
2. 247°M.
3. 067°M.
4. 255°M.

Question 392: Without an onboard GPS, a pilot flies over the Peterborough aerodrome on his way to Plevna/Land O'Lakes. After some time he becomes "uncertain of his position". Which of the following would not be a suitable way of finding his position?

1. To take bearings off Coehill and Watertown VORs.
2. To ask Kingston FSS to provide him with a DF steer.
3. To contact Trenton Terminal on 128.4 MHz and ask the controller to locate him on radar.
4. Squawk 7400 (meaning "aircraft lost") and listen on a frequency of 121.5 MHz for instructions.

Question 393: How far is it from the Lindsay aerodrome (N44 21 53 W78 47 02) to the Midland/Huronia aerodrome (N44 41 00 W79 55 42) and what is the track between these two aerodromes?

1. 52.6 SM, 303°T.
2. 52.6 NM, 303°T.
3. 52.6 NM, 303°M.
4. 52.6 SM, 303°M.

Question 394: You pass over the Lindsay aerodrome (N44 21 53 W78 47 02) at 1635Z on your way to Midland/Huronia (N44 41 00 W79 55 42). At 1644Z you fly over the eastern shoreline of Lake Simcoe. What is your groundspeed, and at what time do you expect to be over Midland/Huronia?

1. 113 knots, 1713Z.
2. 113 knots, 1703Z.
3. 113 mph, 1703Z.
4. 103 knots, 1713Z.

Question 395: You pass over the Lindsay aerodrome (N44 21 53 W78 47 02) on your way to Midland/Huronia (N44 41 00 W79 55 42). At the altitude you are flying, you find you need to maintain a heading of 315°M to fly the track of 303°M. The weather ahead of you is deteriorating and you decide to turn around and return to Lindsay. What would be a reasonable heading to adopt initially?

1. 140°M.
2. 111°M.
3. 123°M.
4. 135°M.

Question 396: To the west of Kingston airport (N44 13 31 W76 35 49) there are large figures 1^1. This means that, within the rectangle of latitude and longitude,

1. it is safe to fly at 1,100 ft ASL.
2. there is no terrain higher than 1,100 ft ASL.
3. there is no known terrain or obstacle higher than 1,100 ft AGL.
4. there is no known terrain or obstacle higher than 1,100 ft ASL.

Question 397: Close to the top-left-hand corner of the rectangle of latitude and longitude identified in question 396, there is a dot with the associated number 675. This dot indicates that

1. a mast rising to 675 ft ASL is situated at that position.
2. there is a Dialed Remote Communications Outlet (DRCO) at that location that can be activated on 675 kHz.
3. triangulation point 675, used when creating the map, is located at that position.
4. the highest known point in the rectangle is 675 ft ASL.

Question 398: The difference between the track and heading of an aircraft is that

1. the track is the direction in which the aircraft is pointing; the heading is the direction it is travelling across the ground.
2. heading is used in the northern domestic airspace; track is used in the southern.
3. the heading is measured in degrees magnetic; the track is measured in degrees true.
4. the heading is the direction in which the aircraft is pointing; the track is the direction it is travelling across the ground.

Question 399: You have drawn your desired track line on a VNC for a 200 NM trip. When measuring the track it

1. is best to measure close to the centre of the track.
2. is best to measure the track from the departure aerodrome.
3. is best to measure the track into the destination aerodrome.
4. does not matter where the track is measured, it is the same all along the line.

Question 400: An aircraft is flying a heading of 343° and turns 95° to the right. Its new heading is

1. 248°.
2. 095°.
3. 438°.
4. 078°.

Question 401: Airport A lies directly south of airport B. Airport A's latitude is N45 36 and airport B's latitude is N46 40. What is the distance and track from A to B?

1. 64 statute miles, 360° True.
2. 64 nautical miles, 360° True.
3. 104 nautical miles, 360° True.
4. 64 nautical miles, 360° Magnetic.

Question 402: You intend to fly VFR to an aerodrome for lunch. You estimate that the outgoing flight will take 1 hour 20 minutes. You then intend to spend 40 minutes on the ground before flying back. The return trip should take 1 hour 10 minutes. The estimated time *en route* that you should enter on your flight plan is

1. 3 hours 30 minutes.
2. 2 hours 30 minutes.
3. 1 hour 20 minutes.
4. 3 hours 10 minutes.

Question 403: An aircraft is equipped with a mode C transponder, an ADF, a VOR receiver capable of receiving a localiser and glide slope, a VHF radio and a handheld GPS. This would be entered into the equipment code box of a VFR flight plan as

1. S/C.
2. SA/C.
3. SG/C.
4. S/T.

Question 404: You are flying a 150 nautical mile west-bound cross-country along a great circle. After 45 minutes you are 100 NM from your departure point, but 6° north of your intended track. If this error is only because the wind was not as forecast, which of the following techniques could you use to get back on track?

1. The half-track estimation method: turn right 6°.
2. The double track error method: turn left 12°.
3. The opening and closing angle method.
4. The double track error method: turn right 12°.

Question 405: Given the true heading and track that an aircraft is flying, and its groundspeed and true airspeed, a wind triangle can be used to find

1. the calibrated airspeed of the aircraft and the speed of the wind.
2. the speed of the wind and the magnetic track of the aircraft.
3. the speed and direction of the wind.
4. the direction of the wind and the magnetic heading of the aircraft.

8.5 Navigation Computers

Question 406: Consider the upper winds forecast for Jasper, Alberta, given in figure B.7 on page 94. You will pass over Jasper at 1800Z on the 23rd of the month and will need to fly a track of 090°T at 6,000 ft ASL. Your aircraft has a true airspeed of 115 knots. What heading should you fly and what groundspeed can you expect to achieve?

1. 087°T and 115 knots.
2. 031°M and 58.5 knots.
3. 031°T and 58.5 knots.
4. 090°T and 115 knots.

Question 407: An aircraft is flying a heading of 120° at 100 KIAS. Its track is 115° and it has a groundspeed of 112 knots. Which of the following might be the direction of the wind?

1. 090°.
2. 010°.
3. 210°.
4. 120°.

Question 408: You are flying at 140 knots true airspeed along a track of 100°M with a heading of 095°M. You decide to reduce your airspeed to 100 knots. To maintain the same track you will need to

1. turn to the right.
2. continue on the same heading.
3. turn to the left.
4. turn through 180°.

Question 409: You need to fly a track of 120° true and the upper winds at your altitude are forecast to be from 320° true at 25 knots. You fly at a true airspeed of 105 knots. What heading should you use, and what groundspeed will you achieve?

1. A heading of 115° and airspeed of 128 knots.
2. A heading of 125° and groundspeed of 128 knots.
3. A heading of 128° and groundspeed of 115 knots.
4. A heading of 115° and groundspeed of 128 knots.

Question 410: You are flying at a pressure altitude of 6,500 ft, the outside air temperature is −12°C and your calibrated airspeed is 95 knots. Your true airspeed is

1. 102 knots.
2. 105 knots.
3. 88 knots.
4. 95 knots.

Question 411: You have just flown between two checkpoints, 25 NM apart, in 14 minutes. Your groundspeed is

1. 107 knots.
2. 107 miles per hour.
3. 104 miles per hour.
4. 179 knots.

Question 412: Your groundspeed is 115 knots. How long will it take to fly between two checkpoints 38 NM apart?

1. About 25 minutes.
2. About 20 minutes.
3. About 15 minutes.
4. About 28 minutes.

Question 413: With the mixture properly leaned, your aircraft burns 7.2 gallons of fuel per hour. You plan to cruise for 256 NM at a groundspeed of 107 knots. How much fuel do you expect to burn in cruise?

1. 17.2 gallons.
2. 16 gallons.
3. 14.8 gallons.
4. 10.7 gallons.

Question 414: An airport is at 300 ft ASL and its sea-level pressure is 30.35 inches of mercury and the temperature is −20°C. What are the pressure and density altitudes of the airport?

1. 94 ft below sea level; 4,614 ft below sea level.
2. 694 ft ASL; 3,610 ft below sea level.
3. 694 ft below sea level; 4,614 ft below sea level.
4. 94 ft below sea level; 3,100 ft below sea level.

Question 415: You are cruising at a pressure altitude of 6,500 ft, the outside air temperature is −8°C and your calibrated airspeed is 99 knots. What is your true airspeed?

1. 91 knots.
2. 99 knots.
3. 111 knots.
4. 107 knots.

Question 416: Consider the CFS entry for Fort Cushing given in figure B.11 on page 98. You are approaching Fort Cushing and learn from the METAR at a near-by airport that surface winds are 290° at 15 knots. What headwind and cross-wind can you expect when landing on runway 25?

1. 12 knot headwind and 10 knot crosswind from the left.
2. 12 knot headwind and 10 knot crosswind from the right.
3. 14 knot headwind and 5 knot crosswind from the right.
4. 14 knot headwind and 5 knot crosswind from the left.

8.6 Pre-Flight Preparation

Question 417: Consider the CFS entry in figure B.10 on page 97. Before departing on a flight to Bear Lake Lookout in winter, whom would you contact to get a report on the condition of the runway?

1. The township of Bear Lake Lookout.
2. Flight services.
3. Reg, the owner of the aerodrome.
4. Air traffic control at CYXZ.

Question 418: The types of NOTAM are

1. National, Control Zone and Aerodrome.
2. National, Flight Information Region and Aerodrome.
3. North Atlantic, Flight Information Region and Aerodrome.
4. National, IFR and VFR.

Question 419: You are planning a night VFR flight and estimate that it will take 16 minutes to climb to cruise altitude with a fuel burn of 10 US gals/hr. Cruise and descent will take a further 1 hour 45 minutes with a fuel burn of 7 US gals/hr. What is the minimum total fuel you need on board when you take off?

1. 17.5 US gallons.
2. 20.3 US gallons.
3. 23.2 US gallons.
4. 15.0 US gallons.

Question 420: You are planning a 350 NM westbound flight and realise that the centre of a low pressure system is likely to lie very slightly to the north of the direct route. During your flight planning you should plan

1. to fly south of the centre of the low pressure.
2. to fly north of the centre of the low pressure.
3. to fly directly through the centre of the low pressure.
4. not to depart until the low pressure fills.

Question 421: For this question and question 422, consider the following NOTAM:

```
090070 CYTZ TORONTO/CITY CENTRE
CYTZ LDG RWY 15 AND TKOF RWY 33 NOT AUTH
0905011108 TIL APRX 0908041600
```

The term TIL APRX in the NOTAM indicates

1. that the time at which the NOTAM will be cancelled will not be known until 0908041600.
2. that you should assume the NOTAM is in effect for a period of 1 hour after 0908041600.
3. that a cancelling NOTAM will have to be issued.
4. that the NOTAM does not come into effect until approximately 0908041600.

Question 422: Landing on runway 15 is not authorised after

1. 0905Z on November 1st, 2008.
2. 0905Z on November 8th, 2001.
3. 1108Z on May 9th, 2001.
4. 1108Z on May 1st, 2009.

Question 423: The entry from the CFS in figure B.10 on page 97 indicates that the lighting on runway 22 consists of

1. threshold lights showing green on approach with medium intensity runway edge lights.
2. sequenced flashing white lights leading to the runway.
3. blue runway edge lights.
4. lights along the centre of the runway.

Question 424: For a night VFR flight, the amount of fuel to be carried in a light, propeller-driven aircraft must be no less than that required to complete the flight, taking into account anticipated delays and then to fly at cruise speed for ______ minutes.

1. 45
2. 30
3. 60
4. 90

8.7 Radio Theory

Question 425: The following radio frequencies are used in the area around Winnipeg: 248 kHz, 115.5 MHz, 118.3 MHz and 1575.42 MHz. Respectively, they are used for

1. NDB, Talking to Tower, VOR, GPS.
2. NDB, Glide Slope, VOR, GPS.
3. NDB, VOR, Talking to Tower, GPS.
4. GPS, VOR, Talking to Tower, NDB.

Question 426: The main advantage of using VHF rather than HF radio equipment in an aircraft for communications is that it

1. can be driven from the aircraft's DC power supply.
2. allows voice rather than just Morse code to be transmitted.
3. is generally smaller and lighter.
4. allows particular frequencies to be tuned digitally.

Question 427: The VHF frequency of 121.5 MHz is used for

1. air-to-air chat.
2. making position reports.
3. contacting flight service stations.
4. emergency communications.

Question 428: Which of these statements about radio waves is false?

1. Radio waves travel in straight lines.
2. Higher frequency signals tend to have a longer range.
3. Shorter wavelengths are associated with lower frequencies.
4. Radio waves travel at the speed of light.

8.8 VHF Omnidirection Range (VOR)

Question 429: Before using a VOR for navigation, its integrity should be checked by ensuring that

1. it is the only VOR within a radius of $1.23\sqrt{h}$ nautical miles where h the altitude of the aircraft.
2. the OFF flag disappears when the VOR is tuned.
3. the aircraft is pointing to within 15° of the VOR.
4. the Morse code identifier is the same as the value printed on the map.

Question 430: A pilot is flying directly to a VOR with the CDI centred. She can detect when she passes over the VOR by observing

1. the needle that has been pointing directly upwards rotating to point directly downwards (the 6 o'clock position).
2. when the Morse code signal changes as a result of the Doppler shift.
3. the TO/FROM flag switching.
4. when the CDI moves to the full left position on the display.

Question 431: A pilot is flying 10 NM directly to the east of a VOR in the southern domestic airspace on a heading of 045°M. He tunes and identifies the VOR and turns the rotating course card to place 280° at the top. The CDI and flag will read

1. left deflection, FROM.
2. left deflection, TO.
3. right deflection, FROM.
4. right deflection, TO.

Question 432: A pilot is flying directly south of a VOR in the southern domestic airspace on a heading of 120°M. She tunes and identifies the VOR and centres the CDI with a TO flag showing. The value shown at the top of the rotating course card (OBS) is

1. 180.
2. 120.
3. 300.
4. 360.

Question 433: Consider the map provided with this book. You are within range of the Simcoe (N44 14 W79 10) and Coehill (N44 40 W77 53) VORs. With the CDI centred, Simcoe displays a FROM flag when 110° is placed at the top, and Coehill displays a TO flag with 040° at the top. Over which lake are you flying?

1. Rice Lake.
2. Round Lake.
3. Lake Simcoe.
4. Chemong Lake.

8.9 Automatic Direction Finder (ADF)

Question 434: A Cessna 150 is flying on a heading of 360° and is 55 nautical miles south of a VOR and 25 miles south of an NDB. The pilot has tuned and identified both transmitters and has adjusted her VOR receiver to centre the CDI with a TO flag. She makes a 180° turn to fly directly south. How will the indications change?

1. The CDI moves to full-scale deflection to the right with flag changing to FROM; the ADF needle moves to 6 o'clock.
2. No change on either the VOR or ADF.
3. No change on the VOR; the ADF needle moves to 6 o'clock.
4. No change on the CDI, but the flag switches to FROM and ADF needle moves to 6 o'clock.

Question 435: When homing to an NDB using an ADF, the integrity of the NDB signal can be determined by

1. checking the ADF flag to see whether it has flipped to OFF.
2. continuously monitoring the Morse code.
3. switching the ADF periodically to the BFO position and checking that the needle moves.
4. ensuring that the ADF needle remains pointing upwards.

Question 436: A pilot is flying on a heading of 045°M and tunes and identifies an NDB with her fixed card ADF. The ADF needle points to 170°. To fly directly away from the NDB she should turn to a direction of

1. 035°M.
2. 270°M.
3. 315°M.
4. 090°M.

Question 437: A pilot flies on a heading of 360° directly over an NDB that she has tuned and identified. As she passes over the NDB

1. the ADF needle will swing from pointing directly upwards to directly downwards.
2. the ADF needle will swing from pointing directly downwards (6 o'clock) to directly upwards (12 o'clock).
3. the ADF's TO/FROM flag will switch to FROM.
4. the ADF needle will move from pointing directly upwards to directly downwards and then swing to point upwards again.

8.10 Global Navigation Satellite System (GNSS)

Question 438: The basic principle on which the GPS operates is that the device in the aircraft

1. transmits a signal which is retransmitted by one or more satellites. The delay allows the unit to calculate its position.
2. receives signals from a number of geostationary satellites, each transmitting position information.
3. receives signals from a number of non-geostationary satellites, each transmitting the time.
4. receives signals from a number of non-geostationary satellites, each transmitting position information.

Question 439: A GPS receiver in an aircraft cannot measure

1. airspeed and heading.
2. groundspeed and altitude.
3. groundspeed and track.
4. altitude and track.

Question 440: The Wide-Area Augmentation System (WAAS)

1. is the improved algorithm used by modern GPS receivers to allow them to find the GPS satellites more rapidly when they are first switched on.
2. increases the range of GPS receivers by relaying the information from the GPS satellites through geo-stationary satellites.
3. provides correction signals to GPS receivers to make their calculated positions more accurate.
4. is the system whereby the GPS satellites can be seen from different points on the earth, including the southern hemisphere.

Question 441: Which of the following is not a genuine concern when navigating by GPS?

1. The signals from the GPS satellites can only be received if the sky is clear—cloud above the aircraft means that the signals cannot be received.
2. The locations of aerodromes and navigation beacons are sometimes incorrectly placed in the GPS database.
3. Occasionally insufficient GPS satellites are above the horizon for the GPS receiver to be able to calculate an accurate location.
4. Occasionally, although sufficient GPS satellites are above the horizon, their relative positions make it impossible for the GPS receiver to be able to calculate an accurate location.

8.11 Other Radio and Radar Aids

Question 442: A mode C transponder operates by

1. transmitting the altitude of the aircraft and the number dialled into the transponder when interrogated by secondary radar.
2. continuously transmitting the aircraft's altitude and position from the on-board GPS receiver.
3. continuously transmitting the altitude of the aircraft and the number dialled into the transponder.
4. transmitting the identity of the aircraft and the number dialled into the transponder when interrogated by secondary radar.

Question 443: VHF Direction Finding (DF) Assistance is

1. the service that ATC provides to locate aircraft fitted with transponders on request of the pilot-in-command.
2. an enhancement to GPS sometimes known as the Wide-Area Augmentation System.
3. a system provided by some Flight Service Stations by means of which the location of an aircraft can be roughly determined.
4. using VORs transmitting in the VHF range to navigate.

Question 444: At St John's International Airport, Newfoundland where the local time is UTC-3$\frac{1}{2}$, suitable local times for testing an ELT would be

1. 1125 to 1130 for no more than 5 seconds.
2. 1130 to 1135 for no more than 5 seconds.
3. 1155 to 1200 for no more than 5 seconds.
4. 1200 to 1205 for no more than 5 seconds.

Question 445: What is the difference between primary and secondary radar?

1. Primary radar is an interrogation of the aircraft's transponder, whereas secondary radar bounces radio waves off the metal of an aircraft and measures the time for them to reflect back to the transmitter.
2. Primary radar is radar used in the *en route* system, whereas secondary radar is lower-powered radar used by tower controllers.
3. Primary radar is a military system, whereas secondary radar is used to detect civil aircraft.
4. Primary radar bounces radio waves off the metal of an aircraft and measures the time for them to reflect back to the transmitter, whereas secondary radar is an interrogation of the aircraft's transponder.

Question 446: A mode C transponder obtains the aircraft's altitude for transmission from

1. an encoding altimeter that measures pressure altitude.
2. the time it takes for the interrogation signal to reach it.
3. the aircraft's altimeter, the reading being adjusted by the pilot setting the correct local pressure.
4. the aircraft's GPS receiver.

Question 447: When activated, an emergency locator transmitter

1. continuously broadcasts the aircraft's identity on 406 MHz and emits a "chirping" signal on 121.5 MHz.
2. broadcasts the aircraft's identity on 406 MHz and emits a "chirping" signal on 121.5 MHz whenever a SARSAT satellite is within range.
3. broadcasts the aircraft's identity on 121.5 MHz and emits a "chirping" signal on 406 MHz whenever a SARSAT satellite is within range.
4. continuously broadcasts the aircraft's identity on 121.5 MHz and emits a "chirping" signal on 406 MHz.

Chapter 9

Human Factors

Contents

9.1 Aviation Physiology

Question 448: When flying a light aircraft and looking for other aircraft, the best scanning technique is a

1. scan where the pilot's eyes focus on the windscreen itself, attempting to align a fixed point with the horizon.
2. continuous scan from the ten o'clock to the two o'clock position and back again.
3. scan from side to side where the pilot's eyes stop, focusing on each part of the sky in turn.
4. continuous scan from top to bottom of the windscreen while looking straight ahead.

Question 449: Which of the following statements about fatigue is true?

1. The effects of fatigue can be reduced by flying westward across time zones.
2. The effects of fatigue can be reduced by lowering the oxygen level in the blood.
3. Fatigue tends to make a pilot fix his attention on just a few things, excluding other important conditions.
4. Acute fatigue is a long-term phenomenon caused by an extended period without sleep.

Question 450: A pilot is used to landing on a wide and well-lit runway at a major airport. When landing on a narrow, poorly lit runway at night he must be aware that he might have the illusion of

1. being too low and therefore landing short of the runway.
2. being too low and therefore landing a long way down the runway.
3. being too high and therefore landing short of the runway.
4. being too high and therefore landing a long way down the runway.

Question 451: Which of the following statements about hyperventilation is not true?

1. Hyperventilation can be helped by slowing the breathing rate to 12 breaths per minute.
2. Hyperventilation often causes numbness or tingling in the hands, feet and lips.
3. Hyperventilation is caused by the reduced oxygen level in the atmosphere above 10,000 ft ASL.
4. Hyperventilation can be induced by stress.

Question 452: Hypoxia, as experienced by pilots flying at altitude,

1. can be cured by slowing the breathing rate to 12 breaths per minute.
2. causes a feeling of nausea.
3. cannot occur below 10,000 ft ASL.
4. is almost impossible for the affected pilot to detect.

Question 453: A pilot who smokes has

1. a decreased tolerance to positive and negative Gs.
2. an increased risk of injury when flying following SCUBA diving.
3. an increased risk of hypoxia at lower altitudes.
4. an increased chance of hyperventilation.

Question 454: Which of the following is a vestibular illusion?

1. When returning to straight flight after a prolonged turn in cloud, the aircraft appears to be banking in the opposite direction.
2. When landing on a narrow runway, the pilot has the illusion that she is too high.
3. When pulling out of a steep descent, the pilot's body appears to be much heavier than normal.
4. When banking close to the ground in a strong crosswind, the aircraft appears to be slipping when it is co-ordinated flight.

9.2 Operating Environment

Question 455: Which of the following does not result from consuming an alcoholic drink?

1. The eyes become more sensitive, possibly leading to pain in bright sunlight.
2. The body's reaction to hypoxia is exaggerated, causing hypoxic symptoms to appear at lower altitudes.
3. The fluid in the inner ear is affected, causing imbalance.
4. The brain is affected, causing impaired reaction time.

Question 456: A pilot has purchased an over-the-counter medication advertised as "100% natural" to treat a mild stomach upset. What action does she need to take if she intends to use the medication shortly before acting as pilot-in-command?

1. She should use the internet to make sure that the medication is genuinely 100% natural.
2. She should ensure that at least 8 hours passes between taking the medication and acting as pilot-in-command.
3. No special action is required as the medication is 100% natural.
4. She should consult her aviation medical examiner.

Question 457: The pilot of a light aircraft flying at 3,500 ft ASL is feeling dizzy, slightly nauseous and light-headed. A possible cause is

1. carbon monoxide from the engine's exhaust system leaking into the cabin.
2. hypoxia caused by the increased level of oxygen.
3. carbon dioxide from the engine's exhaust system leaking into the cabin.
4. hyperventilation caused by stress.

9.3 Aviation Psychology

Question 458: A low-time VFR pilot is using ATC's flight following service and has flown into deteriorating weather. He has now entered cloud and ATC has just called him. He needs to respond to ATC's call, concentrate on avoiding a spiral dive, tune the nearby VOR and devise a plan to get back into VFR conditions. Which of these four activities are the most and least important?

1. Avoid the spiral dive; respond to ATC.
2. Devise a plan; respond to ATC.
3. Avoid the spiral dive; tune the VOR.
4. Respond to ATC; tune the VOR.

Question 459: The steps in Benner's DECIDE model for decision making are

1. Determine Change, Evaluate Options, Choose Best Option, Implement Best Option, Drive Evaluation, Expedite Evaluation.
2. Determine Change, Evaluate Significance, Choose Possible Actions, Identify Required Outcome, Do the Best Action, Evaluate Result.
3. Determine Change, Evaluate Significance, Choose Outcome, Identify Possible Actions, Do the Best Action, Evaluate Result.
4. Determine Change, Evaluate Significance, Choose Outcome, Implement Outcome, Drive Evaluation, Expedite Evaluation.

Question 460: A pilot is flying towards deteriorating weather and has to decide whether to make a precautionary landing in a field. If he were to apply Benner's DECIDE model, what might be suitable for C: "Choose Outcome"?

1. The aircraft and occupants to be safe.
2. Selecting a field in the general area, turning 180° and returning to better weather, slowing the aircraft down, descending to the MOCA.
3. Recognising that the weather is deteriorating to a point where he is not comfortable.
4. The situation becoming significant rapidly.

Question 461: While doing his pre-flight checks in a Cessna 172, a pilot finds a large bolt lying on the ground under his aircraft. He decides to ignore it "because it's unlikely that it came from his aircraft and, even if it did, it is unlikely to be critical". The hazardous attitude he is primarily demonstrating is

1. invulnerability.
2. resignation.
3. anti-authoritarian.
4. impulsivity.

Question 462: It is often said that the last words of many pilots are "just watch this, I'll show you something spectacular". Such pilots may be demonstrating

1. an impulsive attitude.
2. a macho attitude.
3. a resigned attitude.
4. an anti-authoritarian attitude.

9.4 Pilot - Equipment Relationship

Question 463: Consider the section of the VNC included in this book. A pilot is flying to the Ottawa VOR (N45° 26.6', W075° 53.8') and thence to Kingston NDB (N44° 17.8', W76° 36.3'). When entering these waypoints into her GPS, the appropriate identities to select from the database would be

1. CYOW, CYGK.
2. YOW, YGK.
3. YOW, CYGK.
4. CYOW, GK.

Question 464: The altimeter in figure B.13 on page 99 is currently reading

1. 180 ft.
2. 1,180 ft.
3. 10,180 ft.
4. 200 ft.

Question 465: Consider the magnetic compass shown in figure B.12 on page 98. To turn to a heading of 180°M, the aircraft should be turned

1. 160° to the left.
2. 16° to the right.
3. 16° to the left.
4. 160° to the right.

Question 466: You have now reached the last question in the main part of this book. How do you feel about that?

1. The pilot-in-command.
2. Ready to take the practice examination in this book, and then sit the formal Transport Canada examination while everything is still fresh in my mind.
3. Hypoxic.
4. 1,200 ft ASL on a track of 365°M.

Chapter 10

Sample Examination

Please treat the following 100 questions as you would a genuine examination. Allocate three uninterrupted hours to complete them and do not have any materials available other than those you would have with you in the real examination.

10.1 Air Law and Procedures

Exam Question 1: Two powered aircraft, one single-engined and one twin-engined, are arriving to land at an uncontrolled airport. Which of the following best describes the landing priority?

1. The twin has priority over the single.
2. The single has priority over the twin.
3. The aircraft at the lower altitude has priority.
4. The faster of the two aircraft has priority.

Exam Question 2: A pilot has filed a VFR flight plan with Flight Services. It is not necessary to contact Flight Services to update the flight plan when the

1. destination aerodrome has changed.
2. duration of the flight has changed.
3. altitude being flown has changed.
4. route of the flight has changed.

Exam Question 3: The minimum flight visibility required for a day VFR flight in uncontrolled airspace at 900 ft AGL (2,300 ft ASL) is

1. 2 miles.
2. not important as long as the aircraft remains clear of cloud.
3. 1 mile.
4. 3 miles.

Exam Question 4: Unless the area is floodlit, an aircraft parking area used at night must be marked with fixed lights or retro-reflective markers. These lights or markers must be coloured _______ and be placed at intervals not exceeding ________.

1. blue; 60 metres
2. red; 60 metres
3. white; 100 metres
4. red; 100 metres

Exam Question 5: It is unnecessary for an aerodrome to have a wind sock (wind direction indicator) if the

1. aerodrome only has grass (unpaved) runways.
2. aerodrome is restricted to use by privately-registered aircraft.
3. aerodrome has a single runway and that runway is less than 3,000 ft in length.
4. direction of the wind at the aerodrome can be determined by the direction of smoke in the air.

Exam Question 6: Which of the following is not a type of registration as recorded on an aircraft's certificate of registration?

1. A civil aircraft owned by and exclusively used in the service of a government in Canada.
2. A commercial aircraft.
3. A private aircraft.
4. A military aircraft.

Exam Question 7: For the purposes of logging flight time, "night" means

1. the time when the sun is below the horizon and there is no moon visible.
2. the time between the beginning of morning civil twilight and the end of evening civil twilight.
3. between 2100 and 0600 local time in summer and between 1600 and 0700 local time in winter.
4. the time between the end of evening civil twilight and the beginning of morning civil twilight.

Exam Question 8: An aircraft is departing VFR from an uncontrolled airport which is located with a Flight Service Station (FSS). The pilot nneds the permission of the FSS representative before departure

1. only when the visibility is below 3 statute miles by day, or 5 statute miles by night.
2. if the ESCAT plan has been implemented.
3. at all times if the airport has a Mandatory Frequency.
4. at all times if the airport is within a class E control zone.

Exam Question 9: Under which of the following conditions must a flight plan be filed for a VFR flight?

1. If the flight enters the ADIZ.
2. If the flight is of more than 25 nautical miles from the point of departure.
3. If the flight is international.
4. If the flight will enter controlled airspace.

Exam Question 10: A pilot had several alcoholic drinks 12 hours ago and now feels only a very minor effect of the alcohol. May he act as a member of a flight crew?

1. Yes, but not as pilot-in-command.
2. Yes, but only if there is at least one other flight crew member.
3. No.
4. Yes.

Exam Question 11: Following a flight, the entry in the pilot's personal log book does not need to include

1. the air time.
2. the flight time.
3. the point of departure and landing.
4. whether the flight was by day or night.

Exam Question 12: Which of the following is a "class" of aircraft as defined in the Canadian Aviation Regulations?

1. Single-pilot.
2. Cessna 172.
3. Single-engined.
4. Jet-powered.

Exam Question 13: Amphibian aircraft A is taxiing in a northerly direction on a lake and a float plane, B, is taxiing towards the north-west at A's 3 o'clock position. Which aircraft is required to give way to the other?

1. The aircraft that is taxiing more slowly must give way to the faster aircraft.
2. The smaller aircraft must give way to the larger.
3. Aircraft B must give way to aircraft A.
4. Aircraft A must give way to aircraft B.

Exam Question 14: Which of the following is not correct regarding entering the circuit for landing at an uncontrolled airport in an MF zone?

1. If flying a downwind leg, the pilot must broadcast as the aircraft enters downwind.
2. The pilot can enter the circuit straight into final.
3. A landing clearance must be obtained before landing.
4. A special VFR clearance is needed to enter the MF zone if the visibility is below 3 miles.

Exam Question 15: The minimum reported visibility required to depart VFR from an aerodrome in a class E control zone is

1. 3 miles unless a Special VFR clearance is obtained, then 1 mile.
2. 3 miles by day, 5 miles by night.
3. 1 mile by day, 3 miles by night.
4. 5 miles.

Exam Question 16: For a night VFR flight in controlled airspace, an aircraft must carry sufficient fuel to fly to the destination aerodrome and thereafter for

1. 45 minutes at cruising speed.
2. 30 minutes at cruising speed.
3. 30 minutes at best endurance speed.
4. 45 minutes at best range speed.

Exam Question 17: In order to carry passengers at night, it is necessary that the pilot-in-command has completed _______ night takeoffs and _________ night landings within the previous ________ months.

1. 5; 5; 6
2. 6; 6; 6
3. 6; 6; 5
4. 5; 5; 5

Exam Question 18: A single-engined aircraft cruises at 100 knots. The maximum distance from shore that it may be flown over water without life rafts on board is

1. 100 nautical miles.
2. 50 nautical miles.
3. 25 nautical miles.
4. its gliding range at the altitude being flown.

Exam Question 19: An aircraft flying VFR within a terminal control area has been "radar-identified" by the terminal controller. The responsibility for maintaining separation between this aircraft and other aircraft in the terminal control area lies with

1. flight services.
2. the tower controller.
3. the pilot-in-command.
4. the terminal controller.

Exam Question 20: A renewal of an aviation medical certificate is valid from

1. the day of the medical examination.
2. the day on which the pilot receives the updated medical certificate from Transport Canada.
3. the day Transport Canada receives the renewal request from the doctor following the medical examination.
4. the first day of the month following the medical examination.

10.2 Navigation and Radio Aids

For questions 21 to 39 consult the enclosed section of the Toronto VNC. You are planning a VFR flight in a Piper Cherokee from Peterborough (N44° 14' W78° 22') to Brockville (N44° 38' W75° 45').

Exam Question 21: Which of the following would be a suitable cruise altitude for this flight?

1. 7,500 ft AGL.
2. 7,500 ft ASL.
3. 6,500 ft ASL.
4. 7,000 ft ASL.

Exam Question 22: Examining the NOTAMs before your departure, you find the following NOTAM for Peterborough:

```
090111 CYPQ PETERBOROUGH
CYPQ OBST LGT U/S TOWER 440828N 782835W
(APRX 7 NM SW AD) 250 FT AGL 1225 MSL
TIL APRX 0910151400
```

This means there is

1. an unlighted American tower about 7 nautical miles southwest of the aerodrome.
2. a tower about 7 nautical miles southwest of the aerodrome obscured by terrain.
3. a tower about 7 nautical miles southwest of the aerodrome at 250 ft ASL.
4. a lighted but unused tower about 7 nautical miles southwest of the aerodrome.

Exam Question 23: The dashed box around the name Peterborough on the map means that

1. the airport is within an MF zone.
2. the airport cannot be used at night.
3. prior permission is required to land at the airport.
4. customs is available at the airport.

Exam Question 24: The dashed circle of radius 5 nautical miles around Peterborough airport indicates

1. an area of class F (advisory) airspace.
2. the area within which a tower controller at Peterborough can issue a clearance.
3. a class E control zone.
4. a class D control zone.

Exam Question 25: The star immediately to the left of the L in the description of Peterborough aerodrome indicates that

1. the aerodrome is certified (and is therefore an airport).
2. the aerodrome has a rotating beacon.
3. the aerodrome has a hard surface runway.
4. services are only available during limited hours.

Exam Question 26: Which of the following would be the most suitable set-heading point for this flight?

1. The Peterborough NDB.
2. Hastings, at the northern tip of Rice Lake.
3. The southern tip of Chemong Lake.
4. Port Hope on the shore of Lake Ontario.

Exam Question 27: You decide to use Peterborough airport itself as your set-heading point, climbing and departing over the airport. What is the distance and track from there to Brockville?

1. 115 statute miles on a track of 088°T.
2. 115 statute miles on a track of 088°M.
3. 115 nautical miles on a track of 088°M.
4. 115 nautical miles on a track of 088°T.

Exam Question 28: At the altitude you select for cruise, your true airspeed is 119 knots and the winds are forecast to be 320°M at 25 knots. Your heading and time from the set-heading point to destination will be

1. 077°T and 34 minutes.
2. 088°T and 34 minutes.
3. 078°T and 52 minutes.
4. 078°M and 52 minutes.

Exam Question 29: As you fly over Peterborough airport, you tune and identify the Campbellford VOR which is on your line of flight. You turn the OBS to centre the CDI. Which of these is a possible combination of TO/FROM flag and course indicator at the top of the VOR display?

1. FROM, 089°.
2. FROM, 27°.
3. TO, 269°.
4. FROM, 269°.

Exam Question 30: You pass over Peterborough as your set-heading point at 1411Z and pass over the Campbellford VOR at 1425Z. What is your estimated time of arrival at Brockville?

1. 1500Z.
2. 1525Z.
3. 1507Z.
4. 1528Z.

Exam Question 31: Your aircraft consumes 8.6 US gallons of fuel per hour at the altitude at which you are cruising. Given the revised groundspeed calculated in question 30, how much fuel will you burn during the cruise portion of this flight (from set-heading point to destination)?

1. 4.8 US gallons.
2. 7.9 US gallons.
3. 8.3 US gallons.
4. 6.0 US gallons.

Exam Question 32: You decide to use your ADF to assist with your navigation and you tune it to the Brockville NDB by selecting a frequency of

1. 391 MHz.
2. 683 kHz.
3. 38 kHz.
4. 391 kHz.

Exam Question 33: The elevation of Brockville aerodrome is

1. 402 ft ASL.
2. 450 ft ASL.
3. 683 ft ASL.
4. 402 ft AGL.

Exam Question 34: On your track, just to the west of the Campbellford VOR, is a tower marked "964 (328)". The base of this tower is at

1. 636 ft AGL.
2. 964 ft ASL.
3. 636 ft ASL.
4. 328 ft ASL.

Exam Question 35: While following the correct track to Brockville, you tune and identify the Watertown VOR (N43° 57' W076° 04') and centre the CDI with a FROM flag with the bearing of 324° at the top of the unit. What is the name of the small lake passing by your right-hand window?

1. Lake Ontario.
2. Camden Lake.
3. Beaver Lake.
4. Charleston Lake.

Exam Question 36: Passing north of Kingston you decide to obtain the latest weather reports from Kingston, Watertown and Massena so that you can anticipate the weather you might meet in Brockville. You have no direct weather uplink in your aircraft. Which would be the most useful radio station to contact?

1. Brockville Unicom.
2. Kingston Radio.
3. Québec Radio.
4. Trenton Tower.

Exam Question 37: As you cross V145 at your cruising altitude you are in

1. class G airspace (uncontrolled).
2. class E airspace (uncontrolled).
3. class D airspace (controlled).
4. class E airspace (controlled).

Exam Question 38: During the flight to Brockville you encounter unexpected headwinds. You call flight services and give an updated time of arrival of 1520Z. You land at Brockville and find that the telephone is out of order and your cellular telephone batteries are drained. By what time must you close your flight plan to prevent search and rescue being launched?

1. 1545Z.
2. 1520Z on the following day.
3. 1620Z.
4. 1 hour after the time of arrival that you filed on your flight plan.

Exam Question 39: If the weather had deteriorated to the point where you found it necessary to divert to Kingston airport, what identifier would you have entered on your GPS?

1. CYGK.
2. YGK.
3. 305.
4. KING.

Exam Question 40: An aircraft is flying at an indicated altitude of 6,500 ft with its altimeter set to 30.67 inches of mercury. The calibrated airspeed is 145 knots and the outside air temperature is -3°C. The aircraft's true airspeed is

1. 156 knots.
2. 130 knots.
3. 165 knots.
4. 145 knots.

10.3 Meteorology

Exam Question 41: Consider the GFA in figure B.23 on page 101. The symbols to the right of the point marked Ⓑ indicate moderate

1. convective turbulence between the ground and 3,000 ft AGL.
2. convective turbulence between the ground and 300 ft AGL.
3. mechanical turbulence between the ground and 3,000 ft AGL.
4. icing between the ground and 3000 ft AGL.

Exam Question 42: The blue line (with triangles) along the top of the GFA in figure B.23 on page 101

1. indicates that a mass of colder air is moving southward.
2. is a line joining points where the freezing level is at the same height.
3. is a line joining all points with the same magnetic deviation.
4. indicates that warmer air is over-running cooler air.

Exam Question 43: Consider the following METAR:

```
METAR CYND 191100Z 26002KT 15SM FEW025 02/M01
A3029 RMK SC1 FROIN SLP260=
```

The term FROIN indicates that

1. frost was detected on the indicator.
2. freezing rain was observed in the area.
3. freezing rain was observed to the north.
4. fog was reported overnight.

Exam Question 44: The TAF in figure B.22 on page 100 provides a forecast of the weather for

1. the area covered by radio reception from CYQX (typically about 70 nautical miles).
2. the flight information region centred on CYQX.
3. an area within 5 nautical miles around CYQX.
4. an area within 50 statute miles around CYQX.

Exam Question 45: How has the temperature/dewpoint spread changed over the period covered by the METARs in figure B.20 on page 100?

1. This cannot be deduced from AUTO readings.
2. It has reduced.
3. It has not changed.
4. It has increased.

Exam Question 46: During the period covered by the METARs in figure B.20 on page 100, the wind has

1. veered and weakened.
2. veered and strengthened.
3. backed and strengthened.
4. backed and weakened.

Exam Question 47: According to the TAF in figure B.22 on page 100, the precipitation at CYQX is forecast to change at 0200Z on the 20th of the month from

1. light drizzle to rain.
2. light rain to light drizzle with occasional rain showers.
3. light rain to heavier rain.
4. light rain to snow.

Exam Question 48: The forecast provided in the TAF in figure B.22 on page 100 covers the period

1. 1131Z to 1900Z on the 12th of the month.
2. 1900Z to 2000Z on the 12th of the month.
3. 1911Z on the 31st of the month until cancelled by NOTAM.
4. 1200Z on the 19th of the month to 1200Z on the 20th of the month.

Exam Question 49: The density altitude of an airport is not determined by its

1. atmospheric pressure.
2. humidity.
3. cloud coverage.
4. temperature.

Exam Question 50: The METARs given in figure B.20 on page 100 represent ________ produced by a ________. The latest was issued at ________ on the _______ of the month.

1. observations; human observer; 1200Z, 19th
2. forecasts; meteorologist; 1200Z, 19th
3. forecasts; machine; 1100Z, 1st
4. observations; machine; 1200Z, 19th

Exam Question 51: The conditions required for a thunderstorm to occur include a lifting agent. Which of the following would not normally act as a lifting agent?

1. Orographic effects.
2. A cold front.
3. A temperature inversion.
4. Low-level convergence.

Exam Question 52: The temperature of a standard atmosphere at 10,000 ft

1. cannot be determined without knowing the humidity of the atmosphere.
2. is $-5°C$.
3. cannot be determined without knowing the dry adiabatic lapse rate of the day.
4. is $15°C$.

Exam Question 53: An approaching cold front in summer is often associated with

1. low, stratus ceilings.
2. a line of thunderstorms.
3. a large adiabatic lapse rate.
4. a sequence of cirrus, altostratus and nimbostratus clouds.

Exam Question 54: The wind arrow shown in figure B.5 on page 94 is taken from a GFA. It indicates that the wind

1. at the surface is forecast to be between 25 and 29 knots, gusting to 35 knots, from the south-west.
2. at 5,000 ft AGL is forecast to be 30 knots, gusting to 35 knots, from the north-east.
3. at 5,000 ft AGL is forecast to be 30 knots, gusting to 35 knots, from the south-west.
4. at the surface is forecast to be between 25 and 29 knots, gusting to 35 knots, from the north-east.

Exam Question 55: Which cloud type is least likely to produce noticeable precipitation?

1. cirrus.
2. stratus.
3. cumulonimbus.
4. cumulus.

Exam Question 56: During a climb-out after takeoff, winds will normally

1. weaken and back.
2. strengthen and veer.
3. strengthen and back.
4. weaken and veer.

Exam Question 57: When cool air is blown gently across a lake or river that is much warmer, the lowest layer of air warms and absorbs moisture. As this rises, the water vapour condenses, forming fog. This is a description of

1. advection fog.
2. steam fog.
3. radiation fog.
4. upslope fog.

Exam Question 58: According to the METARs given in figure B.20 on page 100, the visibility at 1115Z was measured to be

1. one statute mile but fluctuating between 300 metres and more than 9 kilometers.
2. one statute mile but fluctuating between 3 and more than 9 kilometres.
3. just over one nautical mile but fluctuating between 300 and 9,000 ft.
4. just over one statute mile but fluctuating between 0.3 and more than 9 statute miles.

Exam Question 59: According to the TAF in figure B.22 on page 100, at 1900Z the ceiling at CYQX is forecast to be at

1. 1,500 to 2,500 ft ASL.
2. 2,500 ft AGL.
3. 1,500 ft ASL.
4. 1,500 to 2,500 ft AGL.

Exam Question 60: Cloud heights in a TAF are given above _______ and cloud heights in a GFA are given above ________.

1. sea-level; sea-level
2. ground level; ground level
3. ground level; sea-level
4. sea-level; ground level

Exam Question 61: If a pilot flies to an area of higher atmospheric pressure without resetting the altimeter, maintaining the same indicated altitude, the aircraft's actual altitude above sea-level will

1. decrease.
2. remain as indicated on the altimeter.
3. decrease unless the pressure was originally greater than 29.92 inches of mercury.
4. increase.

Exam Question 62: An inversion is the condition when

1. atmospheric pressure increases with altitude.
2. temperature increases or remains constant with altitude.
3. temperature decreases or remains constant with altitude.
4. intense instability occurs in the atmosphere.

Exam Question 63: A high environmental lapse rate is an indicator of

1. possible atmospheric stability.
2. higher than normal temperatures aloft.
3. the appearance of stratus cloud.
4. possible atmospheric instability.

Exam Question 64: Consider the 1600Z METAR for Bear Lake Lookout given in figure B.17 on page 100. By how many degrees would the temperature have to drop for the air to become saturated?

1. 20°C.
2. 2°C (36°F).
3. 22°C.
4. 2°C (4°F).

Exam Question 65: The relative humidity of a parcel of air can be increased by

1. increasing its temperature while keeping its moisture content the same.
2. increasing its moisture content while keeping its temperature the same.
3. increasing its temperature while keeping its pressure the same.
4. increasing its pressure while keeping its moisture content the same.

Exam Question 66: The saturated adiabatic lapse rate is less than the dry adiabatic lapse rate because

1. condensing water vapour adds energy to the atmosphere in the form of heat.
2. saturated air requires less expansion to cause it to condense.
3. condensing water vapour extracts latent heat from the atmosphere.
4. the environmental lapse rate is greater when the air is saturated.

Exam Question 67: Wind tends to blow from a _______ pressure to a _______ and, in the northern hemisphere, is deflected to the _______.

1. low; high; left
2. high; low; left
3. low; high; right
4. high; low; right

Exam Question 68: Wind strength can be estimated by examining a surface analysis chart and noting

1. how close the isogonals are: the further apart, the stronger the wind.
2. how wide the isobar lines have been drawn: the wider, the stronger the wind.
3. how close the isogonals are: the closer, the stronger the wind.
4. how close the isobars are together: the closer, the stronger the wind.

Exam Question 69: Consider the GFA in figure B.23 on page 101. The forecast freezing level at the point marked Ⓐ is

1. between 10,000 and 12,500 ft AGL.
2. somewhat greater than 12,500 ft ASL.
3. between 10,000 and 12,500 ft ASL.
4. slightly below 10,000 ft AGL.

Exam Question 70: Consider the GFA in figure B.23 on page 101. For what date and time will the next regularly-issued GFA be valid?

1. 1200Z on 21st September 2009.
2. 0600Z on 21st September 2009.
3. 1800Z on 22nd September 2009.
4. 0600Z on 22nd September 2009.

10.4 Aeronautics and General Knowledge

Exam Question 71: A pilot is flying at an indicated altitude of 4,500 ft with an altimeter setting of 29.92 inches of mercury. The pilot gets a local altimeter setting of 30.20 inches of mercury and adjusts the altimeter accordingly. Before the pilot changes altitude, the altimeter will read

1. 4,757 ft.
2. 4,220 ft.
3. 4,243 ft.
4. 4,500 ft.

Exam Question 72: How does a turn co-ordinator measure changes of pitch?

1. By having its gyroscopic axis mounted at the longitudinal axis of the aircraft.
2. By averaging the roll and turn rates.
3. By relying on the gradual precession of the gyroscope caused by the rotation of the earth.
4. It does not measure changes of pitch.

Exam Question 73: A turbo-charged engine

1. uses a turbine to pressurise the intake air to the engine.
2. reduces the amount of fuel in the fuel/air mixture at higher altitudes.
3. can only be used with jet fuel.
4. increases the amount of fuel in the fuel/air mixture at higher altitudes.

Exam Question 74: Applying carburetor heat

1. causes the mixture to become leaner.
2. causes the fuel to be warmed before it reaches the carburetor.
3. causes the mixture to become richer.
4. should never be performed below 3,000 ft ASL.

Exam Question 75: For this question and question 76 refer to the CFS entry for Bear Lake Lookout given in figure B.10 on page 97. At Bear Lake Lookout the outside air temperature is 15°C, the altimeter setting is 29.20 inches of mercury and the winds are 260°M at 12 knots.
The pressure and density altitudes at Bear Lake Lookout are

1. 602 ft and 2,000 ft.
2. 602 ft and 1,322 ft.
3. 1,996 ft and 2461 ft.
4. 1,322 ft and 2,115 ft.

Exam Question 76: Under the conditions given in question 75, the takeoff distance chart in figure B.1 on page 93, indicates that the ground roll distance and distance to clear a 50 foot obstacle when departing Bear Lake Lookout in a Cessna 172M loaded to 2300 lbs would be

1. 934 ft and 1,649 ft.
2. 1,038 ft and 1,833 ft.
3. 1,073 ft and 1,789 ft.
4. 1,073 ft and 1,896 ft.

Exam Question 77: Consider the CFS entry for Fort Cushing given in figure B.11 on page 98. In the winter when the local wall-clock (time zone) time is 0830, the UTC (Zulu) time is

1. 1530Z on the same day.
2. 0830Z on the next day.
3. 0130Z on the same day.
4. 0130Z on the next day.

Exam Question 78: The Ⓟ at each end of the runway in the CFS entry for Bear Lake Lookout (figure B.10 on page 97) indicates the

1. position of flashing beacons.
2. position of the runway displacement.
3. parking positions for aircraft during run-up checks.
4. location of precision approach path indicators.

Exam Question 79: Many light aircraft are provided with a radio (or avionics) master switch. This switch is designed to

1. provide a single point of failure for all the aircraft's avionics.
2. provide power to the alternator windings during engine start.
3. protect delicate avionics during engine start and stop.
4. connect the pilot's microphone to the radio to allow an outgoing call to be made.

Exam Question 80: The primary danger associated with the accumulation of ice on the wing of an aircraft is that

1. any landing lights positioned in the wings will become obscured.
2. the gross weight of the aircraft may exceed its allowed limit.
3. the stall speed of the aircraft may decrease.
4. the stall speed of the aircraft may increase.

Exam Question 81: During a descent, the pitot tube blocks with ice. How may this affect the altimeter?

1. It will cause the altimeter to freeze at its current value.
2. It will not affect the altimeter.
3. It will cause the altimeter to over-read.
4. It will cause the altimeter to under-read.

Exam Question 82: The empty weight of an aircraft is 1405 lbs and its moment is 120,970.5 lb-in. Arms are as follows:

- the pilot and front seat passenger: 85.5 inches
- back seat passengers: 118.1 inches
- fuel: 95.0 inches
- oil: 32.5 inches
- baggage: 150.0 inches

The aircraft is loaded with a pilot and front seat passenger, together weighing 320 lbs, two backseat passengers totalling 300 lbs, 40 lbs of baggage, 15 lbs of oil and 50 US gallons of fuel. Consider the chart given in figure B.25 on page 103. The aircraft

1. is loaded safely for the normal category but not for the utility category.
2. is loaded safely for the utility category.
3. has its centre of gravity behind the permitted limit.
4. is too heavy.

Exam Question 83: The wind is reported by the tower controller to be 320° at 25 knots at an airport where the magnetic variation is 10°E. A pilot landing on runway 01 should expect a crosswind from the

1. left of 16 knots and a headwind of 19 knots.
2. right of 19 knots and a headwind of 16 knots.
3. left of 19 knots and a headwind of 16 knots.
4. left of 19 knots and a tailwind of 16 knots.

Exam Question 84: What is the general relationship between the speed of an aircraft and the drag it experiences?

1. As speed increases, both induced and parasitic drag decrease.
2. As speed increases, induced drag increases and parasitic drag decreases.
3. As speed increases, induced drag decreases and parasitic drag increases.
4. As speed increases, both induced and parasitic drag increase.

Exam Question 85: A pilot is used to flying out of an aerodrome with a runway that is 75 ft wide. She is approaching a large airport with runways 200 ft wide. On final approach she should anticipate an illusion of being ________ and therefore landing _______.

1. too low; a long way down the runway
2. too high; a long way down the runway
3. too low; short of the runway
4. too high; short of the runway

Exam Question 86: The point at which an aircraft stalls depends on its

1. angle of attack.
2. attitude.
3. angle of incidence.
4. speed.

Exam Question 87: An aircraft is in level flight at a constant speed of 100 knots. In this condition

1. its thrust is equal to its drag.
2. its drag is less than its thrust.
3. its weight is less than its lift.
4. its thrust is equal to its lift.

Exam Question 88: Which of the following statements about wheelbarrowing is not true?

1. Wheelbarrowing can cause an aircraft to yaw uncontrollably.
2. Wheelbarrowing can be mitigated by braking hard.
3. Wheelbarrowing can occur if an aircraft lands with a sideways motion.
4. Wheelbarrowing does not occur on tail-wheel aircraft.

Exam Question 89: The primary instrument for differentiating between a spiral dive and a spin when in IMC is the

1. airspeed indicator.
2. altimeter.
3. heading indicator.
4. attitude indicator.

Exam Question 90: A runway is fairly short and has a row of trees at the departure end. What would be a suitable speed to fly after takeoff until the trees are cleared?

1. V_{PD}.
2. V_a.
3. V_x.
4. V_y.

Exam Question 91: When activated, a 406 MHz ELT

1. alerts the pilot when its signal has been received by Search and Rescue.
2. transmits a unique identifying code when it receives an interrogation from an over-flying satellite.
3. transmits the 4-digit number dialled into the front of the unit by the pilot when interrogated by the TCAS of an over-flying aircraft.
4. continuously transmits a unique identifying code.

Exam Question 92: If the horizontal tail of a Cessna 172 were to stall because of a build-up of ice while the aircraft was in level cruise flight, the aircraft would

1. roll to the right.
2. pitch nose-down.
3. not be affected.
4. pitch nose-up.

Exam Question 93: The CRFI of a runway at an airport is reported to be 1.0. This means that

1. the braking action on the runway is equivalent to that of a clear, dry runway.
2. conditions are conducive to hydroplaning.
3. there is no effective braking on the runway.
4. there is at least 1mm of standing water on the runway.

Exam Question 94: The pressure altitude of an aerodrome can be most easily found when an aircraft is parked on the ramp by

1. setting the altitude displayed to the altitude of the aerodrome and reading the pressure.
2. setting the altimeter to the local sea-level pressure and reading the altitude displayed.
3. setting the altimeter to the local station pressure and reading the altitude displayed.
4. setting the altimeter to 29.92 inches of mercury and reading the indicated altitude.

Exam Question 95: While in cruise flight, a RAIM error occurs. Which navigation instrument will this affect?

1. The magnetic compass.
2. The ADF.
3. The GPS receiver.
4. The VOR receiver.

Exam Question 96: An aircraft stalls in level flight at 50 knots. During an aerobatic exercise, it experiences a load factor of 4. At this point its stall speed is

1. 200 knots.
2. 25 knots.
3. 12.5 knots.
4. 100 knots.

Exam Question 97: Hypoxia is caused by

1. a lack of carbon dioxide in the blood.
2. a lack of oxygen in the air being breathed.
3. an exposure to a cold environment.
4. a lack of carbon monoxide in the blood.

Exam Question 98: The boundary layer on an aerofoil is

1. a thin layer of air close to the aerofoil that moves backwards relative to the incident air.
2. the area between the leading edge and the point of maximum thickness of the aerofoil.
3. a thin layer of air close to the aerofoil that does not move relative to the wind.
4. a thin layer of air close to the aerofoil that does not move relative to the aerofoil.

Exam Question 99: Ground effect is caused by a decrease in

1. parasitic drag.
2. induced drag.
3. thrust.
4. weight.

Exam Question 100: The green arc on a conventional airspeed indicator shows the range of

1. speeds at which flaps may be fully extended.
2. speeds at which the aircraft can be flown with one engine inoperable.
3. normal cruising speeds.
4. speeds between the no-flap stall speed and V_a.

Appendix A

Notes on the Questions

Question 1. The answer referring to the technical logs is wrong—they *must not* be carried on board. The certificate of registration is one of the documents that *must* be carried on board. (CAR 202.26)

Question 2. There is no such thing as a "flight training registration" and, given that flight training is a commercial operation, it is unlikely that a private registration would be adequate. (CAR 202.17)

Question 3. It is said that the origin of the phrase "socked in" (meaning bad weather) applied to the practice in times past of taking in the wind socks when the aerodrome was unusable. That no longer happens but the CARs do demand that the wind socks be removed from an aerodrome as soon as it is closed down. (CAR 301.06)

Question 4. This is another question for which you either know the answer (because you have flown at night) or you have to learn it. You should be familiar with the whole of section 301.07 of the CARs. (CAR 301.07)

Question 5. Like much of air law, this is yet another of those questions for which you just have to learn the answer. You should be familiar with the whole of section 301.07 of the CARs. (CAR 301.07)

Question 6. Runway markings are again something you have to learn, although in this question there is one answer that can be eliminated immediately: the answer about the glide slope makes little sense. In principle a red sign could be used to indicate that the runway is out of operation; however, it is not.

Question 7. These are the hold-short lines for a runway with an instrument approach. The dashed lines are on the runway side.

Question 8. The correct answer is the yellow cross. This can be a surprise because, in practice, many taxiway closures are actually marked with white crosses but section 300.01 of the CARs is quite clear: "...is in a single contrasting colour, white on runways and yellow on taxiways, that is visible from an aircraft flying at an altitude of 300 m (1,000 ft) above the marking." (CAR 301.04 and 300.01)

Question 9. An aerodrome is "any area of land, water (including the frozen surface thereof) or other supporting surface used, designed, prepared, equipped or set apart for use either in whole or in part for the arrival, departure, movement or servicing of aircraft and includes any buildings, installations and equipment situated thereon or associated therewith." An owner of an aerodrome may apply for registration (in which case the aerodrome will appear in the CFS) or for certification. Certification makes it an airport. (CAR 302.02)

Question 10. This is a difficult question because she will have her 40th birthday two years after getting her medical. The rules say that, for a person over 40 years old, a class 3 medical can validate a Private Pilot Licence for 2 years. Thus, she will need a new medical on her 42nd birthday. (CAR 404.04)

Question 11. This is the recency requirement most forgotten by pilots. To fly VFR (or IFR), it is necessary to have completed a "2-year recurrency". This can be achieved by:

- completion of a flight review by a flight instructor
- attending a safety seminar conducted by Transport Canada
- successfully completing a recurrent training programme that has been approved by the Minister
- completing the self-paced study programme produced annually in the Transport Canada Aviation Safety Newsletter
- completing a training program or Pilot Proficiency Check as required by Parts IV, VI or VII of the CARs
- completing the skill requirements for issue or renewal of a pilot permit, licence or rating, including night rating, VFR over-the-top rating, instrument rating, multi-engine class rating, flight instructor rating, landplane or seaplane rating
- completing the written examination for a permit, licence or rating.

(CAR 401.05)

Question 12. The holder of a PPL may carry out many responsibilities as pilot-in-command, including acting as pilot-in-command of *any* aircraft if the flight is for training purposes and is under the supervision of a qualified instructor. However, an additional rating is required to fly twin-engined aircraft unless the flight is for training purposes. (CAR 401.26/28)

Question 13. In the past a student was the pilot-in-command during a flight test. This changed in 2017 and the examiner is now the pilot-in-command. (CAR 401.19)

Question 14. Like much of air law, this is simply one of those things that you have to learn (and may immediately forget after the examination). While on the subject, the pilot will not be allowed to act as PIC until at least 6 weeks after the birth of her child. (CAR 404.06)

Question 15. Most students remember the "8 hours bottle to throttle" but forget the second part of the requirement: that there be no residual influence of alcohol. So, if you drink heavily 10 hours before flying and there is still alcohol in your blood stream, you may not act as a crew member. (CAR 602.03)

Question 16. The designator CYA means that this is class F advisory airspace and the letters in brackets stand for Training and Soaring (gliding). Had this been restricted airspace, the designator would have been CYR rather than CYA.

Question 17. This is class F *advisory* airspace, therefore no clearance or permission is required to enter. As gliding and training are likely to be in progress, it is important to keep a good look-out for other traffic.

Question 18. VFR flight is, of course, allowed in class C airspace; otherwise almost all large airports would be inaccessible to VFR traffic. However, it does require an implicit or explicit clearance to enter. A special VFR clearance is required in any control zone if the visibility drops below normal VFR minima. (CAR 601.08)

Question 19. Northbrook is in no specifically designated airspace. It is not under an airway, it is not within any class F, it is not close to any major airport and so the airspace above it is uncontrolled: class G. This holds true for all low-level airspace (up to 18,000 ft, above which it becomes class A).

Question 20. All that is required is to have established two-way radio communications with a controller: "Montréal Terminal, this is Cessna 172 Golf Alfa Bravo Charlie". "Alfa Bravo Charlie, go ahead." The interesting condition (for armchair lawyers) is the situation that arises when the exchange goes: "Victoria Terminal, this is Cessna 172, Golf Xray, Yankee, Zulu", "Xray, Yankee, Zulu, remain clear of class D airspace". In this case, two-way radio communication has been established (and so the aircraft can enter the class D) but has been given an instruction to remain out of the class D (and therefore can't enter). (CAR 601.09)

Question 21. The *Designated Airspace Handbook* really does exist and is freely available from the internet. It makes fascinating reading because it defines the precise outlines of every piece of non-class G airspace in Canada. Class F restricted (as opposed to advisory or danger) airspace cannot be entered without the permission of the user agency as defined in that document.

Question 22. At first glance, this *does* look like another ring of class D airspace (as are the first two rings). However, close examination shows that there is no D designator inside the ring and the label reads "Transpondeur Mode C Requis 6500 ASL". It's not clear why this is written in French but the meaning is clear (even to an Anglophone like me): it's transponder airspace above 6,500 ft ASL.

Question 23. Kaladar lies directly under a low-level airway (V104). The airway starts at 2,200 ft AGL, i.e., at $2200 + 900 = 3100$ ft ASL. The airspace is uncontrolled (class G) below this. The airway itself is class E and becomes class B at 12,500 ft.

Question 24. The other answers are wrong: class E, for example, is controlled airspace but a VFR pilot needs no clearance or permission to enter (otherwise it would be impossible to fly a cross-country that intersected low-level airways—class E). The airspace above 18,000 ft ASL (up to FL600) is class A airspace over most of Canada but is not the only controlled airspace.

Question 25. The CFS entry shows that Fort Cushing is an uncontrolled airport (no tower frequency), not in an MF zone (no MF frequency). It also does not say that circuits are flown right-hand; therefore they must be flown left-hand. This excludes one answer immediately. Crossing the aerodrome from the south at circuit height would also imply a right-hand circuit for runway 25 and therefore another answer can be excluded. As there is conflicting traffic in the area that will be arriving at the downwind leg at approximately the same time as the aircraft in the question, entering directly into downwind is not allowed: excluding another answer. The pilot will have to get across to the upwind side of the aerodrome and cross over from the north to enter mid-downwind for a left-hand circuit. (AIM, RAC 4.5.2)

Question 26. The CFS entry for Bear Lake Lookout indicates that it is situated at 1,322 ft ASL. The aircraft must overfly at least 2,000 ft above ground—at or above 3,322 ft ASL. (CAR 602.96)

Question 27. Again one of those things you just have to learn. You can remember it by noting that it is the same visibility needed to fly VFR in a control zone. (CAR 602.27)

Question 28. Dropping items from aircraft is allowed as long as it doesn't endanger people on the ground. Otherwise parachute drops and "flour-bombing" competitions at flying clubs would not be permitted. (CAR 602.23)

Question 29. Unless there is an emergency, priority is never based on speed or weight. At most aerodromes, no radio calls are required. (CAR 602.19)

Question 30. The station pressure is incorrect (unless the aerodrome happens to be at sea level) as setting the altimeter to station (rather than sea-level) pressure should make the altimeter read zero on the ground. 29.92" is also wrong—even in the standard pressure region the local aerodrome altimeter setting is used on the ground. Setting an altitude rather than a pressure is correct only if no altimeter setting is available—it is better to set the pressure setting and then check that the aerodrome elevation is correctly displayed. (CAR 602.35)

Question 31. The regulation says that, "No person shall start an engine of an aircraft unless (a) a pilot's seat is occupied by a person who is competent to control the aircraft or (b) precautions have been taken to prevent the aircraft from moving." In this case, his wife being familiar with the aircraft means that she is competent to control it. Either chocks or a rope around a tree are OK as long as he has a way of removing them once in the pilot's seat. (CAR 602.10)

Question 32. This is the sort of question that is an examination-setter's dream. There is no way to work out the answer—either you know it or you don't. (CAR 602.14)

Question 33. Again, the rules are clear and, for examination purposes, you must simply learn them. (CAR 602.28)

Question 34. The standard pressure region is in the far north of Canada (for example, Churchill, Manitoba, is south of the standard pressure region) where there are few weather observation stations to provide an altimeter setting. In this area, a standard pressure of 29.92 inches of mercury is used for cruise flight (i.e., aircraft fly at flight levels). Taking off, the climb to cruise altitude, the descent for landing and the landing itself, however, are performed with the local aerodrome altimeter setting. (CAR 602.35/36)

Question 35. It would make no sense to have these altitudes as heights above ground level because there is no instrument in most aircraft (apart from a GPS) that can display height above ground. If you remember that odd altitudes plus 500 ft are used for flights towards the east (you could remember "you must be odd to want to go to England"), the question is really whether the altitudes are based on track or heading. The purpose of the specified altitudes is to avoid head-on collisions and that would not be possible if headings were used. So they must be based on track. (CAR 602.34)

Question 36. There is no *controller* at an aerodrome in an MF zone. It is not necessary to fly a complete circuit at an aerodrome in an MF zone (as all aircraft will have radios, unlike those at an uncontrolled aerodrome without an MF zone), so joining the circuit on base or straight-in final is allowed. (CAR 602.97 to 103)

Question 37. The briefing must contain the location and means of operation of emergency and normal exits; the location and means of operation of safety belts, shoulder harnesses and restraint devices; the positioning of seats and the securing of seat backs and chair tables; the stowage of carry-on baggage; where the aircraft is unpressurised and it is possible that the flight will require the use of oxygen by the passengers, the location and means of operation of oxygen equipment; any prohibition against smoking; the location and use of first aid kits and survival equipment and, in small aircraft (i.e., one with a maximum takeoff weight below 5,700 kg), any ELT. (CAR 602.89)

Question 38. ADIZ is certainly an acronym for Air Defence Identification Zone. Don't confuse it with ATIS. The ADIZ is only situated around those borders through which Canada has never been invaded. (AIM, RAC 2.13 and CAR 602.145)

Question 39. One proposed answer is meaningless because there is no way of transmitting through a VOR receiver. Squawking 7500 might alert ATC to the fact that you have been hijacked but not that you have lost communications. Flying triangles in controlled airspace is not a good idea because it would certainly be unexpected by ATC. The correct answer is to leave the class D airspace either by landing at the airport (if the class D is a control zone around an airport) or by flying out of the airspace. (CAR 602.138)

Question 40. There is reference in the rules to 50 nautical miles from land but they state that life preservers have to be on board either if the aircraft will be more than 50 nautical miles from land **or** if it will be out of gliding distance from land. In the case of a Cessna 172, it would have to be very high to give it a gliding range of 50 nautical miles. There is no mention in the regulation about life preservers having to be worn (just them being on board). (CAR 602.62)

Question 41. The requirements are for 30 minutes of cruise fuel during the day or 45 minutes of cruise fuel at night. Note that, when calculating the fuel to reach the destination, you need to take account of taxiing and foreseeable delays prior to takeoff, meteorological conditions, foreseeable air traffic routings and traffic delays and any other foreseeable conditions that could delay the arrival of the aircraft. (CAR 602.88)

Question 42. A flight itinerary (rather than a flight plan) can be used for all flights except international ones. If the flight is to enter the Air Defence Identification Zone (ADIZ), then the flight itinerary or flight plan must be filed with Flight Services (or a community radio station or ATC) but otherwise all non-international flights can use a flight itinerary left with a responsible person. (CAR 602.73)

Question 43. One answer is clearly wrong because it would result in a collision. The other three answers would at least avoid the collision. (CAR 602.19)

Question 44. Jets have no priority over other traffic, so one answer is incorrect. The higher priority for the lower altitude traffic only applies when landing and that eliminates another answer. It also makes sense that passing aircraft, not the one being passed, must give way. An aircraft in an emergency situation, however, has priority over all other traffic. (CAR 602.19)

Question 45. VFR flight normally *must* be flown with visual reference to the ground. The exception to this is when flying VFR over-the-top. This rating permits a pilot to fly the cruise portion of a journey above an undercast but does not permit the pilot to enter cloud. (CAR 421.44)

Question 46. This question is often raised by newly-qualified pilots. There is a belief that VFR flight is not permitted above *any* cloud layer. This is not true: as long as there are sufficient gaps to allow "operation" (the CARs are not clear about what "operation" means but it presumably includes the ability to navigate) with reference to the ground, then VFR flight is permitted. (CAR 602.114)

Question 47. VFR flight is not allowed in controlled airspace if the visibility is less than 3 miles. A VFR Over-the-Top clearance would be of no use because the aircraft is arriving to land and flying above the cloud layer based at 5,000 ft would be of no use. The 3 mile visibility answer has a ring of truth—in general, it is true of controlled airspace but control zones are special: if the pilot requests it, ATC may issue a *special VFR* clearance that allows a pilot to fly in 1 mile visibility as long as the ground is in sight. ATC cannot suggest the special VFR clearance—the request has to come from the pilot. ATC does, however, sometimes drop strong hints: "Visibility is 2 miles. Is there anything *special* you would like?". (CAR 602.117)

Question 48. This is a strange condition: a landing light is only needed when carrying passengers. Landing on an unlit runway at night is always illegal. (CAR 605.16)

Question 49. Seat belts or other restraints (e.g., a child restraint or a restraint for an invalid being carried on a stretcher) must be worn, "during movement of the aircraft on the surface, during takeoff and landing and at any time during flight that the pilot-in-command considers it necessary that safety belts be fastened". Taxiing for takeoff is clearly "movement of the aircraft on the surface". (CAR 605.25)

Question 50. The rules say that if the flight is between 10,000 ft and 13,000 ft ASL, then supplemental oxygen must be used for the whole flight (not just the part after 30 minutes) if the flight at those altitudes is to take more than 30 minutes. (CAR 602.32)

Question 51. The journey log is one of the documents normally required on board the aircraft. However, if the intention is to land back at the departure aerodrome without an intermediate stop, then it is not required to be on board. (CAR 605.95)

Question 52. Appendix A of CAR 625 contains a list of items considered to be "elementary maintenance". The list is exhaustive so that, if the work is not on the list, it is not "elementary" and requires a sign-off from an AME. (CAR 625, Appendix A)

Question 53. CAR 605.04 clearly says that "No person shall conduct a takeoff in an aircraft ... unless ... the aircraft operating manual is available to the flight crew members at their duty stations". On many light aircraft, the Operating Handbook is tucked into a document bag inaccessible to the pilot. This is not permitted. (CAR 605.04)

Question 54. Amazingly, if you are only flying in uncontrolled airspace you do not need an altimeter that can be adjusted for the local atmospheric pressure—that is only needed for flight in controlled airspace. The other instruments are all needed. It would actually be very difficult to buy an altimeter that cannot be adjusted for local pressure. (CAR 605.14)

Question 55. Again, this is something that just needs to be learned. The GEN section of the AIM seems to be rarely read by students but contains some fascinating information. (AIM GEN 3.3.1)

Question 56. Even though the flight data and cockpit voice recorders should be "preserved and protected" as far as possible, the wreckage of an aircraft should not be disturbed to extricate them. (AIM GEN 3.4.1)

Question 57. The "conflict resolution" service can be requested in this type of condition. The controller can see the position of both your aircraft and the oncoming aircraft and, work-load permitting, can provide you with directions to avoid the other traffic—either by recommending that you turn to a particular heading or that you climb or descend. Remember that ATC has no obligation to provide VFR traffic with advisories about the proximity of other aircraft (or to provide IFR traffic with advisories about VFR traffic)—it is the responsibility of VFR pilots (and IFR pilots in VMC) to look out of the window and see and avoid other aircraft.

Question 58. To prevent runway incursions, all hold short instructions (e.g., Alfa Bravo Charlie, taxi Bravo, hold short of runway 32) must be read back to the controllers. When flying VFR, other instructions and clearances should not be read back—in most cases a simple WILCO (I have understood your transmission and will comply) is sufficient.

Question 59. As you are radar-identified, the controller knows your location better than you do, so you don't need to provide that. However, your altitude is useful so that the controller can confirm the altitude (mode C) readout from your transponder.

Question 60. If an ATC instruction would result in an unsafe situation (e.g., an ATC vector for a VFR pilot that would cause the aircraft to enter cloud), then the pilot must say "Unable" and, if possible, give the reason: ATC: "Alfa, Bravo, Charlie turn left to 120 degrees"; ABC: "Unable: could not remain VFR"

Question 61. Remember that ATC cannot see your heading on the radar, only your track. When ATC calls traffic at your 12 o'clock position, they mean straight ahead as seen on the radar. Since you are crabbing 10° to the left into wind, the traffic is to the right of your "straight ahead" position.

Question 62. In this case the pilot needs to pass the problem back to the controller by saying that she is unable to accept the clearance. The controller will probably vector her around for another landing when there is no traffic on the intersection runway. Attempting to land short, when she is not confident that she can, would be extremely dangerous.

Question 63. This is extremely unlikely to occur in practice but is another good examination question. It presumably means that the controllers have lost their ability to transmit on the radio, but have managed to find their light guns. In general, green lights whether flashing or steady, indicate that you are permitted to do something.

Question 64. This is a straightforward conversion using an aviation calculator. It used to be that at least in Ontario, a nautical mile was a statute mile plus PST and GST. However, the tax rates have changed and no longer total 15%.

Question 65. This question could well have been included in the Air Law section (the lighting requirements for various types of towers are included in section 4 of standard 621.19 of the CARs) but document TP12880E also calls for obstruction marking and lighting to be covered in the Flight Operations section. Like much of air law there is little to do but learn this type of information, although it is reasonable that red lights should be used rather than blue or yellow ones because red light has a greater range.

Question 66. There is no need to learn these directions if you think why the controls are being held in specific ways—it's to prevent the wind getting under the tail or wing and lifting it up. With the wind coming from behind the aircraft as in this question, it is reasonable not to lift the elevator or the wind could get under it and tip the aircraft onto its nose. Similarly, with the wind coming from the left side, if the left aileron were raised, the wind could again get underneath and lift the wing.

Question 67. While E-15 is a map, it is not a VNC. The VNC is indicated by A5014: the Prince George VNC.

Question 68. The point to note here is the length of the displaced threshold.

Question 69. Runway 19 points (within a few degrees) to 190°M (it must be a magnetic bearing as it doesn't have the letter T after it). The other end will be 180° from this: 010°M. For runway numbering, the final digit is dropped, leaving the runway number as 01 (or, in the USA, simply 1).

Question 70. The strength and readability levels need to be learned (although in practice anything other than 1 or 5 is rarely used):

- The readability scale is 1—unreadable; 2—readable now and then; 3—readable with difficulty; 4—readable; and 5—perfectly readable.
- The strength scale is 1—bad; 2—poor; 3—fair; 4—good; and 5—excellent.

Question 71. On aircraft and ships, a red light is mounted on the left (port) side and a green light on the right (starboard). In this case, seeing the right light on the right indicates that the aircraft is approaching head-on. Interception normally involves flashing lights.

Question 72. This is again one of those things that you have to learn (from the COM section of the AIM). If P is pronounced PAPA it is often interpreted over the radio as ALFA—the correct pronunciation is "pah PAH".

Question 73. This is a PAPI (see question 83) and the more red lights, the lower you are. A perfect glide slope would always show two white and two red lights. It is a pilot "joke" that when the lights appear green you are much too low and you're seeing them through the grass.

Question 74. There is no such thing as "Local North", so that answer is clearly wrong. Runways in the northern domestic airspace are numbered in accordance with true north (and have a T after the number, e.g., runway 23T) because magnetic headings are of little use in areas where the magnetic dip is very large.

Question 75. The formula is $s = 9 \times \sqrt{p}$, where p is the tire pressure in psi and s the minimum speed in knots at which hydroplaning should occur. In this case $s = 9 \times \sqrt{25} = 9 \times 5 = 45$ knots.

Question 76. Wheelbarrowing only occurs with nose-wheel aircraft. It happens when the pilot applies down elevator and thereby places too much weight on the nose wheel. In some cases, directional control is lost and propeller strikes are not unknown. The normal corrective action is to apply up elevator to remove the extra load from the nose wheel.

Question 77. This is the sort of question that is an examination writer's dream but which has little or no practical use in flying. A side slip and a forward slip are aerodynamically identical: the aircraft is flying with the ailerons trying to turn the aircraft in one direction and the rudder trying to turn it in the other. In either type of slip, the pitot tube is not pointing directly into the air flow and the static port is not perpendicular to the air flow so the airspeed indicator is inaccurate. The only distinction between a side slip and a forward slip is how the slip is entered: if the pilot maintains track over the ground, the slip is a forward slip. This type of slip is used to lose height on final approach. If the pilot maintains heading, it is a side slip. This type of slip is used to land in a crosswind.

Question 78. With the reduced headwind, the pilot will be arriving at the runway sooner than he would otherwise have expected. To maintain the perfect glide slope, the rate of descent will need to be increased to perhaps 450 or 500 ft per minute (as there will be fewer minutes during the descent).

Question 79. ROGER means, "I have heard and understood your transmission". It therefore makes no sense to respond to the calls about aircraft type or repeating a transmission with ROGER. It would be possible to respond to the heading change with ROGER but a better response would be WILCO: "I have heard and understood your transmission and will comply with it". Remember that, apart from hold-short instructions, there is never a requirement to read back instructions or clearances when flying VFR: it just clutters the radio channel and prevents other calls from getting through. ROGER and WILCO are your friends.

Question 80. Accessing the ATIS first is important as it gives you information about the airport's weather and the runways in use and accessing ATIS after talking to the tower would give you little or no additional information. Terminal controllers handle the area around the airport's control zone and therefore need to be accessed before talking to tower (as tower controllers only control the control zone itself).

Question 81. The weight of a US gallon of AVGAS (about 6 lbs at 15°C) is something that you will need to know for weight and balance calculations. Other answers are for an Imperial (rather than US) gallon and for a litre. The density changes with temperature and, at −40°C, a US gallon of AVGAS weighs 6.41 lbs.

Question 82. The only confusion here is that if one end of a parallel runway is LEFT, then the other end is RIGHT.

Question 83. The Ⓟ on the runway diagram indicates a PAPI (Precision Approach Path Indication). In the LIGHTING section, this is defined to be a P1—a type 1 PAPI suitable for small aircraft.

Question 84. With the single exception of an IFR pilot being vectored by ATC, the pilot-in-command is *always* responsible for ensuring that she doesn't run into the ground.

Question 85. A nautical mile is defined to be the distance between two lines of latitude one minute apart and a knot is a speed of one nautical mile per hour. The answer of 100 ft per minute is also almost correct: 1 knot is about 101.268591 ft per minute and pilots will often refer to a vertical speed of, say, 500 ft per minute as 5 knots.

Question 86. This is a straightforward use of an aviation calculator. Almost all of these calculators have a function to convert between different units used in aviation.

Question 87. 121.5 MHz is the emergency frequency and would be unsuitable for this kind of chat. 114.6 MHz is a VOR frequency and could not be accessed with a VHF communications radio. 126.7 MHz is the *en route* frequency and is also inappropriate for chat. In the Southern Domestic Airspace, 122.75 MHz is designated for air-to-air communications (123.45 MHz in the Northern Domestic Airspace).

Question 88. Altitudes below 18,000 ft should be stated as "X thousand Y hundred feet" rather than "X hundred".

Question 89. This calculation requires a number of steps:

1. Calculate the pressure altitude of the aerodrome. The actual elevation is given at 2622' ASL and the pressure is 30.60" Hg. A flight calculator gives the pressure altitude at being 2,000 ft ASL (a very convenient number!). If you prefer to use the rule of thumb that says that 1" Hg is approximately 1,000 ft, then $30.60 - 29.92 = 0.68$ and so the aerodrome's pressure altitude is about 680 ft lower than its actual altitude: 1942'. The actual difference in takeoff distance will be small but, if you prefer this method then you will need to interpolate into the table (i.e., estimate a value between two values from the table).
2. Calculate the headwind that will be met during takeoff. Presumably, with the wind from 280°M, you will use runway 25 and so, by the flight calculator, the cross-wind will be 10 knots and the headwind 18 knots.
3. With this basic information, we can look into figure B.1. There is a row for a pressure altitude of 2000' but unfortunately no column for 15°C, meaning that we will have to interpolate between the 10° and 20° columns. So the ground roll, before we make the necessary corrections, will be $\frac{1000+1075}{2} = 1037.5$ ft.
4. There is an 18 knot headwind and, according to the note at the top of the table, this allows us to reduce the distance by 20%. This makes the ground roll 830 ft.
5. Close inspection of the CFS entry for Fort Cushing yields additional information that the runway is made of turf. The note at the top of the table tells us that we must increase the distance by 15%, resulting in 955 ft.

Note that the interpolation used to calculate conditions at 15°C is never needed in practice and is rarely needed in an examination. In practice, simply use the more pessimistic number (in this case the 20°C value). It is unlikely that the aircraft that you are flying is perfectly new with a perfectly new engine and it is also unlikely that you will fly a perfect short-field takeoff. If the difference in lengths (37 feet 6 inches) is crucial, then perhaps you should not be thinking of taking off. In an examination, given the multiple-choice nature of the questions, it is common for there to be only one answer within the given range and so it can be chosen without computation.

Question 90. This again requires a number of steps although some of them have been carried out in answering question 89:

1. Calculate the pressure altitude of the aerodrome. This was calculated as 2000' in question 89.
2. Calculate the headwind that will be met during takeoff. Again this was calculated in question 89 and found to be 18 knots.
3. With this basic information, we can look into figure B.1. There is a row for a pressure altitude of 2000' but unfortunately no column for 15°C, meaning that we will have to interpolate between the 10° and 20° columns. So the distance to clear the obstacle, before we make the necessary corrections, will be $\frac{1770+1895}{2} = 1832.5$ ft.
4. There is an 18 knot headwind and, according to the note at the top of the table, this allows us to reduce the distance by 20%. This makes the distance 1,466 ft.
5. Close inspection of the CFS entry for Fort Cushing yields the additional information that the runway is made of turf. The note at the top of the table indicates that we must increase the distance by 15% of the ground roll figure. This is where many students fall into sin: they simply reduce the distance to the obstacle by 15% but, once the aircraft has left the ground, the fact that the runway was turf does not affect its climb. So a headwind will affect both the roll and distance to climb but the runway surface will only affect the roll. In this case, the answer to question 89 gave the increase in ground roll as $955 - 830 = 125$ ft. So we must add 125 ft to 1,466 to get 1,591 ft.

Question 91. The notes in figure B.1 give the corrections for wind for headwinds and tailwinds up to 10 knots. In this case, the tailwind will be 18 knots and therefore it is impossible to calculate the ground roll distance. If you try to take off in this condition, then you are effectively an uninsured test pilot: Cessna does not guarantee the performance of the aircraft.

Question 92. The following steps need to be performed, luckily some of them have already been done for question 89:

1. Calculate the pressure altitude of the aerodrome. This was calculated as 2000' in question 89.
2. Calculate the headwind that will be met during landing. Again this was calculated in question 89 and found to be 18 knots.
3. With this basic information, we can look into figure B.2. There is a row for a pressure altitude of 2000' but unfortunately no column for 15°C, meaning that we will have to interpolate between the 10° and 20° columns. So the distance to clear the obstacle, before we make the necessary corrections, will be $\frac{1300+1335}{2} = 1317.5$ ft and the ground roll distance will be $\frac{550+570}{2} = 560$ ft.
4. There is an 18 knot headwind and, according to the note at the top of the table, this allows us to reduce each of the distances by 20%. This makes the distance to clear the obstacle 1,054 ft and the ground roll distance 448 ft.

5. Close inspection of the CFS entry for Fort Cushing provides the additional information that the runway is made of turf. The note at the top of the table tells us that we must increase the distances by 45% of the ground roll figure. In this case, 45% of the ground roll figure is 201.6 ft and therefore both distances must be increased by 201.6 ft. The distance to clear the obstacle is 1,255.6 ft and the ground roll is 649.6 ft.

Question 93. First it is necessary to find the pressure altitude associated with an indicated altitude of 6,500 ft. The altimeter setting at Fort Cushing was 30.60" Hg and a flight calculator will allow you to find that the cruise altitude is 5,878 ft ASL. As the standard temperature at this altitude is 3°C, the centre column of figure B.6 can be used to find that, at 2,500 rpm, a true airspeed of between 110 knots (6,000 ft) and 111 knots (4,000 ft) should be achieved. These numbers are too close together to make interpolation worthwhile, so 110 KTAS will be used. To calculate the indicated airspeed a flight calculator needs to be used to find that the indicated airspeed will be 101 knots.

Question 94. At a pressure altitude of 6,000 ft, the fuel burn (from figure B.6) would be 7.2 gallons per hour; at 4,000 ft it would be 7.5 gallons per hour. As calculated in question 93, we will be cruising at a pressure altitude of 5,878 ft (equivalent to 6,500 ft indicated). Simple interpolation shows that the fuel burn at this altitude will be $7.5 - \frac{1878}{2000} \times 0.3 = 7.21$—just over 7.2 gallons per hour. If you were in a hurry in the examination, you could argue that you're at a pressure altitude of just less than 6000' and so the fuel burn will be between 7.2 and 7.5 gallons per hour, and probably closer to 7.2 than 7.5.

Question 95. The V speeds that Transport Canada wants you to know for the written examination are listed in the document TP12880E. V_{lo} is one of them. Actually most retractable aircraft have different maximum speeds for lowering and raising their wheels. A Piper Seminole, for example, can extend its gear at 140 knots but must be below 100 knots to retract it.

Question 96. There are rather nasty charts (looking like quarter circles with concentric circles) that allow you to approximate the cross and headwinds for a particular runway, but it is much easier (and more accurate) to use a flight calculator. These give a positive or negative crosswind to indicate whether it is coming from the right or left but, rather than trying to remember which is which, it is better just to visualise it: in this example, imagine being lined up on runway 12 and having the wind come from 150°M. From which direction would the wind be coming? From the right of course.

Question 97. The rule of thumb is that a slope of 1% effectively increases (downslope) or decreases (upslope) the runway length by 10%. Here the upslope will cause additional drag on the aircraft during its takeoff run and so the runway can be considered shorter than the true 3,000 ft—eliminating two of the answers. If you didn't know the rule of thumb in an examination then, after eliminating the two obviously wrong answers, you might have to guess between the other two but one is the more probably: it's unlikely that the topic would be considered if the change in distance was as little as 100 ft.

Question 98. The Canadian Runway Friction Index runs from 1.0 (braking is equivalent to braking on a bare and dry runway) to 0.0 (there is effectively no braking capability). However, it only records reduced braking action caused by ice and snow—not by water. Whether or not the runway should be used for landing is a decision to be made by the pilot-in-command.

Question 99. V_a represents the manoeuvring speed of an aircraft. This is sometimes defined as the speed below which a pilot can use full control deflections without over-stressing the aircraft. In fact, it is really only nose-up control deflections that matter—these are the ones that place stress on the airframe. Basically, at speeds below V_a, the aircraft will stall before damage can occur if the nose is pulled up abruptly; above that speed the stall may not occur and damage may result.

Question 100. V_{NE} is the speed that should never be exceeded because flight above this speed can result in structural damage to the aircraft. In a stall (including a spin—a type of stall) the airspeed is normally not increasingly rapidly so V_{NE} is unlikely to be exceeded. During a steep turn the speed also remains fairly constant. During a spiral dive, however, the speed increases very rapidly.

Question 101. This is one of those things that you either know (probably because you've flown in slow flight) or you don't. If you don't, then you will simply have to learn it.

Question 102. A spin is caused by the fact that the lower wing is stalled more than the upper wing. This is why using ailerons to try to stop the spin is ineffective: it just increases the angle of attack on the lower wing and makes it stall more. In a spiral dive the aircraft is not stalled and the airspeed is likely to be increasing rapidly.

Question 103. V_x is the best angle of climb speed—the speed at which an aircraft gains the most height for the least forward distance across the ground. This is the speed used to clear an obstacle. V_y is the best rate of climb speed—the speed at which an aircraft gains the most height in the least time. This is the speed normally used after takeoff when there are no obstacles.

Question 104. The "cushion of air" concept is quite widely accepted among many pilots. In fact, it is the reduction in induced drag when the wing-tip vortices cannot form properly that causes ground effect.

Question 105. If best endurance were slower than stall speed, then one couldn't fly at best endurance. The best range speed is normally much slower than a typical cruise speed. Best endurance speed occurs at the minimum of the total power curve and best range speed is a little higher.

Question 106. The indicated airspeed of the stall will be the same at any altitude. However, the higher the aircraft is, the more disparity there is between the TAS and the IAS. At 9,000 ft the aircraft will stall more readily (at a higher TAS), but the IAS will be the same.

Question 107. An aircraft can stall at any speed and at any angle with the horizon. Consider an aircraft in a vertical dive at, say 150 knots. If the pilot suddenly pulls the nose-up to avoid hitting the ground, the angle of attack will increase. The aircraft will still be travelling downwards quite quickly and the nose may be well below the horizon but the aircraft might stall. It is only the angle of attack that determines whether an aircraft stalls.

Question 108. By definition, the best *endurance* speed is the speed at which the aircraft will stay in the air for the longest time on a tank of fuel. Normally, the best endurance speed is too slow for normal flight operations and would only be used if the aircraft were running short of fuel while waiting for a nearby airport to become available for landing.

Question 109. Although the weight of the aircraft may be increased by the ice, this is not the primary danger associated with ice. The main danger is that the ice alters the shape of the wing and reduces lift and increases its stall speed.

Question 110. If both aircraft are flying a rate one turn, then they will complete the 360° turn in 2 minutes. So two answers must be wrong. The faster the aircraft is flying, the greater bank angle will be required to maintain a rate one turn so B's bank angle will be greater than A's—eliminating another answer. This leaves one answer: aircraft A will fly at 100 knots for 2 minutes and aircraft B at 150 knots for 2 minutes. Clearly, aircraft B will travel further.

Question 111. One answer can be eliminated immediately: the use of oxygen by the pilot has nothing to do with the aircraft's specification. Unless you know the answer, then it would be difficult to reject any of the other answers. Even if you had remembered that the service ceiling is the height at which the aircraft can only achieve a climb of 100 ft per minute, you may have had difficulty in deciding between the remaining answers. Being able to maintain level flight determines the *absolute ceiling* rather than the *service ceiling* of the aircraft.

Question 112. When the density altitude is lower than normal, the aerodrome appears to be at a lower altitude where the air is denser.

Question 113. This question isn't really the type that you will see on the Transport Canada examination, but it is important to include it because many students (you are, of course, an exception) have trouble with the "balance" portion of a weight and balance calculation. Often they don't really know what they're doing and attempt to go through the motions without really understanding. Doing a balance calculation for an aircraft is very much like the example in this question: given some weights (pilot, passengers, fuel, baggage and the empty aircraft itself) at different positions, where would the aircraft balance if it were to be put on a pivot like the one in figure B.26? This position is called the centre of gravity (or, more correctly, the centre of mass). We find it by calculating moments (force × distance) around a point known as the datum. For Piper aircraft, the datum is often the tip of the spinner at the front of the aircraft; for Cessnas it is the firewall behind the engine. As this example will show, IT DOESN'T MATTER where the datum is taken. Firstly let's take the datum as point Ⓐ in figure B.26. We also have to decide which direction of turning we will count as positive and here it is decided (unilaterally) that clockwise will be positive. There are three weights in this "aircraft": one is 120 lbs at 0 inches from the datum, one is 90 lbs at 150 inches from the datum and the third is 15 lbs 220 inches from the datum. If you imagine putting your finger at point Ⓐ, you will see that each of these will tend to turn the see-saw in a clockwise direction. The total moment is therefore

$$(0 \times 120) + (150 \times 90) + (220 \times 15) = 16800 \text{ lb-inches}$$

So, the question is, given the total force of $120 + 90 + 15 = 225$ lbs, where would that single force have to be to give the same effect? We want a 225 lb force to give a moment of 16800 lb-inches and so it will have to act at $\frac{16800}{225} = 74.7$ inches from Ⓐ. As it will have to rotate the plank clockwise about Ⓐ, it will have to be 74.7 inches to the right of Ⓐ. This is the calculation that you do when you determine the "balance" portion of a weight and balance calculation—where will the centre of gravity lie? It is not important where the datum is and, to prove that, we will do the sums again with the datum at Ⓑ. There are again three weights to take into account: 120 lbs 220 inches from the datum, 90 lbs 70 inches from the datum and 15 lbs 0 inches from the datum. The first two of these are trying to make the plank rotate anti-clockwise about Ⓑ and so their moments will be negative. The total moment is therefore

$$(-220 \times 120) + (-70 \times 90) + (0 \times 15) = -32700 \text{ lb-inches}$$

Again, the total forces acting are 225 lbs and the single force that would have the same turning effect would be one acting $\frac{-32700}{225} = -145.3$ inches from the datum. As this is negative it means that the force must turn the plank anticlockwise about Ⓑ and so must act 145.3 inches to the left of Ⓑ. 145.3 inches to the left of Ⓑ is the same as 74.7 inches to the right of Ⓐ: where ever the datum is placed, the centre of gravity will always be in the same space. If you have trouble with balance calculations, you should read this answer carefully—it will make your life much easier when you understand what you're actually doing. Perhaps you should try taking moments around Ⓒ (or any other point) to prove that you get the same answer again.

Question 114. By definition, the datum is the position from which the arms are measured. The arm of the datum is therefore always zero. In this case, it is the baggage area which has an arm of zero and so that must be the datum.

Question 115. The term *utility category* is used for the range of centres of gravity within which the aerobatic exercises defined in the Pilot Operating Handbook are permitted.

Question 116. This is, of course, not really an experimental aircraft. It is just a Cessna 172 with its datum moved from the firewall to the baggage area to make the arithmetic slightly harder. The point is that it doesn't matter from which point the arms are measured.

Question 117. Some arithmetic shows that the new centre of gravity is 52.14 inches from the datum (if you calculated 52.0 inches then you forgot to subtract the amount of fuel burned from the 38 gallons already on board) rather than the 51.82 inches before. This means that it moved 0.3 inches further from the datum. As the datum is in the baggage area, this means it has moved further forward.

Question 118. This answer is unexpected to many students. Having the centre of gravity outside the limits actually makes it slightly harder to stall (the stall speed reduces). Of course, if the aircraft *does* stall, then recovery is not guaranteed.

Question 119. Gusty winds tend to break up wing-tip vortices (wake turbulence)—the worst conditions occur when there is a light, steady wind to blow the vortices across a neighbouring runway.

Question 120. Wing-tip vortices, the cause of induced drag, form as tubes of rotating air behind an aircraft and can be extremely dangerous for a light aircraft following a heavy one.

Question 121. Wake turbulence tends to drop behind a heavy aircraft. It is therefore best to stay above its glide path. Its wing-tip vortices will stop when the wing is no longer providing lift (i.e., at the point where it touched down). Therefore wake turbulence should not be a factor if you land beyond the point where the heavy aircraft landed.

Question 122. The term *Mayday* (which may dervive from the French m'aider) means that an emergency is taking place where there is imminent danger to life or to the continued viability of the aircraft itself and immediate help is required. In contrast, *Pan Pan* means that there is an urgency on the aircraft but, for the time being at least, there is no immediate danger to anyone's life or to the aircraft itself.

Question 123. One answer can be dismissed immediately because the largest number that can be dialled into a transponder is 7777. The answer 1200 can also be dismissed because it is the code normally used for VFR flight when no other code has been issued by ATC. To decide between the other two answers, you need to remember the code for either hijack and communications failure.

Question 124. If you cannot contact Flight Services to close your flight plan (and perhaps you could try to make contact with an over-flying aircraft to pass the message), then a search will start one hour after the estimated time of arrival on your flight plan. To reduce the cost of the unnecessary search, you should turn on the ELT at that time to make locating you as easy as possible.

Question 125. The problem is that, after the aircraft has been flying at altitude, the fuel has become cold. As the aircraft descends into warmer and moister air, the fuel is still cold and frost or ice forms on the wings around the fuel tanks.

Question 126. Effectively, any surface over which air is designed to flow in such a way as to affect the flight characteristics of the aircraft is designated as a "critical surface". For example, a wing strut on a Cessna 172 is designed to have air flow across it but that flow of air does not affect the aircraft's flight characteristics. The wing struts are therefore not critical surfaces.

Question 127. Composite materials have been used in aircraft for a long time. The first all-composite fuselage was probably that of a Spitfire built in the early 1940s. However, composites have a number of disadvantages over metals: they provide little protection against lightning and must have metal placed inside them to handle this; they cannot be patched in the same way that metal can and their failure modes are poorly understood—where metals crack in a well-understood manner and inspection can determine that repairs need to be carried out before catastrophic failure; composites show no sign of fatigue before failure.

Question 128. Almost all modern aircraft are of monocoque construction: the skin of the fuselage is load-bearing and there is no need for internal frames to provide rigidity and strength. Perhaps the best known example of a monocoque structure is a chicken's egg. Some modern aircraft (e.g., the Steen Skybolt) are primarily of truss-type construction but this is unusual.

Question 129. Because a tail-dragger's centre of gravity is behind the main wheels (unlike a tricycle gear aircraft where it is in front), any sideways motion during landing will tend to grow rather than be damped.

Question 130. The reason that flaps are used during landing is to allow the aircraft to fly more slowly—the stall speed is reduced.

Question 131. The wing span is the distance from wing-tip to wing-tip and this is not altered by extending the flaps. The chord of a wing is the line between the leading edge to the rear-most part of the wing and this is clearly modified when the flaps are lowered—altering the angle of attack if the aircraft is in level flight. The camber of a wing is a measure of how curved the wing is and this, in turn, determines the coefficient of lift. Thus, both the camber and coefficient of lift are increased by extending the flaps.

Question 132. It is unlikely that you had no problem with this question but it's there for a reason. A passenger did once ask some questions during taxiing and that took some time to understand—he believed that the wheels were being driven from the engine, as with a car. Given at least one person confused by this, the question is worth including.

Question 133. With a constant-speed propeller, the manifold gauge is the instrument that reads "engine power". It measures the restriction of airflow through the engine and hence the unused power capacity in the engine. If the throttle is wide open, then as the piston moves downwards on the induction stroke, the pressure in the induction manifold (the pipe from the carburetor) is more or less at atmospheric pressure (unless there is turbo-charging). On the other hand, if the throttle is partly closed, then a negative pressure will build between the throttle and the cylinder as the piston moves downwards, indicating reduced power from the engine.

Question 134. It is the generator or alternator that ensures that the battery remains charged. The battery (or alternator/generator) is responsible for providing the power for the radios. The answer about the spark is complete gibberish.

Question 135. There is only one sequence that makes sense: you cannot compress unless you have previously sucked the fuel/air mixture in (induction). You can't suck the fuel/air mixture in unless you have previously removed the burned gases (exhaust) and exhaust makes no sense unless you have just burned the fuel/air mixture on the power stroke. It would make no sense, for example, to pull fuel/air in (induction) and then immediately exhaust it before burning it to create power.

Question 136. Turbo-charging does reduce the power provided by the engine slightly because some of the engine's power goes into turning the turbine but this is not its purpose; rather it is an undesirable side-effect. The purpose of turbo-charging is to increase the amount of air at higher altitudes so that it's unnecessary to lean the mixture to keep the ratio of air and fuel correct.

Question 137. To some extent, having two magnetos provides both redundancy *and* better fuel burn. However, the answer about better fuel burn is not strictly correct because it is not the presence of the two magnetos that produces better burning—that occurs because of the two sparkplugs in each cylinder and, in principle, it would be possible to have two spark plugs driven from a single magneto. The main purpose of the twin magnetos is to provide redundancy.

Question 138. The mixture control determines the amount of fuel going into the engine's fuel/air mixture. It is normally used to reduce the amount of fuel as the aircraft climbs, thereby compensating for the thinner air at higher altitudes. Two of the answers refer to the carburetor heat control rather than the mixture control.

Question 139. When the engine is running on the left magneto only, the right magneto should be grounded. If it were being grounded, then the engine would only be firing on a single magneto and the engine would slow down slightly (by a few hundred rpm). Since the engine is not slowing down, the magneto is presumably not being grounded. For the purposes of flight, this is not a problem. Once back on the ground, the engine could fire if the propeller were rotated by hand—a dangerous condition.

Question 140. Warm air is less dense than cold air, so applying warm air reduces the amount of air in the fuel/air mixture, making it richer (i.e., increasing the percentage of fuel).

Question 141. As the mixture control is applied, it reduces the amount of fuel in the fuel/air mixture. This causes the mixture to become leaner (that is why we talk of "leaning the mixture") and a lean mixture burns hotter. As he keeps pulling, the mixture goes over its optimal ratio and the temperature starts to drop because there is insufficient fuel in the mixture. Of course, if he keeps pulling, the engine will stop and the exhaust gas temperature drop significantly!

Question 142. Carburetor icing effectively starts to choke the carburetor outlet in much the same way that closing the throttle does. This results in reduced rpm, as shown on the tachometer.

Question 143. At very low temperatures it is unlikely that the air contains sufficient moisture to cause carburetor icing (any water in the air is in the form of ice crystals that pass straight through the carburetor). By applying carburetor heat, the air can be heated sufficiently for the ice to become moisture that can then refreeze in the carburetor.

Question 144. Warmer air is less dense than colder air and so applying carburetor heat and thereby heating the air going into the fuel/air mixture will reduce the mass of air in the mixture (although not its volume). Reducing the air while keeping the fuel supply constant will cause the mixture to become rich. Most people who have flown an aircraft with a carbureted engine will have noticed a drop in rpm when carburetor heat is applied: leading them to the correct answer. If you have never experienced this, then it is worth bearing in mind that, on the ground, the engine is normally running slightly rich: making it richer reduces the power.

Question 145. Reducing the temperature of the mixture would have little effect on its burning and the power going to the spark comes nowhere near the carburetor. Looking at the position that carburetor icing forms—around the throttle valve after the fuel and air have been mixed—makes it clear that its formation slowly constricts the flow of the mixture and, if severe, locks the throttle in place.

Question 146. Changing the speed and temperature of the fuel/air mixture are biproducts of the carburetor, not its purpose. Its purpose is to mix the correct amounts of fuel and air for burning in the cylinders.

Question 147. For the purpose of alternate air, see the answer to question 148.

Question 148. In a fuel-injected engine the fuel is not mixed with air at low pressure, rather the fuel is injected directly into the cylinder or intake manifold close to the intake valve. Because they don't have carburetors, fuel-injected engines don't suffer from carburetor ice. They can, however, suffer from induction ice: ice or snow forming over the induction air filter and blocking it. To guard against this, fuel-injected engines are often fitted with alternate air: warm air taken from under the engine cowling downstream of the normal air intake. As fuel injection requires the fuel to be under high pressure, gravity feed is normally not an option.

Question 149. In most light aircraft, the electrical power to make the spark is generated by a magneto—a system that operates completely independently of the electrical system and so the engine would not stop. If the aircraft's battery is in reasonable condition, the failure of the alternator will have little immediate effect (this is one of its dangers) because the electrical equipment will run on battery power. However, the battery is not being charged from the alternator and will discharge. To preserve battery power, transmitters are the first items to switch off (e.g., the transponder) because they draw a lot of current. All other non-essential electronics should also be turned off. This is where a hand-held radio (with charged batteries!) is really useful.

Question 150. Alternators are generally lighter and smaller than generators of equivalent output. They also provide a better voltage at slow revolution speeds. However, one major disadvantage of an alternator is that it needs some electrical current to kick-start it. Typically, this is supplied by the aircraft's battery and if the battery is drained or has been removed, the alternator will not generate electricity.

Question 151. On answer can be immediately rejected: a motor does not generate electricity, rather it consumes it. The answer about the regulator is unlikely and can also be rejected: why would one want to switch out a voltage regulator? The amount of current drawn by the electronics is negligible compared to the starting current so that answer, while possible, is also unlikely. The main reason is contained in the remaining answer: during the starting of the engine there may be voltage spikes on the power bus until the regulator has taken control of the system. These could damage fragile electronics and, to prevent this damage, the avionics bus, to which the avionics are connected, is disconnected from the main aircraft power.

Question 152. A circuit breaker and a fuse both perform the same basic function—they detect too much current passing through a circuit and interrupt that circuit to break the flow. A fuse is sacrificial—it melts and breaks the circuit and has to be replaced. On the other hand, a circuit breaker detects the over-current and opens the circuit in such a way that it can be reset. There are no substantial timing differences between fuses and circuit breakers: some fuses are designed to blow very quickly, others more slowly. The wire heating and melting is a description of a fuse rather than a circuit breaker. It is the purpose of neither a fuse nor a circuit breaker to carry as much current as possible.

Question 153. Circuit breakers normally cannot be removed and replaced in flight. Continual resetting is dangerous—the breaker presumably tripped because there is an electrical problem and resetting it repeatedly may cause an electrical fire. However, breakers do spontaneously trip sometimes and resetting them once is normal practice and not dangerous.

Question 154. Firstly, the W means "winter". The 20 indicates that the dynamic viscosity of the oil when the temperature is $-15°C$ will be no more than 9,500 milliPascal seconds (centipoises). The 50 means that its kinematic viscosity when it is hot ($100°C$) will be in the range 12.5 to 16.3 square millimetres per second (centistokes). Note that the actual numbers 20 and 50 do not appear in these values: they are just the row numbers into a table of the oil viscosities. Note also that the units of each viscosity is different. You don't need to know the details for the Private Pilot Licence examination—just remember that the numbers are measures of the viscosity at cold (W) and hot temperatures. The ideal oil is, of course, still runny (non-viscous) at low temperatures and still viscous at high temperatures.

Question 155. This is an awkward question to answer. The "examination answer" is that mineral oils and synthetic oils should *never* be mixed; the mineral oil should be completely flushed from the system before synthetic oil is added. However, there seems to be little research that backs this belief, and many articles speak of it as a long-standing fiction—there being no problem with mixing them.

Question 156. Synthetic oil is much better at lubricating and preventing wear than mineral oil. When an engine is first being used, the additional wear that comes from using mineral oil helps seating to occur, and the irregularities on the pistons and cylinder walls to be worn smooth.

Question 157. There are basically two types of lubrication systems for reciprocating engines: wet-sump, where the oil is stored in the sump of the engine and dry-sump, where (as the name suggests) the oil is not contained in the sump but in a separate oil tank. The dry-sump system does not restrict the amount of oil that can be circulated and is therefore suitable for large engines and, as it is pumped under pressure, suitable for aerobatic flight.

Question 158. If oil were being lost from the engine, then it is probable that the oil temperature would be rising. If there had been an electrical failure that could affect the oil temperature and pressure gauges, then both would drop to zero. The most probable cause is a failure of the pressure indicator but you should still land as soon as possible.

Question 159. Oil dilution is very rarely used these days but it does appear on Transport Canada examinations from time to time. The idea was to reduce the viscosity of the oil when starting the engine on a cold day by pouring fuel into the oil. As the oil heated up after the engine started, the fuel would simply vapourise and disappear. On light aircraft, the mixing of fuel into the oil was manual but on larger aircraft there were mechanisms built into the engines to introduce the correct amount of fuel. With modern multigrade fuels, oil dilution is no longer needed.

Question 160. The primary purposes of oil in the engine are that it lubricates the moving metal parts, carries away impurities that result from combustion and cools the engine by carrying the heat away from the cylinders. It is this last function that many pilots don't appreciate—the primary cooling mechanism of a piston engine is the oil.

Question 161. The purpose of bonding the truck and aircraft is to ensure that static-electrical charges cannot cause a spark during the fuelling. The other answers are effectively meaningless.

Question 162. The colouring of fuel was particularly important when there was a choice of octane ratings: 80/87 which was coloured red, 100/130 which was coloured green and 100LL which was (and is) coloured blue. As only 100LL is widely available now, the colour coding is less important. It can also be used to determine whether the "fuel" being drained from a tank is pure water, but this is a very uncertain test as even water will acquire a blue colour when present in a tank that has held 100LL.

Question 163. There are two related but independent concepts: pre-ignition is the early burning of the fuel before the sparking plug has fired. Detonation occurs after the sparking plug has fired, but before the controlled flame front (the flame moving across the cylinder) has burned all of the fuel/air mixture. Both of these can cause substantial damage to a piston and cylinder. A high octane rating will tend to suppress rather than encourage detonation and pre-ignition and detonation tends to occur if the engine is run too "lean" (and therefore becomes hotter than normal).

Question 164. The primary problem with MOGAS is its volatility. At altitude, it tends to vapourise and form vapour locks in fuel feed lines. MOGAS contains much *less* lead than AVGAS: about 100 times less than 100 low lead AVGAS! Answers about higher octane ratings and freezing points may be true for certain MOGAS but, even if true, they are advantages rather than disadvantages.

Question 165. Many people erroneously believe that using a higher octane fuel will cause their engine to produce more power. This is not the case. The octane rating is a measure of the fuel's resistance to pre-ignition: firing as a result of the high temperature caused by compression, rather than as a result of a spark from the spark plug. The higher the octane rating, the less the fuel is prone to pre-ignition.

Question 166. Oxygen forms the same fraction of the atmosphere by day and night. Even if it didn't, it's hard to see what the ionisation of the upper atmosphere would have to do with it. While a lack of oxygen may result in hypoxia, it is unlikely by itself to result in hypothermia (caused by cold temperatures). The answer about density altitude is also wrong—a density altitude has nothing to do with day or night. That leaves one answer: night vision is particularly affected by the reduced amount of oxygen available to the retina, and therefore supplemental oxygen is recommended from 5,000 ft at night for non-smokers and from the surface for smokers.

	Normally	Blocked Pitot	Blocked Static
5000' ASL	P - S	P - S	P - S
3000' ASL	P - S	P - S	P - S
1000' ASL	P - S	P - S	P - S

P = Pitot pressure
S = Static pressure

Figure A.1: Explanation for Questions 172 and 173

Question 167. There is (or should be!) no connection between the static and vacuum systems. It is unlikely that the gyroscopes in both instruments have toppled and, even if they have, that would not normally cause a blockage that would increase the suction. If the vacuum pump had failed then there would be no vacuum pressure recorded. That leaves one answer—the vacuum pump is sucking against a blockage, thereby creating a slightly higher pressure (actually "lower" as this is a vacuum but pilots normally speak of a "higher" vacuum pressure) at the pump.

Question 168. Turning on the pitot or carburetor heat is unlikely to have any effect on the static port. If alternate static is available it should be used and, as a last resort, if it is not available, the VSI can be broken to allow cabin air into the system. Note that this does not work in pressurised aircraft.

Question 169. The only instrument connected to the pitot tube is the ASI, so it must be the only affected instrument.

Question 170. The three static port instruments are the ASI (which compares the pressure at the static port with the dynamic pressure at the pitot tube), the altimeter (which is a barometer and measures the static pressure) and the VSI (which measures the rate at which the static pressure is changing).

Question 171. If the cabin is pressurised, then it makes no sense having the static port inside the aircraft because there it will record the cabin pressure rather than the atmospheric pressure.

Question 172. It is better not to try to remember the answers to these questions where "the static port or pitot tube blocks"—work them out as required. In this case two answers can be dismissed immediately and the only difficulty is to differentiate between the other two. It can be argued as follows (see figure A.1):

- The ASI displays the difference between the pressure at the pitot tube (P) and the pressure at the static port (S)
- Near the ground, both S and P are large and the ASI displays their difference
- As the aircraft climbs, both S and P get smaller but, within limits, the difference P - S remains the same
- When the pitot tube blocks, P remains the same as the aircraft climbs (the pressure inside the pitot tube is locked in place) but S continues to decrease so the difference being displayed becomes too big

The ASI therefore over-reads.

Question 173. See the advice at the top of the solution for question 172 and figure A.1. In this case two answers can be dismissed immediately and the only difficulty is to differentiate between the other two. It can be argued as follows:

- The ASI displays the difference between the pressure at the pitot tube (P) and the pressure at the static port (S)
- Near the ground both S and P are large and the ASI displays their difference
- As the aircraft climbs, both S and P decrease but, within limits, their difference remains the same
- When the static port blocks, S remains the same as the aircraft climbs (the pressure inside the static system is locked in place) but P continues to decrease so the difference being displayed becomes too small

The ASI therefore under-reads.

Question 174. The range of speeds at which the flaps may be deployed is indicated by a white arc. V_{NE} is indicated by a red line. V_{MC} is indicated by a short red line. It would not be possible to put manoeuvring speed as a mark on the ASI because it changes with weight.

Question 175. The CAS is basically a correction needed because of the way the pitot tube and static ports are mounted on a particular airframe. CAS is not a calculated number—it is a number to be found in the Pilot Operating Handbook.

Question 176. The only way to do this calculation is to use a flight calculator.

Question 177. Before the blockage, the VSI was measuring the rate at which air left a container through a controlled hole as the atmospheric pressure outside the aircraft decreased. Because of the blockage, the external pressure is no longer changing. The VSI interprets this as meaning that the aircraft is no longer climbing or descending. It therefore displays level flight.

Question 178. The microprocessor answer must be wrong because VSIs were around a long time before microprocessors. VSIs were also around long before transponders. It is a radar altimeter that fires radio energy downwards; these only work below about 2,500 ft and only when there is clear ground or water below.

Question 179. As the VSI has no connexion with the pitot tube, the pitot tube blocking cannot affect its operation.

Question 180. The altimeter responds to changing external pressure at the static port. Because the static port is blocked, the external pressure appears not to change. The altimeter will therefore assume that the aircraft is still at the altitude where the blockage occurred.

Question 181. On a cold day, the atmospheric pressure drops more rapidly with height than on a standard temperature day. Unfortunately, altimeters assume standard temperatures and therefore over-read at altitude on cold days. To compensate for this, Nav Canada publishes cold weather correction tables in the General Pages of the Canada Air Pilot.

Question 182. The term "blind" indicates that the altimeter does not have a display (this is an illogical use of the term since it is not the altimeter that is blind but the person trying to use it). Encoding altimeters (whether blind or not) do not need to be set to the local atmospheric pressure—they always record pressure altitude (i.e., altitude for an altimeter setting of about 29.92 inches of mercury).

Question 183. The current pressure recorded on the altimeter is about 29.92 inches of mercury. Changing it to 30.10 inches of mercury is effectively asking, "Where is the pressure 0.18 inches of mercury greater than it is here?" The answer, of course, is "lower than here, where there is a greater amount of atmosphere above (actually about 180 ft lower than here)." The answer must be that a lower altitude would be displayed. Note that the pressure altitude is displayed when the pressure is set to 29.92 inches of mercury.

Question 184. The altimeter is not connected to the pitot tube, so a pitot tube blockage cannot affect it.

Question 185. Bouncing radio waves off the ground describes a radar altimeter (a device that only works at heights of less than about 2,500 ft AGL, and that only measures height above ground rather than height above sea-level). An airspeed indicator measures the pressure difference and a vertical speed indicator measures the rate of pressure change. An altimeter is simply a barometer measuring atmospheric pressure.

Question 186. Acceleration and deceleration compass errors are caused by magnetic dip, and so would not occur at the equator. They are worst near the magnetic poles. Compasses do not register climbs and, in the context of the question, tumbling is unlikely. The *aide-memoire* here is ANDS—acceleration gives a northerly error, deceleration a southerly error.

Question 187. Magnetic dip is the phenomenon that causes most compass errors. It occurs because the lines of the earth's magnetic field are parallel to the surface of the earth only at the equator; they are almost vertical near the magnetic poles and so compass needles point downwards in the northern hemisphere.

Question 188. This is really a matter of air law—compass swings (i.e., checking the compass for accuracy and re-issuing the compass correction card) must be carried out at least once per year and whenever an event occurs (e.g., a lightning strike) that might cause the compass to become unreliable.

Question 189. This question is ostensibly about the northerly and southerly turning errors in a magnetic compass (the compass leads the aircraft's turn on southerly headings and lags behind the turn on northerly headings). However, when the aircraft is flying due east or west there is no northerly or southerly turning error and the compass reads correctly. Of course, once the turn is under way, the aircraft will now have a northerly component, and the compass will start to lag but its initial display will be correct.

Question 190. The only device ambiguous in the possible answers is the strikefinder. This sferics device has the option of having a (solid state) gyroscope fitted so that, as the aircraft turns, the dots on the screen indicating lightning can be moved to their new positions. Otherwise, encoding altimeters, transponders and VOR receivers have no use for gyroscopes.

Question 191. Gyroscopic action cannot really be described without using a significant amount of mathematics. What makes gyroscopes so fascinating (and useful) is that they are so unpredictable. If you have ever ridden a bicycle you are familiar with the basic concept as the bike's front wheel is a gyroscope. As you ride along, lean the bike slightly to the left. Instead of falling over (as might be expected), the front wheel turns to the left and the bike turns a corner. This is an example of a gyroscope moving at right angles to the applied force (strictly the term should be "torque" rather than "force"). Some people talk about a gyroscope being "rigid in space". It actually isn't, it's just that the movement it makes is not in the direction one would anticipate. For this question, one answer is clearly wrong, another is part of the description of a so-called "solid-state gyroscope": a clever device with no moving parts (other than a light beam), and another describes a magnetic compass.

Question 192. Heading indicator gyroscopes are normally powered by an electric motor or by a stream of air from the vacuum or pressurisation system hitting indentations (known as "buckets") on the rim of the gyroscope. Of these, by far the most commonly seen in light aircraft is a flow of air from the vacuum system.

Question 193. The gyroscope in a heading indicator is mounted horizontally along the longitudinal axis of the aircraft (i.e., nose to tail, although able to move left and right) so that, when the aircraft turns to the left or right (i.e., around the vertical axis), the gyroscope "precesses" at right angles to this motion and appears to remain fixed. Having a gyroscope that remains fixed while the case of the heading indicator moves with the aircraft, allows the change in heading to be displayed. Mounting the gyroscope vertically would have no effect when the aircraft turned to the left or right. Mounting it horizontally across the aircraft (from wing-tip to wing-tip) would work, but not be as sensitive at the front-to-back mounting. It is the gyroscope in a turn co-ordinator that is mounted on a slant.

Question 194. Heading indicators (in common with other gyroscopic instruments) will tumble and lock up if the bank or pitch angle becomes too great. This angle is typically about 55°. For this reason, it is normal to "cage" (i.e., lock) the gyroscope before carrying out aerobatics.

Question 195. Precession occurs when a force is applied to the rotating gyroscope, and the gyroscope turns in a direction at right angles to the applied force. The rotation of the earth does contribute, and such precession is proportional to the sine of the latitude, making it worse towards the poles. Most heading indicators contain a "latitude nut" so that, if an aircraft is mainly flown around one latitude, then it can be adjusted so that it doesn't drift at that latitude. Most aircraft in North America have their latitude nuts set for 45°N. However, the friction in the bearings of a gyroscope provides a greater force than the earth's rotation, and this is the major cause of precession.

Question 196. The aircraft's right wing is shown to be below the horizon and its left wing above the horizon, so the aircraft must be banked to the right. The white dot in the centre of the display is on the horizon, so the aircraft's nose is neither pitched up or down.

Question 197. The major markings around the edge of the display are at 30° intervals (there are three of them between 12 o'clock and 3 o'clock). So the minor increments are 10°. The triangle points between 10° and 20°, somewhat closer to 10° than 20°.

Question 198. This is the cause of the "black-hole" accidents. Taking off on a dark night over unlit terrain, the pilot concentrates on the attitude indicator. If the nose of the aircraft drops slightly, the aircraft accelerates and the attitude indicator displays a pitch-up. This causes the pilot to push the nose down, causing the aircraft to accelerate more. This can result in the aircraft hitting the ground a few miles off the end of the runway.

Question 199. This is why holding patterns are race-tracks rather than circles. After the aircraft has been flying in circles for some time, the attitude indicator displays stright flight.

Question 200. This is basically the same question as question 192. The flow of air created by the vacuum system passes over the edge of the gyroscope and hits against indentations (buckets). This causes the gyroscope to turn. The answer about providing a baseline is meaningless.

Question 201. The Attitude Indicator has to react to both roll and pitch. Having the gyroscope mounted horizontally along the longitudinal axis would allow it to detect changes of pitch but not roll. If it were mounted around the lateral axis, then it could detect roll but not changes of pitch. Two answers can therefore be excluded. Either of the other two answers could actually work for an Attitude Indicator, but in fact the gyroscope is mounted vertically. In modern aircraft with glass cockpits, a solid-state gyroscope with no moving parts is used in the representation of the Attitude Indicator.

Question 202. Students in their early flight training are told to "step on the ball" to get the aircraft back into co-ordinated flight. In gliders this is particularly important and a piece of yaw string is fitted to the windshield to indicate how the aircraft is cutting through the air. In this case the pilot has applied too much right rudder and so needs to apply left rudder to get back into co-ordinated flight. The slip ball must therefore be to the left.

Question 203. Refer to question 201's explanation for the reason why some answers are wrong. The gyroscope *could* be mounted vertically but, in practice, it is mounted angled upwards at about 35° relative to the longitudinal axis of the aircraft.

Question 204. This is a particularly important difference between the two instruments—to some extent the turn co-ordinator lies because it confuses turn (a change of heading) with roll (one wing going down). Normally, these two things happen together and so the error is not serious but in unusual flight conditions a roll may happen without a turn or a turn without a roll. A turn and bank indicator *only* registers a turn and doesn't move if the aircraft is just rolling (and therefore the inclusion of *bank* in its name is wrong—in Europe, it's known as a turn and slip indicator which makes more sense). A turn co-ordinator registers both because its gyroscope is mounted at an angle to the axis of the aircraft.

Question 205. The slip ball in figure B.15 is in the middle so it is clear that the pilot is in co-ordinated flight. That eliminates two answers. According to figure B.14, The aircraft is in level flight while banking to the right (the right wing-tip in the figure is below the horizon). This is also true of Turn and Bank Indicator B in figure B.15.

Question 206. The attitude indicator is the primary instrument in these conditions although it is important to make sure that you don't fixate on it—keep the scan going. If the attitude indicator fails, then the second-best instrument would be either the turn co-ordinator (but remember that it works in a manner contrary to the attitude indicator—the aircraft symbol moves, rather than the horizon) or the GPS. Although many handheld GPSs now have a primitive attitude indicator, remember that this is based on your rate of turn rather than your bank angle.

Question 207. The attitude indicator and heading indicator contradict each other while the compass and turn co-ordinator seem to be in agreement. This implies that the source of power for the attitude indicator and the heading indicator (typically the vacuum system in a small aircraft) is at fault. This should be confirmed by checking your suction gauge.

Question 208. If the aircraft were in a spin then the airspeed would not be increasing rapidly. In a nose-down condition with the airspeed increasing it is unlikely that the aircraft is about to stall (although it may stall if the nose is pulled up too abruptly).

Question 209. Once in a spiral, applying up-elevator effectively moves the nose further into the centre of the spiral, tightening it. Eventually the stresses on the aircraft are likely to cause structural damage.

Question 210. The first thing to remember is that the aircraft doesn't know that it's in cloud; it won't fly any differently than it did in VMC. Certainly, if pitot heat is fitted it is worth turning it on but this is not urgent—30 seconds won't make a big difference. Squawking 7700 may be useful in the long term, but ATC cannot help the pilot fly the aircraft. Slowing the aircraft down might be useful if the route ahead isn't known, but again a few seconds delay would probably not hurt. The first thing to do is clearly nothing. And once that is complete, start a thought-through process to find better visibility: perhaps a gentle 180° turn, perhaps a turn to where the sky seems lighter. Sometimes, climbing through a stratus layer is the quickest way out of cloud. However, the pilot needs to note the heading being flown and then create and fly a plan.

Question 211. This is a straightforward application of Newton's third law. It is the same principle that applies when a person in a canoe uses a paddle to push water backward, causing the canoe to move forward.

Question 212. The statement about fluids passing through a constriction a statement of Bernoulli's principle—basically a restatement of the law of conservation of energy. If it is anything, the answer about heat flow is a simplified statement of the second law of thermodynamics.

Question 213. The aircraft's load factor is greater than 1 and so it is more likely to stall. Its stall speed will therefore be greater than 65 knots and that immediately eliminates two of the possible answers. To calculate the new stall speed we have to multiply 65 knots by the square root of 1.3. Looking at the possible answers given, it is not necessary actually to perform the calculation.

Question 214. The lift to drag ratio of an aircraft is a measure of how much lift is produced by the wing for how much drag. A Cessna 152 creates a lot of drag for a relatively small amount of lift and so its lift to drag ratio is low: about 7. At the other extreme, a competition sailplane is designed to produce very little drag as it flies and its lift to drag ratio is likely to be about 70. The Boeing 747 lies between the two extremes with a lift to drag ratio of about 17.

Question 215. As discussed in the notes to question 216, induced drag is a measure of the amount of work a wing has to do in order to generate the necessary lift. If the aircraft is heavier, more lift is needed and therefore more induced drag is generated. Unless the extra weight has been strapped onto the outside of the aircraft (and there is no indication in the question that it has), the shape of the aircraft moving through the air is unchanged so the parasitic drag will be unchanged.

Question 216. Induced drag can be thought of as the extra work a wing has to do to create the necessary lift to keep the aircraft in the air. The slower the aircraft flies, the more "work" the wing has to do and the more induced drag will result. Putting flaps down assists the wing in creating lift and so the wing will not be working as hard, reducing the induced drag.

Question 217. Parasitic drag is caused by the aircraft being forced through the air—it increases with speed (and in fact doubles if the speed increases by 41%) and cleaning the bugs may reduce parasitic drag, but it won't change induced drag, the drag caused by lift. At low speeds where the wing has to work harder to create lift, the lift-induced drag (induced drag) is larger.

Question 218. Before the time of Newton, you might have been excused if you believed that, if no net force acts on a body, it will stop. This Aristotelean view held sway for about 1900 years but Newton's first law of motion turned science on its head and said that, "Unless a net force acts on a body, the body will remain in a state of rest or, if already moving, will continue to move in a straight line at a constant speed".

Question 219. This is really question 218 expressed slightly differently. If the aircraft is in straight and level flight at a constant speed then there is no net force acting on it—it is in equilibrium. Its weight must equal its lift and its drag must equal its thrust. If the drag were less than the thrust, the aircraft would be accelerating and if the lift were greater than the weight then it would be climbing.

Question 220. The force applied by gravity to a body is called *weight* and *power* is not a force, it's a rate of doing work.

Question 221. This question can be answered either by a little mathematics or by a little thought. Let's start with some thought. When an aircraft is banking, some of the lift is acting horizontally to pull the aircraft around the corner. If the aircraft is to maintain altitude, then 2,300 lbs of lift must be acting upwards and some amount must be acting towards the centre of the circle (see notes on question 222). In total more than 2,300 lbs of lift must be being generated and there is only answer that satisfies this requirement. Speaking mathematically, the load required is $\frac{W}{\cos\theta}$, where W is the weight of the aircraft and θ is the bank angle. In this case $W = \frac{2300}{0.5} = 4600$.

Question 222. If there were no net force acting on the aircraft then, by Newton's first law, it would be travelling at a constant speed in a straight line. Its speed is constant but it's certainly not travelling in a straight line. If the thrust were greater than the drag, the aircraft would be speeding up. This leaves two answers. Consider the earth moving in a circle (actually an ellipse, but very close to a circle) around the sun: the sun's gravity holds the earth in its orbit by pulling the earth in towards the centre. The aircraft turns because of a similar force acting towards the centre of the turn. In the aircraft's case, the force comes not from gravity but from a component of the lift acting towards the centre because of the aircraft's bank.

Question 223. The angle of incidence is the angle between the chord of the wing and the longitudinal axis of the aircraft. Lowering the flaps changes the angle of the chord of the wing and thereby changes the angle of incidence. Banking, changing the angle of attack and changing the trim have no effect on the angle of incidence.

Question 224. The weight of the aircraft acts through the centre of gravity and so that answer can therefore be immediately eliminated. The centre of pressure changes for different angles of attack (although on a symmetrical aerofoil it does lie about 25% of the way back and only changes a little with the angle of attack). There are two points that aerodynamics engineers use to characterise the point where lift occurs: the aerodynamic centre and the centre of pressure; the simpler of these to understand is the centre of pressure.

Question 225. There are various ways of reducing wing-tip vortices (and therefore induced drag). The most effective condition is to have very long and thin wings (i.e., wings with a large aspect ratio). This is not always possible in heavy aircraft (although it is very common in gliders) because of the need for structural strength in the wing. However, winglets can be fitted to the ends of the wing to simulate a longer wing.

Question 226. The lift generated by an aerofoil (in this case, a wing) is given mathematically by:

$$L = \frac{C_L \times \rho \times v^2 \times A}{2}$$

where ρ is the density of the air, v is the speed of the aerofoil through the air, A is the area of the wing and C_L is the coefficient of lift—a simple number determined by the shape of the wing. If you don't like mathematics, then don't worry: the formula simply means that, if the air is more dense, then the wing will produce more lift (obviously) and that, if the area of the wing is larger, then it will produce more lift (again fairly obvious). The interesting factor is the v^2 because this means that, if the speed increases, the lift (reasonably) increases and that doubling the speed will cause the lift to increase by a factor of 4.

Question 227. Certainly, when an aircraft slows down and maintains altitude its angle of attack has to increase to generate the same amount of lift at a lower airspeed. However, a particular angle of attack can be achieved at any airspeed. Consider an aircraft in a vertical dive at 150 knots. If the pilot suddenly pulls back hard on the control column, the nose of the aircraft will come up but the aircraft continue downwards under its own momentum. The angle of attack can be very large (certainly large enough to cause a stall) even though the airspeed is high (see question 107).

Question 228. A constant speed propeller does not attempt to keep the airspeed of the aircraft constant; it keeps the speed of rotation of the propeller constant (in rpm). When the aircraft starts to climb, the propeller, having more work to do, would normally slow down. The constant-speed propeller compensates for this by changing to a finer pitch, thereby speeding it up again.

Question 229. If an engine fails on a multi-engined aircraft, it is important to set the propeller on the failed engine in such a way that it causes as little drag as possible. A freewheeling propeller causes a great deal of drag and is very undesirable. The feathered propeller is set so that the blades face sideways-on into the airflow: the blade is over-coarse and its pitch angle is 90°.

Question 230. If you inspect a fixed pitch propeller you will notice that its pitch is much finer at the tip than at the root—the definition of "wash-out". This is because, when the propeller is turning, the tip is moving much faster than the root and so can generate the same "lift" from a much smaller angle of attack. Propellers are certainly affected by icing as are all aerofoils on the aircraft.

Question 231. This is one of those questions where you can immediately eliminate two of the proposed answers: there is no way that the efficiency of a propeller can be influenced by the groundspeed of the aircraft. A propeller is an aerofoil creating "lift" that moves it forward rather than upwards. Imagine a propeller rotating at, say, 2300 rpm while at rest (e.g., during the run-up on the ground). All of the lift of the propeller is moving air backwards. Now, imagine the same propeller travelling through the air at 100 knots. The air it is trying to move backwards is already moving (relative to it) at 100 knots and it will be less efficient at accelerating it backwards (more formally, the angle of attack of the propeller has reduced). This is why propellers (and turboprops) are used for low-speed aircraft and jets for higher-speed ones.

Question 232. Wash-out and wash-in are mechanisms whereby the wing chord twists: if the wing is viewed from the wing-tip it appears to be twisted. As the wing twists, the angle of incidence changes along the wing. The idea of wash-out is to make the angle of attack higher at the root of the wing than at the tip. This means that, as the aircraft slows towards a stall in straight and level flight, the root will stall slightly before the tip. This makes the stall more controlled, and also means that ailerons keep their effect for a little longer (although putting an aileron down will increase the angle of attack much more than the wash-out reduces it).

Question 233. If you can't remember which formula to use, then a bit of dimensional analysis will help, but the easiest technique is probably to sketch a simple, rectangular wing. If the span is 6 and the chord is 2, then the area is 12 and the aspect ratio is $\frac{6}{2} = 3$. Of the answers given, only one gives the correct value (although one will give its reciprocal—at least the units will be correct). Sometimes, the aspect ratio is defined as the wing span divided by the mean chord but the chord can be very difficult to measure. Remember that the wing area is not the area of the metal that goes into its manufacture—it's the area of the shadow of the wing on the ground when the sun is directly overhead.

Question 234. Paradoxical as it may sound, vortex generators are designed to break up the smooth flow of air across the top of the wing. And, yes, they do increase parasitic drag. It may sound surprising that, after the wing designer has gone to great trouble to make the top of the wing smooth and make the air flow smoothly across it, that items would be fitted to break up that smooth flow. However, as was predicted as long ago as 1904 by Ludwig Prandtl, at low speeds the air very close to the wing surface becomes "tired" (his word). This boundary layer of air breaks away very readily as the aircraft approaches the stall and, by re-energising it by generating vortices, this break-away can be delayed. This gives the aircraft better flying properties at low speed. Preventing the air flow to the wing-tip is the purpose of a wing fence (which also generates vortices). Stall strips (and wash-out) are used to ensure that the root of a wing stalls before the tip. There are many things that increase the camber of a wing, including flaps.

Question 235. The centre of pressure is the line on the wing where the lift has no tendency to pitch the aircraft nose-up or nose-down. As the angle of attack increases (as the nose goes up in level flight), this line moves forward on the wing. As the stall occurs, the aircraft's nose drops and the centre of pressure moves towards the trailing edge. Insofar as it describes anything, the 25% answer describes the aerodynamic centre and the answer about the aircraft's CofG is nonsense.

Question 236. An equilibrium is said to be *unstable* if a small deflection causes the object to keep moving away from its equilibrium position. This would be the case with the pencil: if it were touched, then it is would presumably fall over. *Stable* equilibrium is when, after a small displacement, the system returns to its equilibrium position. An example would be a pendulum. *Neutral* equilibrium is the state where a small displacement causes the system neither to return to, nor move away from, its equilibrium position—e.g., a ball lying on a table top. The "graphitic" term is meaningless and was invented for this question on the assumption that anything to do with pencils should have an answer related to graphite.

Question 237. Lateral stability means stability in roll (i.e., around the longitudinal axis—see the explanation for question 238) and so an aircraft is laterally stable if, when a roll starts, the tendency of the aircraft is to recover to a wings-level attitude. Dihedral, having a high wing and having a swept back wing all contribute to this stability.

Question 238. The three axes of an aircraft are longitudinal (front to back), lateral (wing-tip to wing-tip) and vertical. Confusingly movement around the longitudinal axis is known as roll or lateral movement. Movement around the lateral axis is known as pitch or longitudinal motion. The vertical axis is easy: movement around it is called yaw.

Question 239. Longitudinal stability is stability around the lateral axis (yes, it's confusing) and so means the nose moving up or down. This movement changes the angle of attack of the aircraft's wing.

Question 240. The primary purpose the horizontal tail of the aircraft is to provide pitch stability: on most aircraft, the centre of lift lies behind the centre of gravity and without a tailplane the aircraft would pitch nose-downwards. The tailplane is a wing fitted "upside down" to provide negative lift: a force downwards. This balances the aircraft in pitch: i.e. around the lateral axis. As it creates a downward force, it doesn't add to the lift produced by the wing or reduce the wing loading. Attitude around the longitudinal axis is roll and roll is controlled by the ailerons—eliminating another possible answer.

Question 241. This is a nice, easy question. If you move the controls towards a surface (the horizontal stabiliser or the ailerons), then that surface goes up. Having both ailerons move in the same direction would be a disaster (although it does occur from time to time after maintenance—remember to do the "controls free and *correct*" check before takeoff).

Question 242. The wing with the down-going aileron has the greater lift and therefore the greater induced drag. Without some form of compensation, adverse yaw would occur. Differential (and Frise) ailerons are designed to counteract this yaw. Differential ailerons are arranged so that the up-going aileron moves through a greater angle than the down-going one, creating more drag. This compensates for the drag on the other wing.

Question 243. Control horns may be provided on the rudder and elevator to provide dynamic balance: both can be seen on a Cessna 172. The idea is to have part of the control surface in front of the hinge so that it moves into the airflow in the opposite direction to the main surface. The answer about warning people, although nice, is untrue—there are no aircraft fitted with a warning horn for pedestrians. Some older aircraft have a venturi system fitted to the outside (typically in front of the passenger door) which some (ignorant) people think of as a warning horn because it resembles a horn on antique cars.

Question 244. This question is often asked on an examination because it tests your understanding of the operation of the elevator. As the notes for question 240 explain, the horizontal tail is a "wing" mounted upside down to give negative lift. To make the aircraft's nose move up, the downward lift of the horizontal tail needs to be increased (if there were no horizontal tail—or it were to stall because of a build-up of ice—then the aircraft's nose would move downwards). Increasing this lift means moving the elevator to create more downwards "lift". To do this, the trim tab needs to move down. In an examination, the answers including "neutral" and "rudders" can be eliminated immediately.

Question 245. The troposphere is that part of the atmosphere from the surface up to the tropopause. The actual height of the tropopause varies from place to place and from season to season but it is typically at about 36,000 ft ASL. It is in the troposphere that the temperature of the atmosphere drops with height. This drop stops at the tropopause and reverses above it in the stratosphere.

Question 246. If you selected an answer including the adiabatic lapse rate then you have misunderstood the concept of lapse rates and need to reread that section of a textbook or ask an instructor for help. The environmental lapse rate is the rate at which the temperature of the atmosphere decreases with altitude throughout the troposphere. At the tropopause, this decrease stops (hence the term "pause" as used in "menopause" and other words to mean a cessation), and temperature is no longer lost with height: the lapse rate becomes zero or even negative. The dry and saturated adiabatic lapse rates are nothing to do with the temperature of the atmosphere—rather they are measures of how a rising (and therefore expanding) packet of air loses temperature as it rises.

Question 247. Apart from very localised effects such as inversions (that typically stop at a few thousand feet AGL), temperature and pressure both drop with altitude. This is fairly obvious for pressure as, at higher altitudes, there is less atmosphere above pressing down. It is slightly less obvious for temperature as many people think that the atmosphere is heated by the sun and, at higher altitudes, there is less atmosphere above to filter the sun's rays. Actually, the troposphere is heated mainly from below—from the earth—and so its temperature drops with height.

Question 248. Most people are familiar with the concept of a gas heating as it is compressed (think of the end of a manual bicycle pump getting hot as you compress air in it). Similarly, when a gas expands, it cools. As a parcel of air rises through the atmosphere, the pressure outside it drops and it expands. And, as it expands, it cools.

Question 249. Methane cannot exist in any quantity in the earth's atmosphere (think what would happen every time you lit a match). The primary constituents are nitrogen (about 78%), oxygen (about 21%), argon (about 1%), carbon dioxide (about 0.04%) and water vapour (about 1%). Of these, the ones important to aviation are oxygen and water vapour but the two dominant constituents are nitrogen and oxygen.

Question 250. The word isobar comes from the Greek word "isos", meaning "equal", and bar, the unit of pressure (as in millibar). In principle, it would be possible to join points with the same station pressure but it would not be useful—if one station were at the top of a mountain and a nearby station were much lower in a valley, then their pressures would be very different but not because of the atmospheric conditions.

Question 251. A hectoPascal is the same as a millibar. All three units given in the question appear on charts, reports and forecasts for pilots.

Question 252. Station pressure is the actual pressure measured at the recording station. As A is much higher than B, it has less weight of atmosphere pushing down on it. Its station pressure will therefore be lower than B's. The sea-level pressure is the station pressure corrected for the altitude of the station—it's the pressure that the atmosphere would create at the bottom of a well dug down to sea-level. If the calculations have been done correctly, the pressure corrected to sea-level should be the same at A and B.

Question 253. This is a straightforward application of a flight calculator if you understand that "setting the altimeter to 29.92" means "displaying the pressure altitude". So this question really asks for the pressure altitude of Bear Lake Lookout aerodrome. Given its actual altitude from figure B.10 and the current altimeter setting from figure B.17, it's easy to calculate the pressure altitude. If you use the simplified rule-of-thumb where 1 inch of mercury is approximately equivalent to 1,000 ft of altitude, you will get 1,782 ft—the 1,751 answer is still the closest.

Question 254. This is another straightforward application of a flight calculator.

Question 255. A high density altitude means that, as far as the aircraft is concerned during the takeoff roll, the aerodrome is at a high altitude. The air is therefore thinner and a longer takeoff roll will be needed.

Question 256. The pilot has been flying from an area of higher to lower pressure. This is the dangerous direction as it will cause his altimeter to over-read. Two answers can therefore be dismissed immediately. Using a flight calculator, it will be found that the pressure altitude at Bear Lake Lookout will be 1,639 ft if the altimeter is at 29.58" Hg and 1,751 ft if the altimeter is at 29.46" Hg—a difference of 112 ft. So the altimeter will be reading 112 ft too high and $1322 + 112 = 1434$. If, instead of using a calculator, you used the rule of thumb that 1" Hg is roughly equivalent to 1,000 ft, the difference would be about 120 ft and the answer 1,434 would still be the closest.

Question 257. The sun's rays pass through the atmosphere from above without significantly warming it. The energy reaches and warms the earth which then re-radiates the heat at a different wavelength—a wavelength that the atmosphere can absorb.

Question 258. The difference between a particular temperature in degrees Celsius and a difference in temperature in Celsius degrees is something that catches a lot of people out. Newspapers will sometimes report that the "temperature rose rapidly by $-12°$C" and wonder how they got that number until you realise that the reporter has translated an article from the USA where the temperature was said to have risen 10 Fahrenheit degrees and plugged 10°F into a calculator to convert it to Celsius). So, to recap:

- to convert a temperature from Fahrenheit to Celsius, subtract 32, multiply by 5 and divide by 9. In this case, 10 minus 32 multiplied by 5 and divided by 9 results in -12.2.
- to convert a temperature range from Fahrenheit to Celsius, forget the 32 and just multiply by 5 and divide by 9. In this case, 10 multiplied by 5 and divided by 9 results in 5.55.

Question 259. Inversions prevent convection (see question 270) and this prevents particles of dust and other pollutants in the air from escaping. If the inversion is prolonged, say a day or two, smog forms below the inversion and the visibility reduces.

Question 260. Inversions can be caused by several meteorological conditions. The idea is to get cooler air under warmer air. This can occur when cool air over water gets blown gently onto warm land or when a cold front is passing. However, one very common cause is radiation cooling of the ground on a clear, cool night following a hot day. The ground cools and thereby cools the atmosphere close to it, leaving cooler air underlying warmer air.

Question 261. The temperature of a standard atmosphere drops with altitude at the rate of about 1.98°C per 1,000 ft until the tropopause is reached. Under some actual conditions (see question 260), an inversion can form and the temperature remains constant or even increases with altitude, typically for a few thousand feet.

Question 262. The temperature of a standard atmosphere drops at 6.5° per kilometer until the tropopause is reached. This does not reflect the actual drop in temperature in the real atmosphere at a particular place at a particular time.

Question 263. The temperature is the same (20°C) at each airport, but the dew point is much higher at CYXA. There is a simple rule of thumb for calculating the relative humidity given the temperature and dew point: $R = 100 - 5 \times (T - T_d)$. Using this formula for the two aerodromes in the question, the relative humidity at CYXA is about 90% and the relative humidity at CYXB is about 60%. The athlete needs to able to sweat to be comfortable; a very humid atmosphere such as the one at CYXA prevents this.

Question 264. The pressure altitude is governed by the actual altitude of the airport and the atmospheric pressure at the airport. These are the same for CYXA and CYXB, so one answer is incorrect. Cloud heights in a METAR are given as heights above ground so the lowest cloud at CYXA is at 7,000 ft AGL (i.e., 8,000 ft ASL), eliminating another answer. The sea-level pressure is 29.88 inches of mercury or 1011.7 hectoPascals (or 1011.7 millibars) and that leaves only one possible answer, but many density altitude calculators only take into account pressure altitude and temperature, omitting humidity. Using a calculator that takes humidity into account, the density altitude at CYXA is 2,139 ft and at CYXB is 2,046 ft.

Question 265. Water vapour *condenses* out of the air as the temperature drops and becomes cloud or fog. On a cold night, water vapour may go directly from the gaseous state to a solid state (frost) without going through the water stage—this is known as deposition. The change from frost directly to water vapour, again without passing through the liquid state, is known as sublimation.

Question 266. The adiabatic lapse rates (saturated and unsaturated) have nothing to do with the rate at which the temperature of the atmosphere drops with height—that's the environmental lapse rate. The term "adiabatic" means "if heat is neither gained nor lost". It refers to a parcel of air rising through the atmosphere and meeting lower and lower external pressures. The parcel of air therefore expands and cools. If the air is not saturated, then it cools at about 3°C per 1,000 ft. If it is saturated, then it still cools at 3°C per 1,000 ft but, the condensation of the water vapour also releases latent heat (the heat that went into vapourising the water in the first place). This extra heat offsets the 3°C somewhat and the saturated adiabatic lapse rate is normally between 1.2°C and 2.2°C per 1,000 ft.

Question 267. The dew point is the highest temperature at which the parcel of air is saturated with water vapour. So, if the pressure doesn't change, it is the temperature to which an unsaturated parcel of air must be cooled to make it saturated, and the temperature to which a saturated parcel of air must be warmed so that it is no longer saturated. The dew point forms the boundary between the air being saturated and unsaturated at a given pressure. In this question the parcel of air must be saturated and in need of warming to get it to its dew point (as none of the other answers make sense). Answers can be eliminated by remembering that we can never warm air to cause it to become saturated and the dew point is a temperature, not a pressure.

Question 268. A cold front, localised heating and up-hill winds represent good lifting agents. A cold front undercuts the warmer air mass and forces it aloft. Local heating (e.g., of a black road surface) causes the air in contact to become warmer than the surrounding air and start to rise. Wind blowing on a hillside is forced to rise. However, it is difficult to see how a layer of stratus cloud is likely to cause air to rise.

Question 269. When lifted, unstable air tends to continue to rise. It therefore forms clouds with vertical development—cumulus clouds.

Question 270. The answer about the saturated, adiabatic lapse rate can be eliminated immediately—it is a constant and doesn't change from day to day—see the explanation for question 266. The stability of the air is defined by the environmental (i.e., actual) lapse rate with altitude on the particular day. When there is a temperature inversion, the air does not cool with altitude for at least a few thousand feet. A rising parcel of air will cool at the adiabatic lapse rate and, if the environmental lapse rate is low, will find itself cooler than the surrounding air. It will therefore stop rising. The same effect occurs if the environmental lapse rate is low (i.e., the air doesn't drop in temperature very quickly with altitude). To get unstable air and convection, a large environmental lapse rate is needed.

Question 271. Once lift has started (e.g., by local heating or by a cold front), unstable air continues to lift. An inversion is a temperature profile, not a description of an air mass (and an inversion normally causes stable rather than unstable air).

Question 272. The Latin term "nimbus", when associated with cloud names (e.g., nimbostratus, cumulonimbus), means "rain bearing".

Question 273. Any liquids ejected in the exhaust of a jet engine immediately form ice crystals and spread out to form a continuous layer of cloud. The keywords "high", "continuous" and "ice crystals" indicate cirrostratus cloud.

Question 274. Two answers can be eliminated immediately: cirrus clouds are very high clouds made from ice crystals and they produce no precipitation; cumulonimbus clouds are associated with thunderstorms rather than drizzle. Cumulus clouds have vertical development and are more likely to produce rain than drizzle. However, stratus clouds, cover the sky and often produce drizzle.

Question 275. There are a lot of clues provided in the description; "high" probably means some form of cirrus while "layer" implies some form of stratus. The layering certainly excludes thunderclouds and any form of cumulus except stratocumulus (a contradiction in terms). The fact that the cloud is "almost transparent" means that it is unlikely to be rain-bearing and so answers with "nimbus" are also excluded. The remaining answer contains both the term "cirrus" and the term "stratus".

Question 276. If you take the word "cumulonimbus" apart you find "cumulo" meaning vertical development (caused by unstable air) and "nimbus" meaning rain bearing. This eliminates two answers. Steady, light rain is more likely from nimbostratus clouds. Cumulonimbus clouds (abbreviated to CBs) are always associated with thunderstorms.

Question 277. Although virga is normally associated with rain, it can also occur with snow.

Question 278. Cirrus clouds are the highest in the sky. At their altitude, the temperature is such that liquid water cannot exist.

Question 279. This is one of those definitions that you just have to know. If you were unsure in an examination, then you could certainly reject the answer about persistence as being extremely unlikely and the answer about depth as being fairly unlikely. However, it is not possible to deduce whether the definition relates to 1 km or 1 statute mile: in fact it is more likely (but wrong) to assume it would be in statute miles as most other visibility ranges are in statute miles. However, having done this question and read these comments, you should never forget it again.

Question 280. Cirrus cloud is a high level cloud consisting of ice particles—it cannot possibly be at the ground. The same can be said for altostratus—by definition of "alto" it is at a middle level (although the Latin word "alto" means high). This leaves cumulus and stratus in the race and fog forms in a layer across the ground—a stratus effect.

Question 281. One answer is clearly wrong because the dew point cannot be higher than the temperature. In an examination you might conclude that two of remaining answers are effectively the same and if one is correct, then so must the other be. This means that they cannot be correct.

Question 282. Fog occurs when either sufficient moisture is added to the air, or the temperature of the air is sufficiently reduced so that it reaches its dewpoint. The term "advection" means a flow *with* a fluid (in this case the wind) and is normally contrasted with convection. In the case of advection, the wind blows the moist air across the cooler surface and the temperature of the air drops to its dew point, causing fog. With upslope fog, as its name suggests, the cooling is caused by the moist air moving up a slope of a hill and cooling as it expands. Radiation fog occurs on a clear night when the moist air is cooled to the dew point as its heat is radiated into space. All of the above types of fog occur when moist air is cooled to the dew point. Steam fog differs because it occurs when air is blown over a warm lake or river. The air at lake or river level gathers moisture and warmth and rises slightly, cooling and forming fog. This is certainly the most beautiful type of fog and possibly one of nature's most beautiful phenomena.

Question 283. Turbulence is caused when an aircraft flies between two volumes of air travelling at different speeds. Convective turbulence is caused by local heating of the air (for example, by a large expanse of paved road amongst fields when the sun is shining), causing it to rise: to convect. One of the most pleasant places to observe convection in action is in a pint of Guinness™. The beer warms in the centre, rises to the top, cools and descends around the edges. This causes the bubbles to appear to be going downwards—indeed, around the edge they are. Remember as you fly through convective turbulence that glider pilots call it lift and seek it out. The answer about advective turbulence is designed to confuse. Don't be confused: there is no such thing, although it would not be a bad term for horizontal wind shear.

Question 284. The presence of stratus (rather than cumulus) cloud indicates that there are few rising columns of air. This may be partly due to the fact that stratus cloud, once formed, covers the sky and does not allow the sun's rays to reach the earth and create warm areas. Without rising columns of air there should be little or no turbulence.

Question 285. The terms used for reporting turbulence are light chop, light turbulence, moderate chop, moderate turbulence, severe turbulence and extreme turbulence. When considering a PIREP containing a report of turbulence, it is necessary to take into account the type of aircraft reporting it. "Moderate Turbulence" (changes in altitude and/or attitude occur but the aircraft remains in positive control at all times. Some changes to airspeed.) means something different when reported by an Airbus than when reported by a Cessna 150.

Question 286. With a headwind turning into a tailwind, the aircraft's airspeed will decrease and this, in turn, will reduce the lift being generated, causing the aircraft to descend below the optimal glide path.

Question 287. For example, if wind at the ground is reported to be from 120°T and at 3,000 ft it is reported to be from 180°T, it is clear that as you climb from the surface to 3,000 ft, you will encounter some form of wind shear. Wind shear is particularly important for large aircraft when landing. If a headwind suddenly changes to a tailwind, then the time it takes to spool up the jet engines may result in the pilots not being able to react quickly enough and falling below the optimal glide slope.

Question 288. It is very reasonable that the wind should blow from an area of high pressure to an area of low pressure. Indeed, were the earth not rotating, it would blow directly from high to low (as it does initially even on a rotating earth). However, when viewed from the surface of the earth, it appears to be deflected to the right in the northern hemisphere and, at sufficiently high altitudes to avoid friction with the surface of the earth, it almost follows the isobars.

Question 289. As the wind strength has changed from 6 knots to 12 knots, it's clear that it has strengthened, therefore two answers can be eliminated. Remember that the reported wind direction in a METAR (and elsewhere) is the direction that the wind is coming *from.* It was coming from 320°T and is now coming from 300°T. It has therefore moved anti-clockwise, and this type of change is known as "backing".

Question 290. On a summer's afternoon the land would have heated up more quickly than the water of Lake Ontario. The air over the land would therefore tend to rise, creating a small area of low pressure. This will draw in cooler air from over the lake, creating an on-shore breeze. This breeze blows from the south, so runway 19 will be appropriate.

Question 291. The winds at altitude are less affected by friction with the ground. They are therefore stronger and follow more closely the isobar lines. You can remember this for an examination by noting that the winds *back* when you come *back* to the airport to land.

Question 292. Pressure gradient is measured in millibars (or hectoPascals) per mile. If the isobars are close together then it means that there is a large change of pressure over a short distance—the pressure gradient is steep. When the pressure gradient is steep the winds will be strong.

Question 293. Once a low pressure system has properly formed, the winds above a few thousand feet AGL tend to follow the isobars. As far as the clockwise/counter-clockwise part is concerned, remember that, if you stand with your back to the wind, the low pressure is on your left.

Question 294. The adjectives used for air masses are "continental" meaning "dry" and "maritime" meaning "moist". Thus, the continental polar air mass is dry and cold, and the maritime tropical air mass is moist and warm.

Question 295. As described in the notes for question 294, the term "continental" means "dry". And "arctic" is associated with "cold".

Question 296. In the winter in the northern hemisphere, the arctic air mass expands and the arctic front moves south. The polar front does likewise: in the summer it lies around 60° north and in the winter around 30° north.

Question 297. It is confusing that the polar air mass is not at the north *pole* (the arctic air mass is). The polar front is the border between the polar air mass to the north and the Ferrel cell to the south. It is the line along which the jet stream travels.

Question 298. A moist, unstable air mass with an approaching cold front forcing air aloft is unlikely to produce stratus (layer) clouds. The combination of instability, moisture and a rapidly-moving lifting agent is normally a recipe for cumulus clouds with lots of vertical development—leading at least to towering cumulus and possibly to thunderstorms. Cirrus giving way to altostratus and then stratus describes the arrival of a warm front.

Question 299. The pilot is in the cooler air mass so any precipitation above him is occurring in warmer air. If this were hail, it would remain as hail as it fell into the colder air—that answer can therefore be eliminated. "Clear icing" is not a form of precipitation, thereby eliminating another answer. That leaves two answers. If there are ice pellets mixed with the snow at the aircraft's level, there must be some form of moisture above (rain or, more likely, freezing rain) to form ice.

Question 300. This is a question that is very common on examination papers, and the answer just has to be learned, although you can do some analysis by drawing the isobars associated with the front and remembering that the wind aloft tends to follow the isobars. As you fly through a cold front from either side (warmer to cooler or v.v.) the wind veers. To some extent this is only an academic question. Passage through a cold front is not instantaneous as it appears on a weather map: in a slow aircraft you are in the frontal system for some time and during this time there can be significant changes in wind direction. It is not a matter of having a heading of x and it changing abruptly to y. As far as the answers provided for the question are concerned, the answer suggesting no change of heading is unlikely (or the question would not have been set) and a GPS cannot provide heading information, only track. So, if necessary, guess between the other two answers.

Question 301. The term TROWAL is an acronym of "Trough of Warm Air Aloft". The lighter, warm air has been forced aloft by the cold front that has caught up with the warm front. Cold fronts travel more quickly than warm fronts and never meet head-on because that would require one front to be rotating clockwise around the low pressure and the other anticlockwise—this does not occur: in the northern hemisphere the rotation is always anti-clockwise viewed from above. When the low pressure initially forms, the cold and warm fronts are typically stretched out in a line rather than catching up with each other.

Question 302. The type of front is determined by the relative temperature (cooler or warmer) of the air that is moving.

Question 303. The position of the front line on a weather chart (whether a cold or warm front) is the surface position where the two air masses meet.

Question 304. It would seem intuitive (but wrong) that ice would most readily form on blunt surfaces facing the air flow. The reason it doesn't form there first is that air tends to stagnate in front of blunt surfaces, causing a higher ambient pressure and increasing the temperature slightly.

Question 305. Freezing rain occurs when condensation occurs in warm air aloft and the rain falls through cold air below, becoming super-cooled and turning into ice on contact. These conditions are most likely to occur when a warm front is approaching and the warm air rides up over a layer of cold air. The warm air cools as it rises and condensation occurs. The liquid rain drops fall through the cold air below. It is possible for freezing rain to be associated with a cold front (again the cold air lies beneath the warm air) but the violence of a cold front is not conducive to the formation of freezing rain. Because the warmer air is aloft, pilots are often told that, if they enter freezing rain, they should climb. Often this is impossible—most light aircraft cannot tolerate more than a few seconds of freezing rain before they become unable to climb.

Question 306. Rime icing is a result of freezing drizzle and looks like frost in a freezer. It is most likely to form in stratus-type clouds with temperatures between 0°C and −22°C. It rarely occurs by itself, normally being accompanied by clear icing (and then being termed "mixed icing"). Freezing rain is most likely to form clear icing on an aircraft: a layer of clear and smooth ice. Any flight through freezing rain must be avoided because clear ice normally accumulates rapidly and distorts the shape of the aerofoils, making continued flight difficult or impossible.

Question 307. A thunderstorm is defined by the typically anvil-shaped, cumulonimbus cloud. The anvil head forms as the cloud flattens itself against the tropopause. The abbreviations for the various cloud types include CI for cirrus, CS for cirrostratus, CC for cirrocumulus, AS for altostratus, CU for cumulus, TCU for towering cumulus, NS for nimbostratus, ST for stratus, SF for strato fractus, SC for stratocumulus and CB for cumulonimbus.

Question 308. A squall line is a line of severe thunderstorms, normally associated with a cold front providing the lifting agent for the thunderstorms. A squall line contains heavy precipitation, hail, frequent lightning, strong straight line winds and sometimes tornadoes and waterspouts.

Question 309. Many accidents, particularly to airliners, have been caused by a headwind suddenly shifting to become a tail wind. In one incident at Lloydminster, Alberta in 2007 the flight service specialist noticed the wind shift to a 40 knot tailwind as an 18-passenger aircraft rolled for takeoff. By quick thinking, he was able to alert the pilot and have the takeoff aborted just before rotation. Icing and visibility may be issues for an aircraft flying close to a thunderstorm but sudden changes in wind direction are most dangerous during takeoff or landing.

Question 310. Radar (whether ground-based or mounted in an aircraft) detects the reflexion of radio waves from precipitation: rain, snow, hail, etc. Sferics devices detect electrical discharges from lightning (and intense rain where the heaviness of the rain is causing electrostatic activity). Sferics devices also detect welding happening in a hangar as you taxi out.

Question 311. A thunderstorm needs:

- a high environmental lapse rate so that, once a parcel of air starts to rise, it continues to rise, accelerating as it goes. This does not occur if the environmental lapse rate is low or, even worse, negative.
- moist air so that, as it starts to rise, the latent heat released from the condensing moisture will add energy (heat) to the system.
- a lifting agent to start the process. There are many lifting agents, including convection on a sunny day, but the most powerful is an approaching cold front undercutting the warmer, moist air and forcing it upwards. Of course, the air associated with a warm front is also lifted, but normally much less violently than that of a cold front.

To make a thunderstorm really powerful, a wind shear at high altitude is also needed. If there is no wind shear, then the hail forming within the storm tends to fall down inside the storm, impeding the rising air. If there is a significant wind shear, the falling air may be several miles away from the rising air in the core of the thunderstorm.

Question 312. Weak wind-shear aloft generally produces a weak thunderstorm because the ice and hail fall back through the rising air, quenching the thunderstorm. A pulse thunderstorm is a single-cell thunderstorm.

Question 313. A METAR is a record of an observation describing the weather at a particular location—it is a report. A TAF and GFA are both forecasts of weather in the future—the TAF being textual and covering a small area around an aerodrome, and a GFA being graphical and covering a large area.

Question 314. The ATIS is a recorded message, normally updated every hour, transmitted from busy aerodromes to give pilots the basic information they need before contacting a controller. In Europe, the station pressure (known as QFE) *would* be given but not in North America. In North America the sea-level pressure is given. Setting QFE causes the aircraft's altimeter to read 0 on the ground. Setting sea-level pressure causes the altimeter to read the aerodrome's elevation when the aircraft is on the ground.

Question 315. There used to be many FSSs across Canada, each with staff trained to provide fully-interpretive weather briefings. Some years ago, nine FICs were created (Kamloops, Yellowknife, Whitehorse, Edmonton, Winnipeg, London, Québec, Halifax and North Bay) and the staff with the training and authority to interpret the weather were concentrated into those locations. When you dial 1-866-WX-BRIEF to file a flight plan or get weather information you are contacting one of the nine FICs. FSS staff are responsible for taking weather observations, reading forecasts and reports, providing airport advisory services and, if the equipment exists, DF steers.

Question 316. CAR 602.72 says that "The pilot-in-command of an aircraft shall, before commencing a flight, be familiar with the available weather information that is appropriate to the intended flight." Although it might be prudent to speak with a FSS specialist before the flight, there is no specific regulation that demands this. If the pilot is confident with his or her ability to interpret the weather information available from the internet and other sources, self-briefing is adequate.

Question 317. The only subtle part of this question relates to whether the METARs are issued on the Zulu (UTC) hour or the local hour. This is important in Newfoundland where the local time is half an hour different from the time zone time. In fact, METARs are always issued on the Zulu hour.

Question 318. There is no such thing a "routine" SIGMET: significant weather does not occur on a given schedule. In general, if thunderstorms were forecast on the GFA and are isolated, a SIGMET would not be issued. Until late 2013, SIGMETs were issued as corrections to GFAs.

Question 319. SIGMETs are not issued as forecasts—they report weather that is actually occurring.

Question 320. In the days of teletypes transmitting at 10 characters per second, it could perhaps be justified that METARs and TAFs have this highly condensed form. Today, with almost ubiquitous broadband connectivity, it is harder to understand. The sea-level pressure at CYTZ is given in two forms in the METAR: as A3005 and as SLP175. The first of these means that it is 30.05 inches of mercury, slightly higher than the standard 29.92 inches of mercury. The second gives the pressure in millibars (or hectoPascals, which are the same)—the question is what should be prefixed to 175 to get the correct value: either a 9 or a 10 (remember that this is being done to save transmission time on those old teletypes!). In this case 9172 makes no sense and so we should put a 10 on the front to get 10175. Adding a decimal point gives 1017.5, just above the normal value of 1013.4 millibars.

Question 321. The cloud condition in the METAR from CYTZ is given as CLR and in the METAR from CYTR as SKC. This is the difference between an observation made by a human (at CYTR) and an automated machine (at CYTZ). The automated machine cannot reliably detect cloud above 12,000 ft AGL and so in a report from an AUTO station, instead of SKC, the term CLR is used.

Question 322. At CYTZ there is a 3°C difference between the temperature and dew point (22/19), and at CYTR there is only a 1°C difference (20/19). This means that the air is closer to saturation in CYTR than it is in CYTZ—i.e., the relative humidity is greater there.

Question 323. The term CAVOK (pronounced KAV-OH-KAY) is sometimes used in a METAR in the USA (and TAFs outside North America) but it is never used in a Canadian METAR. It does, however, sometimes figure in informal weather reports. It means that there is no cloud lower than 5,000 ft above the aerodrome level, no cumulonimbus precipitation, thunderstorm, sandstorm, duststorm, shallow fog or drifting dust, sand or snow, and a visibility of at least 6 statue miles.

Question 324. The altitude is given as FL025 — flight level 025. A flight level is a pressure altitude (i.e., the indicated altitude when the altimeter is set to 29.92 inches of mercury. The fact that the aircraft type is a Cessna 182 makes it unlikely that it would be flying at 25,000 ft.

Question 325. Note the difference between the time that the NOTAM was issued (1221Z) and the time at which the observation was taken (1220Z).

Question 326. The notation "YVV 180002" means on the 180° radial from the YVV VOR (i.e., due south of it) at a distance of two miles.

Question 327. The indicator "/WV" stands for "Wind Velocity": the direction and speed of the wind. In this case, it is 240006 meaning the wind is coming **from** 240° at 6 knots.

Question 328. An LWIS is a "Limited Weather Information System" that measures the wind conditions, temperature, dew point and altimeter setting and then broadcasts them on the given frequency: 122.55 MHz. The density altitude and visibility are available from a full AWOS (Automatic Weather Observation System) but not from an LWIS.

Question 329. The purpose of the answer related to the transponder is to ensure that you have distinguished between secondary radar (not really radar at all) used to interrogate a transponder and primary radar (which is genuine radar) used to measure the intensity of precipitation. Basically, pulses of radio energy are sent out and the delay and intensity of the reflexions are measured. Heavy rain will reflect a lot of energy, and light snow much less energy. By this means, the intensity of precipitation and the maximum height of precipitation can be estimated.

Question 330. The report given in the question is a special, off the hour, METAR. The report *was* generated by an automated device but that is indicated by the term AUTO rather than the term SPECI.

Question 331. The cloud heights are given as FEW at 4,500 ft AGL and FEW at 24,000 ft AGL. The types of cloud are given as SC1CI1 meaning 1 okta of SC and 1 okta of CI. SC is the abbreviation for strato-cumulus, and it is not unreasonable to have this type of cloud at 4,500 ft AGL. CI stands for cirrus and at 24,000 ft the only types of cloud that would be anticipated are those in the cirrus family.

Question 332. The trick here, of course, is to read not only the A2972 but also the note at the end: PRESRR indicates “Pressure Rising Rapidly”. The METAR given is for 2200Z and the question asks for the pressure at 2100Z. If the pressure has been rising rapidly over the past hour then it must have been less than 29.72 inches of mercury at 2100Z.

Question 333. The winds given in a METAR are *from* a true direction. You can remember this by remembering that “If it’s written down, it must be true”. Wind directions given in METARs, TAFs, FDs and other forecasts and reports are in degrees true. As you approach to land and a tower control tells you that the wind is 320 degrees at 10 knots, then she is giving a magnetic direction—it’s not written down, it’s being spoken.

Question 334. The description *MI* means shallow and the visibility indicator *FG* means fog. The term *MIFG* therefore means *shallow fog*.

Question 335. The METAR is already a correction—it contains a CCA term. If the observer needs to make a further correction, then this will become CCB (and, if another correction is needed, CCC, and so on until the observer is dismissed for incompetence). The term AMD (for “amended”) is used in a TAF when the forecast is amended.

Question 336. To answer this question you need to know three things:

1. GFAs are issued every 6 hours at 0000, 0600, 1200 and 1800 Zulu time.
2. Three GFAs are issued at a time: one for the “current time”, one for 6 hours in the future and one for 12 hours in the future (actually two GFAs are issued for each of these times—one with clouds and weather and one with turbulence and icing).
3. The last picture in each group of 3 contains an IFR Outlook on the right-hand side.

From these three facts, you can deduce that the GFA shown in figure B.8 was the last of the three clouds and weather diagrams in its sequence (because it has the IFR outlook). So the three times must have been 1200Z on the 23rd August, 1800Z on the 23rd August and 0000Z on the 24th August. The next GFA issued will move these all up one place, and have diagrams for 1800Z on the 23rd August, 0000Z on 24th August (as shown in the figure) and 0600Z on 24th August.

Question 337. This is a TROWAL (trough of warm air aloft) where the cold front has caught up with the warm front (as can be seen at the bottom corner of the line where the catching-up is not quite complete). Fronts of this nature emanate from a low pressure.

Question 338. There is an L on the chart at the 9 o’clock position and having an H and an L on a weather forecast really provides a strong clue: H means High Pressure. The cross in the circle indicates the pressure at the centre of the high: 1020 millibars (or hectoPascals—they’re the same thing).

Question 339. This GFA is labelled (in the top right-hand corner) as being the one presenting icing, turbulence and freezing level. The dashed contour lines indicate freezing level. If you are unsure about this in an examination, you can confirm it by checking that the further south you go, the higher the freezing level becomes. The southern-most contour that loops around Lake Ontario shows the freezing level as being at 12,500 ft ASL, and the one further north shows the freezing level at 5,000 ft ASL.

Question 340. The concept of a “station pressure” makes no sense on a GFA because there are no “stations”.

Question 341. The IFR outlook appears towards the bottom right-hand corner of the third of the three GFAs in each set. The text in figure B.8 is, as always, a little cryptic: “CIGS/VIS RA/DZ/FG/BR IN ONSHR FLO HSNBA”. While it might have been possible to defend the use of abbreviations like this for textual reports and forecasts in the days of TELEX machines, as a GFA is an image, full descriptions would not incur additional transmission times. But you should feel lucky that you are studying for your examination at a time when area forecasts are no longer textual. Freely translated, the text means: “ceilings and visibility, rain, drizzle, fog, mist in the onshore flow from Hudson Bay”. Conditions will be IFR because of low ceilings and reduced visibility caused by rain, drizzle and mist.

Question 342. The time group for the issue time is 221130Z which means 1130 Zulu (Greenwich) time on the 22nd of the month. The validity group is 2212/2318 meaning that it is valid for the period from 1200 Zulu on the 22nd of the month (half an hour after the issue time) until 1800 Zulu on the 23rd of the month—a period of 30 hours.

Question 343. A surface layer of 8 oktas or a cloud layer of more than 5 oktas ($\frac{5}{8}$ of the sky) constitutes a “ceiling”. Therefore, a broken (BKN) or overcast (OVC) layer constitutes a ceiling. At the beginning of the forecast period the clouds are expected to be a few at 10,000 ft AGL and these do not constitute a ceiling. However, at 1400Z a broken layer is expected at 7,000 ft AGL—a ceiling.

Question 344. A thunderstorm is indicated in the TAF as TS and the first mention is in the group "PROB40 2214/2220 VRB10G20KT 2SM +TSRA BKN015CB" which means that, between 1400Z on the 22nd of the month and 2000Z on the 22nd of the month, there is a 40% chance of the wind being at 10 knots, gusting 20 knots, with heavy (+) thunderstorms and rain and with broken cumulonimbus cloud based at 1,500 ft AGL.

Question 345. 0700 local (time zone) time is 1200Z (because CYYZ is 5 hours behind Greenwich). There is a clause towards the end of the TAF stating "FM231200 33007KT P6SM BKN020", which can be decoded as: *from 1200Z on the 23rd of the month, the winds will be from 330°T at 7 knots and the cloud will be a broken layer at 2,000 ft AGL.* Note that winds in forecasts (and METARs) are given as degrees true and cloud heights are given as heights above ground level.

Question 346. The local time is 5 hours later than Zulu time (it takes the sun approximately 5 hours to travel from Greenwich, London, UK to CYYZ), and the last line of the TAF reads "Remark: Next Forecast by 1500Z on the 22nd of the month". At 1500Z, the time zone time (i.e., the time on someone's watch) at CYYZ would be five hours earlier—1000.

Question 347. From 1200Z, the wind is forecast to be from 330°T at 7 knots. From 1500Z, it is forecast to be from 030°T at 14 knots. It is clearly increasing in strength so two answers are eliminated. In an examination, if you couldn't remember which direction was veering and which was backing, then guess from the other two answers. In fact the wind has moved clockwise from the north-west to the north-east and this is known as veering.

Question 348. This question is too easy! The key on the right-hand side of the chart indicates that the symbol means moderate turbulence and the symbol has MECH written underneath it. To make it even easier, the annotation on the GFA clearly states that the turbulence is between the ground and 3,000 ft AGL.

Question 349. The notation in question says *BKN* $\frac{160}{60}$ *P6SM ISOLD ACC 200 GVG P6SM -SHRA* or, translated into English, *Broken cloud between 6000 and 16,000 ft, visibility greater than 6 statute miles with isolated altocumulus castellanus 20,000 ft giving a visibility of greater than 6 statute miles in light showers of rain.* All heights in GFAs are given as above sea-level (this is necessary because the GFA covers a large area and the ground level can vary greatly across a GFA) so one answer can be eliminated immediately. It is unlikely that any "alto" cloud will have a base as high as 16,000 ft as "alto" means "middle" and alto clouds normally lie between about 6,500 to 18,000 ft. This eliminates two more answers.

Question 350. While the FDs (upper wind forecasts) do not give the freezing level explicitly, they do provide the information to allow a pilot to work it out. At 0000Z the temperature at 6,000 ft is forecast to be $+8$°C and at 9,000 ft it is forecast to be -1°C. It is therefore reasonable to assume that the freezing level is somewhere in between and much closer to 9,000 ft than 6,000 ft. All altitudes are given ASL.

Question 351. A wind of 99 knots is very unlikely (particularly at 6,000 ft when the wind at 9,000 ft is forecast to be 16 knots), and so two answers would only be used as a last resort. In fact, 9900 is used to indicate that there is no significant wind—it is light and variable in direction.

Question 352. The forecast temperature at 6,000 ft is $+8$°C and at 12,000 ft -9°C. This means the forecast lapse rate is 17°C in 6,000 ft or 2.8°C per thousand feet. This is greater than the standard environmental lapse rate of roughly 1.98°C per 1,000 ft.

Question 353. 3,000 ft ASL is actually underground at Jasper, and the winds don't blow strongly underground (so, to some extent, the forecaster being unable to produce a prediction could also be the correct answer—but it's not the *most* correct answer). In fact, in an FD, the winds and temperatures are not forecast for any level less than 1,500 ft AGL.

Question 354. An easy question, this. The only one of the terms that makes sense for a low pressure area is that it is quasi-stationary—it hasn't moved (much) in the last 6 hours.

Question 355. Another easy question. Sometimes the semi-circles are coloured red.

Question 356. Normally, the symbols used on weather charts just need to be learned for examination purposes: outside the examination room it is adequate simply to have access to a list of them. In this case, you may find these three symbols familiar and, indeed, they should be—they are three of the four symbols described on the edge of every "Clouds and Weather" GFA (see, for example, figure B.8).

Question 357. The upper air charts (which describe the atmospheric conditions at roughly 5,000, 10,000, 18,000 and 34,000 ft ASL) are rarely used by students and questions about them rarely appear on the PPL written examination (although they are explicitly included in TP12880E). Students seem to prefer the surface analysis charts although aircraft don't fly at the surface. All answers given are potentially feasible and the correct answer, height in decametres, is probably the least feasible.

Question 358. This is unfortunately one of those things that has to be learned. Surface analysis charts are issued at 0000Z, 0600Z, 1200Z and 1800Z.

Question 359. Ships tend to sail along rhumb lines, the autopilot maintaining the same heading for a period, and then switching to a new heading. With the advent of GPS it is now possible to fly along great circle routes, the shortest distance between two points. A straight line on a Mercator projection map (a cylindrical projection) is a rhumb line; a fairly short straight line on a conical projection such as a VNC is close to being a great circle. Neither a rhumb line nor a great circle is necessarily the quickest way to fly between two points—that is typically determined by the wind direction.

Question 360. The Prime Meridian is the 0° longitude line. This passes through the observatory in Greenwich, just to the east of London, UK. It is from this line that all longitudes are measured: both east and west. The international date line wriggles but is close to the 180° line of longitude—on the opposite side of the earth from the Prime Meridian.

Question 361. The equator is the line of latitude that encircles the centre of the earth. It is the only line of latitude that is a great circle.

Question 362. Tracks and headings are measured clockwise from the north. If you answered south-west then you are probably a mathematician used to measuring clockwise from the east—forget that convention when flying.

Question 363. The key to this question is understanding that the wind direction is the direction *from* which the wind is blowing. In this question the wind is blowing from the south-east and the aircraft is tracking just south of east. It is therefore experiencing a headwind and its speed across the ground will be less than its speed through the air. Also it will be facing into wind.

Question 364. The sexagesimal system (base 60) is something we can blame on the ancient Sumerians (around 2000 BCE) and the Babylonians after them. Up until well into the middle ages, base 60 was used for most computation and there are many Islamic scrolls calculating trigonometrical tables (sine, etc.) in base 60. However, these days it really only survives in measuring time (60 seconds in a minute, 60 minutes in an hour) and angles (60 seconds in a minute, 60 minutes in a degree). We must all look forward to the day when both time and angles become decimal (10 days in a week, etc.).

Question 365. It is unclear why the VTA is the odd man out—it is a transverse Mercator (i.e., cylindrical rather than conical with the cylinder wrapped around the earth "sideways": touching the poles) projection. Of course, as VTAs cover such small areas, the projection is not really important but it would perhaps have been more consistent to have all the maps with the same projection.

Question 366. The scale of a VNC is 1:500,000 so 10 cm on the map represents $500,000 \times 10 = 5,000,000$ cm on the ground. Five million centimetres is 50,000 metres or 50 km.

Question 367. The great circle must be centred at the centre of the earth. It then provides (by its shorter direction) the shortest distance on the surface of the earth between A and B. The only line of latitude that is a great circle is the equator.

Question 368. It is clear that two answers cannot be correct because lines of longitude get closer and closer together as they converge on the north and south poles. Lines of latitude don't. There are 90 degrees of latitude between the equator and the north pole; so, if a nautical mile were a degree of latitude, it would only be 90 nautical miles from the equator to the north pole. This is clearly wrong—actually it's $90 \times 60 = 5400$ nautical miles.

Question 369. The VTA chart is a transverse Mercator, but not a VNC. With the exception of the VTA chart, all of the charts commonly used by pilots (VNCs, LO Charts, HI Charts) are Lambert conformal conical projections. The reason for using this projection is given in question 371.

Question 370. VNCs do not have an expiry date (LO charts and CFSs do but none of the VFR charts does). The 6 months answer would imply that a particular VNC is current for 6 months. This is not so—sometimes a new version is issued sooner than that and often much later. The correct answer is that you have to go to the Nav Canada web site and check the current editions. This is worth remembering at your flight test as well—one obvious question that the examiner could ask during the ground portion of the test is whether the map you have used to plan the cross-country is current. The answer is, "yes, I checked the Nav Canada web site this morning."

Question 371. This question is meant to uncover two misunderstandings that many students have about the Lambert conformal conical projection: that straight lines are exact representations of great circle routes and that by flying a great circle route (or an approximation thereto), one's heading doesn't change. When flying a great circle route, the heading changes at every instant.

Question 372. If you answered Morrisburg, then you have probably forgotten that longitude increases (from Greenwich in London, UK) from right to left rather than left to right.

Question 373. Again, if you answered Lindsay aerodrome, you have probably forgotten that longitude increases (from Greenwich in London, UK) from right to left rather than left to right.

Question 374. This is a piece of class F airspace; the question is really whether it is restricted or advisory. The label associated with it reads "CYR505 To 1300 cont" indicating that this is restricted (CYR) rather than advisory (CYA) and it reaches from the ground to 1,300 ft continuously.

Question 375. It is unlikely that the military would be using a point that close to a town for target practice. Heliports are marked with the letter H in a circle (or in a square if it is associated with a hospital). A float plane base is almost a possibility, as it is close to the water, but an anchor is used to indicate one of those.

Question 376. If you chose the answer containing W77 08, then you probably haven't realised that, as Canada is to the west of Greenwich, longitude increases from right to left, not left to right. And two answers are wrong because the lake lies between N44 00 and N44 30.

Question 377. Two answers can be dismissed immediately because an agonic line is an isogonal line where the magnetic variation is zero. Here it is 13°W and so this cannot be an agonic line. The magnetic north pole lies in Canada somewhat to the south of the true north pole. When viewed from Eastern Canada (up to points close to the Ontario/Manitoba border), the magnetic north pole appears to the west of the true north pole. In western Canada it appears to the east.

Question 378. The square is the symbol for a DME—distance measuring equipment—and the hexagon a VOR. An NDB would be indicated by a circle surrounded by concentric circles of dots.

Question 379. The symbols *305* [L] *50M 122.5* mean that the airport is 305 ft ASL, has ARCAL-activated runway lights, has a runway of approximately 5,000 ft (4,970 to 5,069 ft) and has a Mandatory Frequency that can be reached on 122.5 MHz.

Question 380. The difference between the radials is 184°: there are therefore 4 degrees to be explained. Looking at the isogonals, it is clear that only about 2 degrees can be attributed to magnetic variation. Almost all of the rest is attributed to the fact that a straight line on a VNC, particularly one running east/west, does not represent a constant track. It is close to a great circle and the track of a great circle changes at every point along it.

Question 381. This question is posed to make sure that you can measure a line longer than your ruler and that you can distinguish between the statute miles and nautical miles scales. To be sure that you're using the correct scale, measure something where you know the distance (e.g., the ring around a VOR is normally 10 nautical miles on a VNC).

Question 382. Travelling from Kingston to Toronto, the aircraft will be flying westwards. The 085° answers are therefore unreasonable. The question is whether the measured value is in degrees true or magnetic. The difference for this trip is about 12° and so, even with a manual protractor, it should be possible to see which answer is correct.

Question 383. An altitude in brackets, whether on a map or in the Canada Air Pilot always means a height above ground. Altitudes without brackets are always heights above sea-level. In this case, the top of the tower is 763 ft ASL and 300 ft AGL. The ground must therefore be at $763 - 300 = 400$ ASL and the tower must be 300 ft tall.

Question 384. The key to the map lists this type of dashed line as the boundary of a class E control zone.

Question 385. The equator is the only line of latitude that has the middle of the earth at its centre, so it is the only line of latitude that is a great circle. The centre of the arctic circle is well to the north of the centre of the earth and so, as a line of latitude, it is not a great circle. All lines of longitude, including the Greenwich meridian and the 76° W line of longitude are great circles.

Question 386. This can be readily calculated. The sun appears to travel around the earth in 24 hours. It therefore travels 360° in 24 hours which is $\frac{360}{24} = 15$ degrees per hour.

Question 387. The CFS entry shows that the local time in Bear Lake Lookout is "UTC-5(4)". This means that it is in the time zone that is 5 hours behind Zulu time but, because of summer time, only 4 hours behind in the summer. At 1300Z in the summer the local time is 4 hours before 1300, i.e., 09:00 local time.

Question 388. In an examination there is really no way to avoid measuring this with a ruler and protractor. If you answered 84.7 miles, then you were using the statute miles rather than nautical miles scale on the ruler. If you answered 055° magnetic, then you hadn't realised that the lines of latitude and longitude on the map align on true rather than magnetic north. In real life, outside the examination room, you would normally find out both the distance and track by using a flight planning program such as CoPilot, Foreflight, WingX or one of the online flight planning applications. Unfortunately you are not allowed to take these into the examination room.

Question 389. Close inspection of the map shows that Peterborough has a class E control zone around it. Even though VFR traffic can fly freely in class E airspace without permission or clearance, it is *controlled* airspace and the requirements for flight in controlled airspace are for at least 3 miles of visibility. The 1 statute mile answer is correct for a day flight in uncontrolled airspace above 1,000 ft AGL and the 2 mile answer is correct for a day flight in uncontrolled airspace below 1,000 ft.

Question 390. This is fairly straightforward as long as you do the measurements correctly. It's about 17 NM from Peterborough to a point abeam of Norwood, and you travelled that distance in 12 minutes. If you travel 17 NM in 12 minutes, you will travel $5 \times 17 = 85$ NM in an hour—you're travelling at 85 knots. It's a further 57 NM to Plevna and, at 85 knots, that will take 40 minutes. 40 minutes after 1242 is 1322Z. In flight (assuming you're doing this because your GPS is broken), it's not necessary to calculate the groundspeed. You could simply argue as follows: "I covered 17 NM in 12 minutes and have 57 NM to go. That will take $12 \times \frac{57}{17} = 40$ minutes". In fact, unless you need groundspeed for some reason, it's not even necessary to measure the distances in nautical miles, measuring centimetres on the map is adequate.

Question 391. The 067° answer is clearly wrong and can be immediately eliminated. The track you need to fly to return to Peterborough is $067 + 180 = 247$ and, as you were having to crab 8° into wind on your outward journey, you will have to crab into wind on your return and so another answer can be eliminated. It's impossible to calculate the correct heading to fly without drawing wind triangles (something that would not be fun to do in the cockpit in deteriorating weather) but a first approximation would be to crab into wind by the same angle as was necessary on the outward trip. You would then correct it later. It appears from the outward crab that the wind is coming from the east, and a first approximation would be to fly a track of 247°M by flying a heading 8° further to the east—239°M.

Question 392. This question presupposes there is no working GPS on board. In this unlikely situation, the pilot's easiest option is probably to contact the controller at Trenton Terminal and explain the situation. The controller will allocate a transponder code and locate the aircraft precisely as soon as the code is dialled in. The controller could then provide vectors to Plevna, probably handing the aircraft off to Montréal Centre somewhere *en route*. Taking VOR bearings is probably a more interesting exercise and one that is very easy to do: tune and identify Coehill and centre the needle with a from flag, noting the radial. Repeat with Watertown and sketch the two lines. The aircraft is close to the intersection points. Asking Kingston for a DF steer is certainly possible but would probably only be done as a joke, given the two better options.

Question 393. As with question 388, in an examination there is really no way to avoid measuring this with a ruler and protractor. If you got the wrong answer, check that you were not using the statute miles rather than nautical miles scale on the ruler.

Question 394. This is fairly straightforward as long as you do the measurements correctly. It's about 17 NM from Lindsay to the shoreline and you travelled that distance in 9 minutes. If you travel 17 NM in 9 minutes you will travel $\frac{17}{9} \times 60 = 113$ NM in an hour—you're travelling at 113 knots. It's a total of 52.6 NM from Lindsay to Huronia and, at 113 knots, that will take 28 minutes. 28 minutes after 1635 is 1703. In flight (assuming you're doing this because your GPS is inoperable), it's not necessary to calculate the groundspeed. You could simply argue as follows: "I covered 17 NM in 9 minutes and the total journey is 52.6 NM. That will take $9 \times \frac{52.6}{17} \approx 28$ minutes". In fact, unless you need groundspeed for some reason, it's not even necessary to measure the distances in nautical miles: measuring centimetres on the map is adequate.

Question 395. The track you need to fly to return to Lindsay is $303° - 180° = 123°$ and, as you were having to crab 12° into wind on your outward journey, you will have to crab into the wind on your return, so one answer is wrong. It's impossible to calculate the correct heading to fly without drawing wind triangles but a first approximation would be to crab into the wind by the same amount as you were having to do on the outward trip. You would then correct it later. It appears from the outward crab that the wind is coming from the north and so a first approximation would be to fly a track of 123°M by flying a heading 12° further to the north—111°M.

Question 396. It used to be possible to answer this question more precisely than we can now—the figure was the highest known obstacle or 100 metres higher than the highest terrain, whichever was larger. The figures are the "Maximum Elevation Figures" (MEF) for the rectangle of latitude and longitude, but that term is no longer well-defined. The answer claiming that it is safe to fly at 1,100 ft ASL is not correct can be seen by moving slightly to the west of the area considered in this question: the MEF for the rectangle containing the CN Tower in Toronto is 2^1 although the CN Tower rises to 2,055 ft ASL. This means that flying at 2,100 ft would, if the altimeter were set correctly, provide 45 ft of clearance. Given that altimeters may be up to 50 ft in error and that altimeter setting are not always accurate, this is not safe flying. Generally, the height of man-made towers is not known to the map makers and they generally round up the heights of the terrain to provide some clearance over obstacles. In Toronto, the height of the highest obstacle is known and so it is used: normally that is not the case.

Question 397. The only really feasible answer here, other than the correct one, is the one about DRCOs. DRCOs are marked on some aviation maps but by a dot within a circle. In this case, a DRCO that was accessed on 675 kHz would be of no use because that frequency is well below the VHF band used for aircraft radios. A mast is wrong because the symbol for a mast is a small Eiffel Tower and the answer about a triangulation point is gibberish.

Question 398. Track and heading are two concepts with which you must become very familiar. Because of the wind, an aircraft normally doesn't travel across the ground in the direction in which it is pointing: imagine rowing a boat across a fast-moving river—to cross the river directly you must point the boat upstream. The heading of the boat is upstream, the track of the boat is directly across the river.

Question 399. A straight line on a VNC is, for a trip as short at 200 NM, close to being a great circle route. On a great circle route, the track changes continuously (a line with unchanging track is called a rhumb line) and so, to get an average track, it is best to measure it somewhere close to the middle. See question 380 for an example of the difference between the track at each end of a line.

Question 400. This is a simple question of arithmetic. Adding 95 to 343 gives 438 but this answer is incorrect because headings (and tracks) must always lie between 000° and 359°. Subtracting 360 from 438 gives the correct answer.

Question 401. One minute of latitude is one nautical mile and there are 60 minutes in a degree. B is 1 degree, 4 minutes of latitude north of A and that converts to 64 minutes—equivalent to 64 nautical miles. As B is north of A, the track must be due north (360°T).

Question 402. Apart from a little sexagesimal arithmetic, the real question here is whether the 40 minutes spent on the ground for lunch should or should not be included in the time. The purpose of entering the *en route* time is so that Flight Services can decide when to launch a search and rescue operation for you. To be able to calculate this, the full time you intend to be away needs to be known. Actually, given the condition in the question, it would probably have been better to file two, separate, flight plans: one for the journey out and one for the journey back. The reasons for this are two-fold:

1. Search and rescue will not be launched until you have been overdue for an hour. If you were to crash 10 minutes after taking off on the journey out, search and rescue will not be launched until one hour after the time you were due back (some 4 hours after you crashed). If you filed the outward journey separately, then the search and rescue would be launched 2 hours and 10 minutes after you crashed—much better.
2. Lunch always takes longer than anticipated! This means that the flight plan has to be modified anyway.

Question 403. The equipment code S (for "standard") means an ADF, a VOR receiver capable of receiving a localiser and glide slope and a VHF radio. The question is whether the GPS should be encoded or not, given that it is not a certified and installed GPS. The answer is that, for a VFR flightplan it *should* be included (for an IFR flightplan it must be omitted). The final C indicates a mode C transponder.

Question 404. Questions about the opening and closing angle method and double track error method are really for examination purposes only. Experienced pilots who have flown light aircraft for several thousand hours accept that, without an autopilot, they cannot fly a heading accurately for an hour or more. Even trying to do so is an intolerable load on any pilot, let alone one studying for a Private Pilot Licence. Remember that these methods *only* work (insofar as they work at all) if you have flown the calculated heading perfectly and the only reason that you are off course is that the wind was not as forecast. Now, to address the question. There is no such thing as the "half-track method". The double track error method, only works in the first half of the journey and you are past the half-way point. That leaves one answer: estimate the closing angle, add it to the 6° you have for the opening angle and turn left that many degrees. In practice, of course, you would probably be following a line on a GPS display and, if not, you would get back onto course by pilotage: pick a distant landmark (lake, town, etc.) that is on your planned route and fly to it. Then take a heading a few degrees to the left of the one you were previously using. By the way, you're about 10.5 miles off course and perhaps should have noticed it earlier.

Question 405. It is not possible to use a wind triangle to convert true headings or tracks to magnetic heading or tracks—so two answers can be rejected. Similarly, calibrated airspeed can only be deduced by referring to the aircraft's Operating Handbook. This leaves only one answer and this calculation is what a GPS unit can do in flight: it already knows the track and groundspeed and, by the pilot entering the aircraft's heading and airspeed, it can calculate the wind direction and speed—very useful if you're making a PIREP.

Question 406. The forecast wind and temperature are given as *9900+06*. The *+06* is the forecast temperature and can therefore be ignored for this question. The wind direction being 99 and speed being 00 implies that the wind is forecast to be light (less than 5 knots) and variable in direction. If this is the case, the aircraft's track will be the same as its heading and its groundspeed will be the same as its airspeed.

Question 407. The aircraft is crabbing to the right to maintain the track of 115°. So the wind must be coming from somewhere between 115° and 295°. However, it has a tailwind and this eliminates all but one of the possible answers.

Question 408. At 140 knots you are crabbing slightly to the left of track (heading 095° with a track of 100°). This means that the wind must be coming from some direction on your left. When you slow down, the wind will have a greater effect on you and you will need to crab even more to the left.

Question 409. I strongly advise against using an E6B circular slide-rule to answer this type of question in an examination (or anywhere else). An electronic flight calculator is much faster and more accurate, particularly in an examination—but you must practise using it.

Question 410. Much as for question 409, this is simply a matter of pressing the correct buttons on an electronic flight calculator.

Question 411. You don't need to do much arithmetic to work out the answer here. 14 minutes is just a little less than a quarter of an hour so you will cover just over $4 \times 25 = 100$ nautical miles in an hour.

Question 412. As with question 411, complex arithmetic is not really required. 38 is roughly a third of 115 and so it will take roughly one third of an hour. To be more precise, it will take $38/115 = 0.33$ of an hour.

Question 413. This is again simple arithmetic. The flight will take $\frac{256}{107} = 2.39$ hours. The fuel burn will therefore be $2.39 \times 7.2 \approx 17.2$ gallons.

Question 414. The pressure is greater than standard and so the airport will appear to be lower than its actual altitude (that's where an airport would have that greater pressure on a standard day) so one answer can be eliminated immediately. Using the rule of thumb that 1 inch of mercury is equivalent to about 1,000 ft, the approximate pressure altitude can be estimated as 130 ft below sea level. This points to two answers as being possibly correct and, using a flight calculator, the answer is found immediately.

Question 415. This is a direct application of the flight computer. In a hurry towards the end of the examination, two answers can be immediately discarded because, as most student pilots know from experience, the airspeed indicator under-reads significantly at altitude.

Question 416. If you answered that the headwind would be 12 knots, remember that the wind direction in a METAR is relative to true north, whereas the runways at Fort Cushing are aligned with magnetic north. Either the wind must be converted to magnetic, or the runway to true.

Question 417. RCR on the CFS entry indicates the source of the Runway Condition Report. In this case, it says "Opr" or "operator". The operator is the township and can be reached on 304-132-4111. And his name is not Reg—that's an indication that the aerodrome is registered (as distinct from certified).

Question 418. National NOTAMs (issued against CYHQ) include topics covering a large part of Canada. Flight Information Region NOTAMs include topics (e.g., a mistake on a map) that are not specific to a particular aerodrome. Aerodrome NOTAMs are concerned with a single aerodrome.

Question 419. CAR 602.88 states that the minimum fuel for a VFR flight at night is the fuel required to get to the destination and then to cruise for a further 45 minutes. In this case the climb will require 2.7 US gallons, the cruise to the destination will require 12.3 US gallons and the 45 minute reserve will need 5.3 US gallons.

Question 420. In the northern hemisphere, wind circulates in an anti-clockwise direction around a low pressure. When travelling westwards, by staying north of the centre of the low, you are likely to have tail winds for most or all of the flight. Making this decision early enough (preferably during the flight planning) adds very little to the flight distance (for example, aiming at a point 50 NM north of the great circle track adds 14 NM (4%) to the trip, and this is likely to be offset by the extra speed provided by the tailwind).

Question 421. Had the term APRX been omitted then the NOTAM would automatically have become ineffective at 0908041600. Because the exact expiration time is not known (hence the APRX), a cancelling NOTAM with the same reference number will have to be issued.

Question 422. This is one of those things that you just have to know. The format used to represent the date/time is YYMMDDHHMM.

Question 423. Runway edge lights are never blue—blue lights are used to mark taxiways. On the CFS entry, the lights for runway 24 are given as "AS(TE ME)". AS means uni-directional flashing strobe lights at the threshold, TE means threshold and runway edge lights and ME indicates medium intensity runway edge lights.

Question 424. The rules state that you must carry at least 30 minutes of reserve for a day VFR flight and 45 minutes of reserve for a night VFR flight.

Question 425. In North America, NDBs transmit on frequencies in the range 190 kHz to 535 kHz. Conversations with the tower and VORs (and localisers) use VHF frequencies with 108.0 to 117.95 MHz reserved for the navigation equipment and frequencies above 117.85 MHz for speech. The GPS satellites broadcast in the UHF band, with 1.57542 GHz being their carrier frequency.

Question 426. VHF equipment is normally significantly smaller than HF equipment. Either HF or VFR radios can be driven from a DC power supply, can be tuned digitally and allow voice to be transmitted.

Question 427. Position reports should be made to a Flight Service Station on 126.7 MHz or, as that frequency is becoming increasingly cluttered with chat and informal position reports, the frequency advertised by the FSS. The air-to-air frequency is 122.75 MHz. 121.5 MHz is reserved for emergency (MAYDAY) and urgency (Pan Pan) communications.

Question 428. If you multiply the frequency of a radio signal by its wavelength, you get the speed of light. So a short-wave signal must have a higher frequency than a long-wave signal: or, to put it the other way around, a low-frequency radio signal (such as that from an NDB) will have a longer wavelength than a higher-frequency signal (e.g., that from a VOR).

Question 429. When flying in the southern part of Canada there are often several VORs within range (indeed this is how VOR navigation is performed, switching over from one VOR to another). The OFF flag disappearing is necessary but not sufficient—you may have accidently tuned the wrong VOR. The answer about heading is crazy because the VOR receiver has no idea of the heading that the aircraft is flying.

Question 430. The answer with the needle rotating is referring to an ADF rather than a VOR and answers about the Morse Code are clearly nonsense. The CDI *will* become very sensitive and, unless the aircraft is being flown very accurately, will move to the fully right or left position. This does not, however, indicate station passage.

Question 431. The aircraft's current heading is irrelevant as the VOR receiver is not influenced by it. If the pilot *were* to fly a heading of 280° then he would be flying TO the VOR and would need to turn left to intercept the extended 280° radial.

Question 432. If the aircraft is directly south of the VOR, then the pilot would need to fly a track of 360° to fly directly (CDI in the middle) to (TO flag) the VOR. The VOR receiver has no idea of the heading or ground track of the aircraft and would display the same result on whichever heading the aircraft was flying.

Question 433. Being on the 110° radial from Simcoe indicates that you are south-east of the Simcoe VOR. Note that, as the bearing is 040° TO the Coehill VOR, your aircraft lies on the $040 + 180 = 220°$ radial: i.e., you are to the south-west of the Coehill VOR. If you sketch the position lines you will find that they intersect over Rice Lake.

Question 434. The ADF is the simpler of the two instruments—its needle simply points to the NDB. Initially, the NDB was directly ahead and the needle would be pointing to the 12 o'clock position. After the turn, the NDB will be behind, so the ADF needle will be pointing downwards, eliminating the answer where it doesn't move. One important point to remember about a VOR receiver is that it has no knowledge at all of the heading of the aircraft. At a range of 55 nautical miles in a Cessna 150, it is unlikely that the aircraft will even move across one radial during the turn (1° at 55 nautical miles is slightly less than 1 nautical mile). So there will be no appreciable change to the VOR reading.

Question 435. The only safe way of ensuring the NDB is still transmitting is to monitor its Morse code signal: if the NDB fails then the Morse code will stop. Most ADFs do not have a flag and keeping the needle pointing upwards is not useful because, if the NDB were to fail, the needle would probably remain where it was: pointing straight up. Switching to the beat frequency oscillator is also not useful.

Question 436. It is probably easier to work out the direction that would take the aircraft directly to the NDB and then invert that figure. As the ADF needle is pointing to 170° (9 o'clock), the pilot would need to turn 170° right to fly directly *to* the NDB—i.e., need to turn to 215°. To fly away she would need to turn to the reciprocal of this: 035°. If you prefer the formula: magnetic bearing to NDB = compass reading + ADF reading. In this case, the bearing to the NDB is $045° + 170° = 215°$ as calculated above simply by looking at the position of the needle.

Question 437. An ADF needle points to the NDB. While flying towards the NDB, the ADF needle will be pointing directly upwards, as the NDB is ahead. Once the aircraft has passed the NDB, the needle will point downwards to indicate that the NDB is behind. An ADF does not have a TO/FROM flag—that is a feature of a VOR receiver.

Question 438. the GPS unit in the aircraft is not a transmitter—it is only a receiver—so one answer can be eliminated. The GPS satellites are non-stationary and can often be seen moving across the sky just after sunset—geostationary satellites, of course, do not move relative to the earth. The satellites transmit highly accurate clock signals and the differences in the received times allow the GPS unit in the aircraft to calculate its position.

Question 439. A GPS receiver can measure the speed and direction at which an aircraft is moving across the ground and its altitude, but it has no information about the direction in which the aircraft is pointing (its heading) or speed at which it is flying through the air (airspeed).

Question 440. WAAS is a system whereby ground stations, whose locations are accurately known, receive the normal signals from the GPS satellites and calculate the error in their positions. Correction information can then be calculated and this is transmitted, via geo-stationary satellites, to the airborne GPS receivers.

Question 441. GPS signals can penetrate cloud but the other inaccuracies listed in the question are real. If you intend to use GPS to fly an instrument approach at a particular airport, you can perform a RAIM (Receiver Autonomous Integrity Monitoring) check for the airport at the time you expect to arrive. This will tell you whether, unless there are unexpected satellite failures, there will be enough satellites sufficiently above the horizon and adequately distributed to give an accurate signal. The databases that come with GPS receivers contain many inaccuracies in the location of airports and navigation aids.

Question 442. Secondary radar, either on the ground or as part of the TCAS system within an aircraft, sends out interrogations, alternately for the number dialled into the front of the unit and for the aircraft's altitude. The transponder replies with the requested information.

Question 443. The DF Steer service is still available at a some aerodromes in Canada (look for the letters DF on the chart). If invoked, the pilot is asked to hold down the push-to-talk switch on a particular frequency while the operator takes a fix. The pilot is then asked to fly a particular heading chosen to be more-or-less at right angles to the path to the station and another fix is taken. This allows the operator to assess the approximate position of the aircraft. In these days of ubiquitous GPS receivers and transponders, it is difficult to imagine it being used, but it seems to be a favourite on Transport Canada examination papers.

Question 444. An ELT may be tested for no more than 5 seconds during the first 5 minutes of any UTC (Zulu) hour. As Newfoundland's local time is $3\frac{1}{2}$ hours ($4\frac{1}{2}$ in the summer) from UTC, the extra half of an hour has to be taken into account.

Question 445. Secondary radar is not really radar as we commonly know it—it does not send out pulses of radio-frequency energy and measure the time for their return. Instead secondary "radar" sends out an interrogation signal to which the transponder on an aircraft responds. Secondary radar therefore cannot detect anything that does not have a transponder. Primary radar is "normal" radar.

Question 446. It comes as a surprise to many experienced pilots to learn that the altitude being transmitted by the transponder doesn't come from the normal altimeter. Somewhere in the aircraft there will be another, so-called "blind", altimeter (one without a display) that encodes the pressure altitude of the aircraft (i.e., the altitude assuming that the altimeter setting is 29.92 inches of mercury). Any correction needed to allow for the actual altimeter setting in a particular area is performed by the receiving unit.

Question 447. The ELT transmits continuously and only the 406 MHz signal is received by the SARSAT satellites; the 121.5 MHz signal is for other pilots to detect using a standard aircraft VHF radio.

Question 448. A continuous scan where the eye never rests on one part of the sky is not particularly effective. The best scan moves across the sky, pausing to focus on each area. Every third or fourth scan should include the flight and engine instruments.

Question 449. Any form of flying across time zones, whether eastwards or westwards, is likely to result in jet lag and even greater fatigue. The answer about reducing oxygen levels also doesn't deserve much attention: hypoxia is a cause of acute fatigue rather than something that mitigates it. There are two types of fatigue: long-term caused by an extended period without proper sleep (known as chronic fatigue) and short-term caused by a recent high work-load. So one possible has it backwards, leaving one correct answer: a fatigued pilot will often concentrate completely on one or two tasks and miss incoming radio calls, descend through assigned altitudes, etc.

Question 450. Don't try to learn these for the examination—they can all be worked out easily. The pilot is used to a wide runway and is seeing a narrow one. When would his normal runway look like that? If he were very high. He will therefore have the illusion of being high. This could lead him to descend prematurely, causing him to land short of the runway.

Question 451. Hyperventilation is "over-breathing", typically brought on by stress in the cockpit. It causes the blood to have too little carbon dioxide which affects the acid/base balance of the blood feeding the brain, causing it to become too alkaline. Ultimately this can, counter-intuitively, reduce the amount of oxygen in the brain, causing hypoxia.

Question 452. Hypoxia (lack of oxygen) due to altitude affects different pilots in different ways. Some people are border-line hypoxic even when at sea-level and should use oxygen at any altitude when acting as pilot-in-command—particularly at night. Smokers are particularly sensitive to hypoxia. Apart from experiencing a general sense of well-being and even euphoria, a pilot cannot detect that she is suffering from hypoxia.

Question 453. Tests show that pilots who smoke are physiologically typically "at 5,000 ft ASL" when actually at sea-level. This means that they need to use supplemental oxygen from 5,000 ft ASL by day or from the ground up at night.

Question 454. The vestibular system is inside the inner ear and controls a person's balance. It can be fooled when a turn is prolonged and the fluid in the vestibular system "catches up" with the turn. When the turn stops, the fluid continues moving, giving the illusion of a turn.

Question 455. Alcohol is a sedative and depressant that affects the brain and also, it is believed, the fluid in the inner ear. It reduces the viscosity of that fluid, making it more difficult for a person to balance: the fluid moves around more than it normally would and this confuses the brain. Alcohol and hypoxia are also additive in their effect on a pilot.

Question 456. There are many very powerful drugs that are "100% natural": Aspirin from the bark of a tree, heroin from poppies, etc. When taking any drug, it is best to consult an aviation medical examiner and confirm that the drug is acceptable for a pilot.

Question 457. The air in the cabin always contains carbon dioxide and a normal level of carbon Dioxide is needed for breathing (hyperventilation is a problem when the level of carbon dioxide falls too low). It is unlikely that the pilot is experiencing hypoxia at 3,500 ft ASL and, even if she is, it doesn't tend to cause nausea. There is no evidence that she is hyperventilating (breathing too often and too shallowly).

Question 458. Certainly tuning the VOR should be at the bottom of the list: if he is enjoying flight following then he is on ATC radar and can rely on ATC for navigation—in an emergency like this, the more tasks that can be offloaded onto ATC the better. Generally, the priorities are to "aviate, navigate, communicate". In this case keeping the aircraft's wings level and avoiding a spiral dive must be the highest priority. And then a plan is needed to get out of the IMC: would it be better to climb (is the cloud a thin layer of stratus?) or turn through 180°, or continue through? Responding to ATC's call can be left until later although, in this case, ATC should certainly be used to provide navigation.

Question 459. Note that this is a very static way of making decisions (and generally when flying there is insufficient time to walk through the steps), and Benner has since updated it, but Transport Canada continues to want students to know about this process.

Question 460. Many students confuse C (choose outcome) with I (identify possible actions). The outcome that pilot wants has nothing to do with whether to land in the field or not; the outcome is to be safe.

Question 461. It could be said that he is displaying all of the hazardous attitudes but primarily he believes that nothing can hurt him—that he is invulnerable. It could, of course, be argued that he also is demonstrating resignation ("what use is it?—if an accident is going to happen then it's going to happen") and possibly even a macho attitude ("I'll show them how to fly an aircraft with a bolt missing!").

Question 462. Macho attitudes are not restricted to men—female pilots also suffer from the "I'll show them" hazardous attitude. The main antidote is possibly to remind oneself about how it would appear in the incident report.

Question 463. It is a common mistake when entering waypoints into a GPS to confuse the airport (e.g., CYOW) with a local navigation device (e.g., YOW for the Ottawa VOR, OW for an NDB near Ottawa). In this case, the VOR is YOW, not CYOW. CYGK is the identifier for Kingston airport, not its NDB. This can be a particular problem in the USA where there is a tendency for the initial letter (K) to be dropped from the airport name, thereby providing confusion between, for example, KART and ART. KART is the Watertown airport and ART its VOR. Sometimes the airport and VOR are a long way apart and it is easy to navigate to the wrong one.

Question 464. Many students always fly below 10,000 ft and rarely look at the "third" hand on the altimeter face. In this case, the third hand is pointing to the "1" meaning 10,000 ft. The altitude being displayed is therefore about 180 ft above 10,000.

Question 465. Magnetic compasses of this type are always confusing (which is why many pilots choose to have a vertical card compass in their aircraft—these look like heading indicators). Looking at figure B.12 it is clear that a turn of about 15° is required so two answers can be eliminated. If you are unsure whether to turn left or right (and you are not alone), then imagine that you are flying a heading of 196°M as shown on the compass face and need to reach 180°M. Clearly that would require a left turn.

Question 466. It is difficult to find the correct answer here. You may certainly be feeling mild hypoxia from the rarefied atmosphere within which you've been working. Being pilot-in-command is, of course, your target. But the best answer is probably your readiness to take the written examination. Do not allow the knowledge and techniques you have gained to start to disappear: book the examination for some time soon, do some last minute preparation by reading around the subject and dive in. We wish you the best of luck.

Appendix B

Reference Material

This appendix contains reference material used in various questions. None of the material in this appendix should be used for actual navigation.

Weight (lbs force)	Pressure Alt (ft)	10°C		20°C	
		Ground Roll (ft)	Total to Clear 50' Obstacle	Ground Roll	Total to Clear 50' Obstacle
Note: Decrease distances by 10% for each 9 knots headwind. For operation with tailwinds of up to 10 knots, increase distances by 10% for each 2 knots. Note: For operation on a dry, grass runway, increase distances by 15% of the ground roll figure.					
2300	Sea Level	835	1475	895	1575
	1000	915	1615	980	1725
	2000	1000	1770	1075	1895
	3000	1100	1945	1180	2085
	4000	1210	2145	1300	2305

Figure B.1: Extract from Cessna 172M Takeoff Distance Table

Weight (lbs force)	Pressure Alt (ft)	10°C		20°C	
		Ground Roll (ft)	Total to Clear 50' Obstacle	Ground Roll	Total to Clear 50' Obstacle
Note: Decrease distances by 10% for each 9 knots headwind. For operation with tailwinds of up to 10 knots, increase distances by 10% for each 2 knots. Note: For operation on a dry, grass runway, increase distances by 45% of the ground roll figure.					
2300	Sea Level	510	1235	530	1265
	1000	530	1265	550	1300
	2000	550	1300	570	1335
	3000	570	1335	590	1370
	4000	590	1370	615	1410

Figure B.2: Extract from Cessna 172M Landing Distance Table

15-33

Figure B.3: Airport Sign

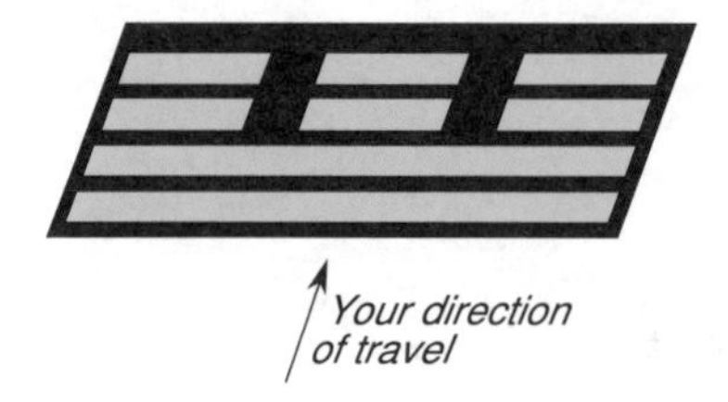

Figure B.4: Taxiway Marking

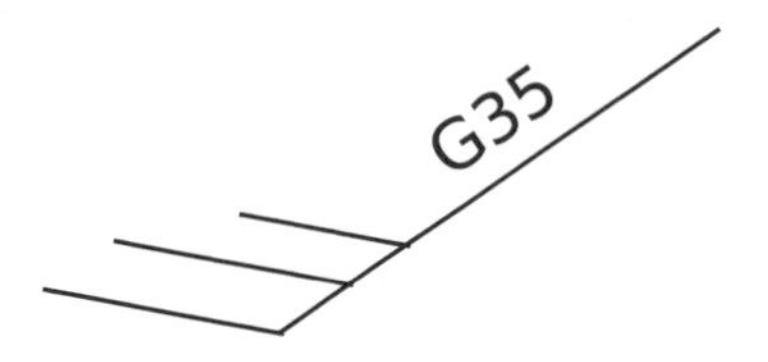

Figure B.5: Symbol from a GFA

Pressure Alt (ft)	RPM	20°C BELOW STANDARD TEMP			STANDARD TEMPERATURE			20°C ABOVE STANDARD TEMP		
		% BHP	KTAS	GPH	% BHP	KTAS	GPH	% BHP	KTAS	GPH
2000	2550	80	114	8.8	75	113	8.2	71	113	7.8
	2500	76	111	8.3	71	111	7.8	67	111	7.5
	2400	68	107	7.5	74	107	7.2	61	106	6.9
4000	2600	80	116	8.8	75	116	8.3	71	116	7.8
	2500	72	111	7.9	68	111	7.5	64	110	7.2
	2400	65	107	7.3	61	106	6.9	58	104	6.7
6000	2650	80	118	8.8	75	118	8.2	71	118	7.8
	2600	76	116	8.3	71	116	7.9	68	115	7.5
	2500	69	111	7.6	65	110	7.2	62	109	7.0
8000	2700	80	120	8.8	75	120	8.3	71	120	7.8
	2600	72	116	8.0	68	115	7.5	65	114	7.3
	2500	65	111	7.3	62	109	7.0	59	108	6.8

Figure B.6: Extract from Cessna 172M Cruise Table

STN YJA - JASPER. ALBERTA	for use	3000	6000	9000	12000	18000
FDCN01 CWAO FCST BASED ON 231200 DATA VALID 231800	17-21		9900+06	2516-02	2524-07	2233-21
FDCN02 CWAO FCST BASED ON 231200 DATA VALID 240000	21-06		2509+08	2519-01	2425-09	2734-18
FDCN03 CWAO FCST BASED ON 231200 DATA VALID 241200	06-17		2107+04	2623-01	2824-04	2728-16

Figure B.7: FDs for Jasper

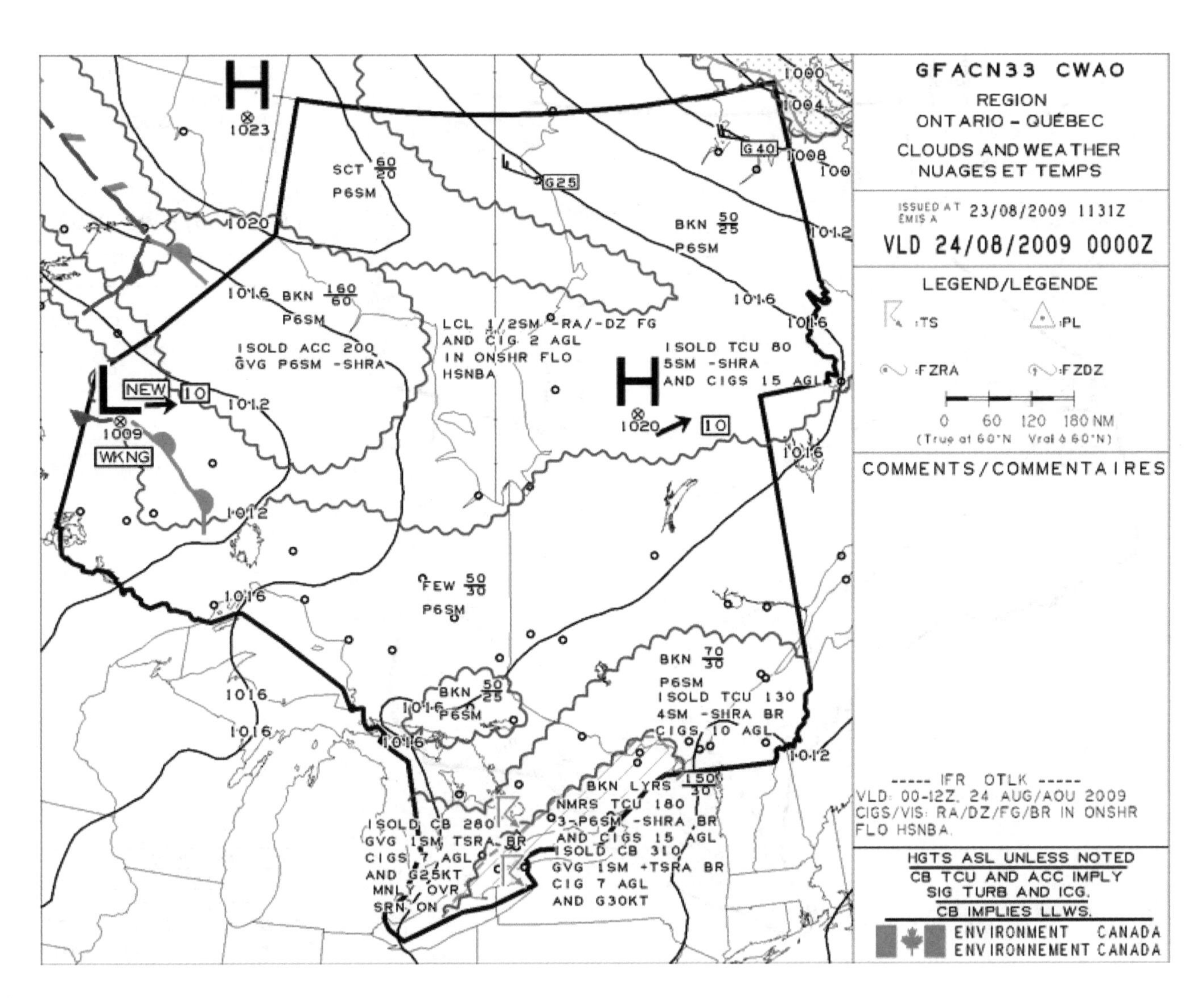

Figure B.8: GFA: Clouds and Weather

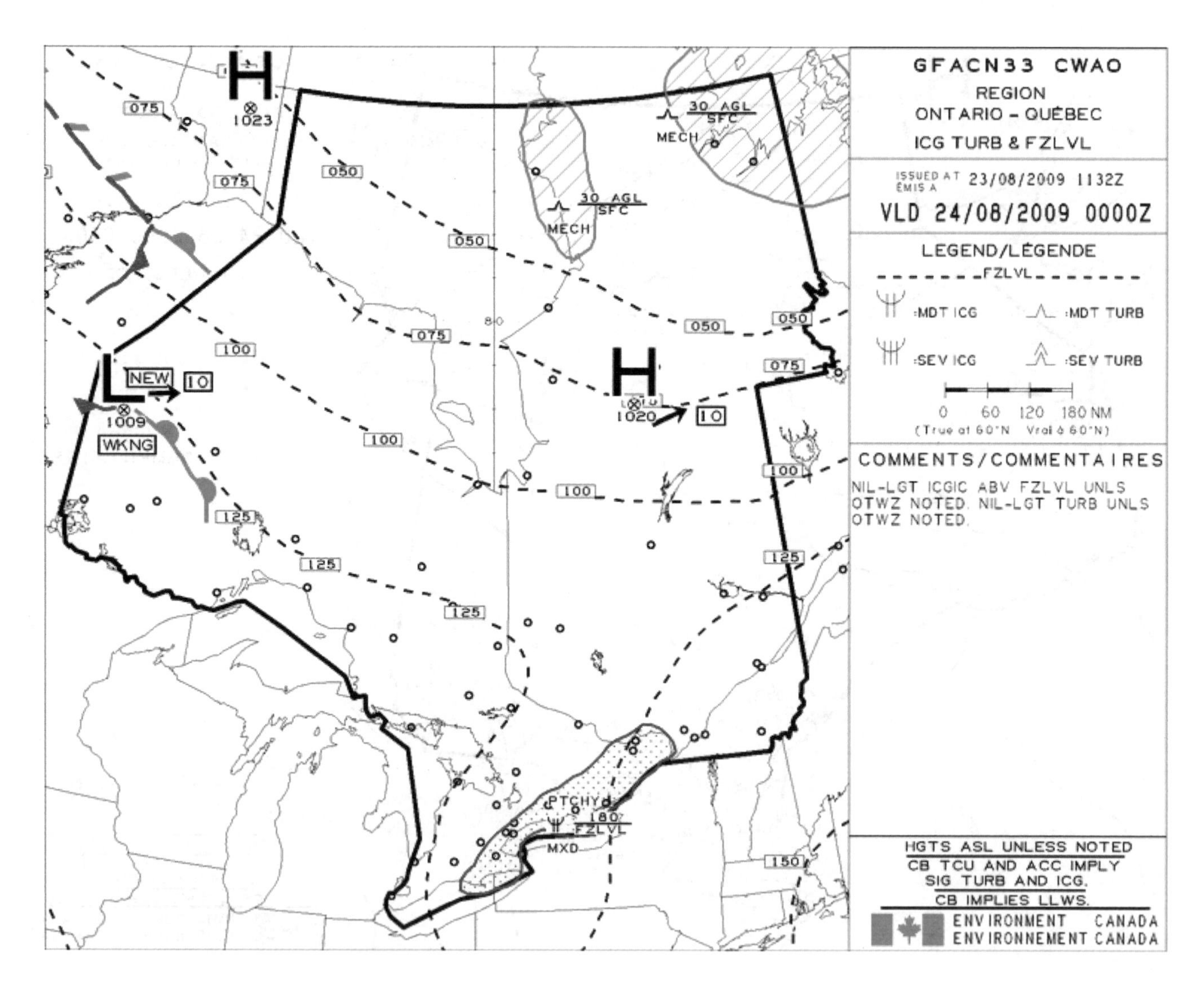

Figure B.9: GFA: Icing, Turbulence and Freezing Level

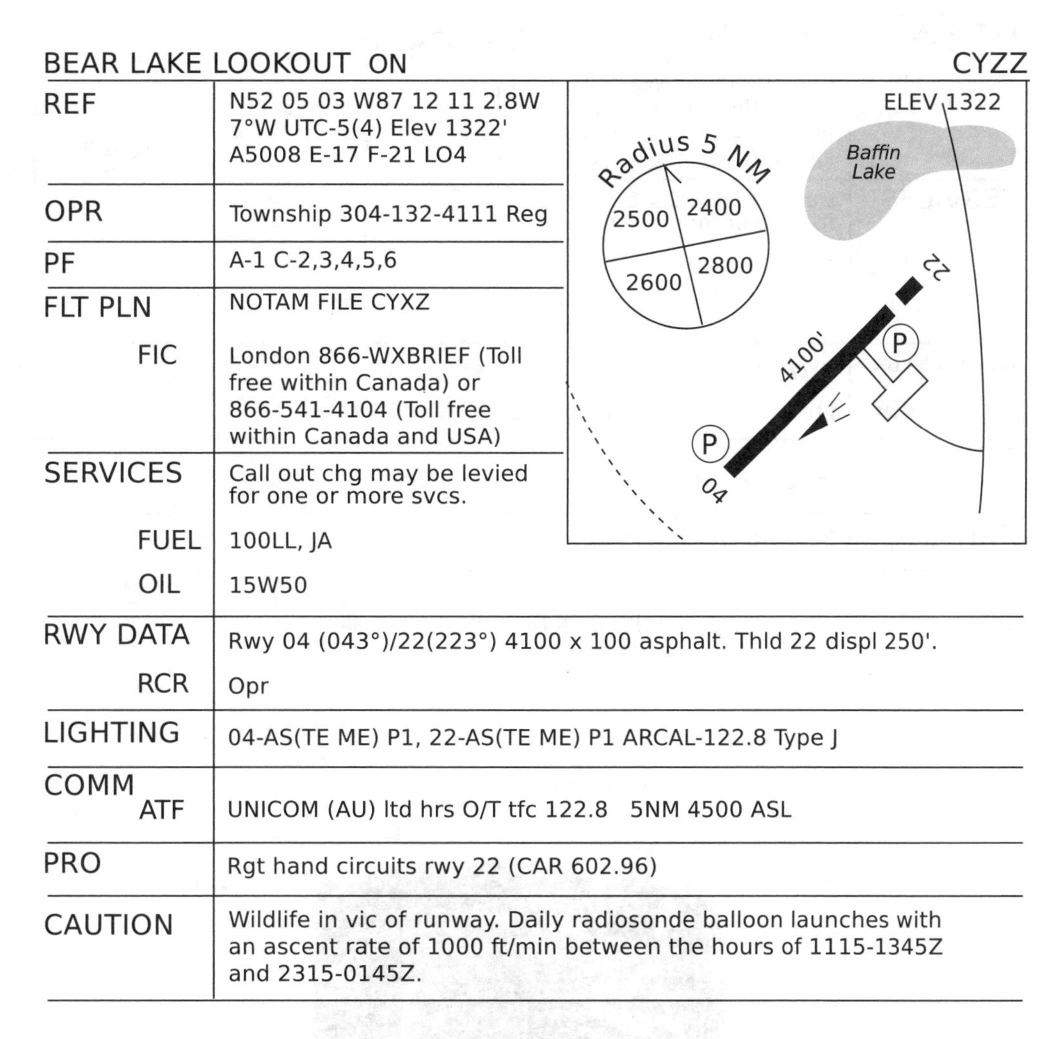

BEAR LAKE LOOKOUT ON CYZZ

REF	N52 05 03 W87 12 11 2.8W 7°W UTC-5(4) Elev 1322' A5008 E-17 F-21 LO4
OPR	Township 304-132-4111 Reg
PF	A-1 C-2,3,4,5,6
FLT PLN	NOTAM FILE CYXZ
FIC	London 866-WXBRIEF (Toll free within Canada) or 866-541-4104 (Toll free within Canada and USA)
SERVICES	Call out chg may be levied for one or more svcs.
FUEL	100LL, JA
OIL	15W50
RWY DATA	Rwy 04 (043°)/22(223°) 4100 x 100 asphalt. Thld 22 displ 250'.
RCR	Opr
LIGHTING	04-AS(TE ME) P1, 22-AS(TE ME) P1 ARCAL-122.8 Type J
COMM ATF	UNICOM (AU) ltd hrs O/T tfc 122.8 5NM 4500 ASL
PRO	Rgt hand circuits rwy 22 (CAR 602.96)
CAUTION	Wildlife in vic of runway. Daily radiosonde balloon launches with an ascent rate of 1000 ft/min between the hours of 1115-1345Z and 2315-0145Z.

Figure B.10: CFS Entry for Bear Lake Lookout

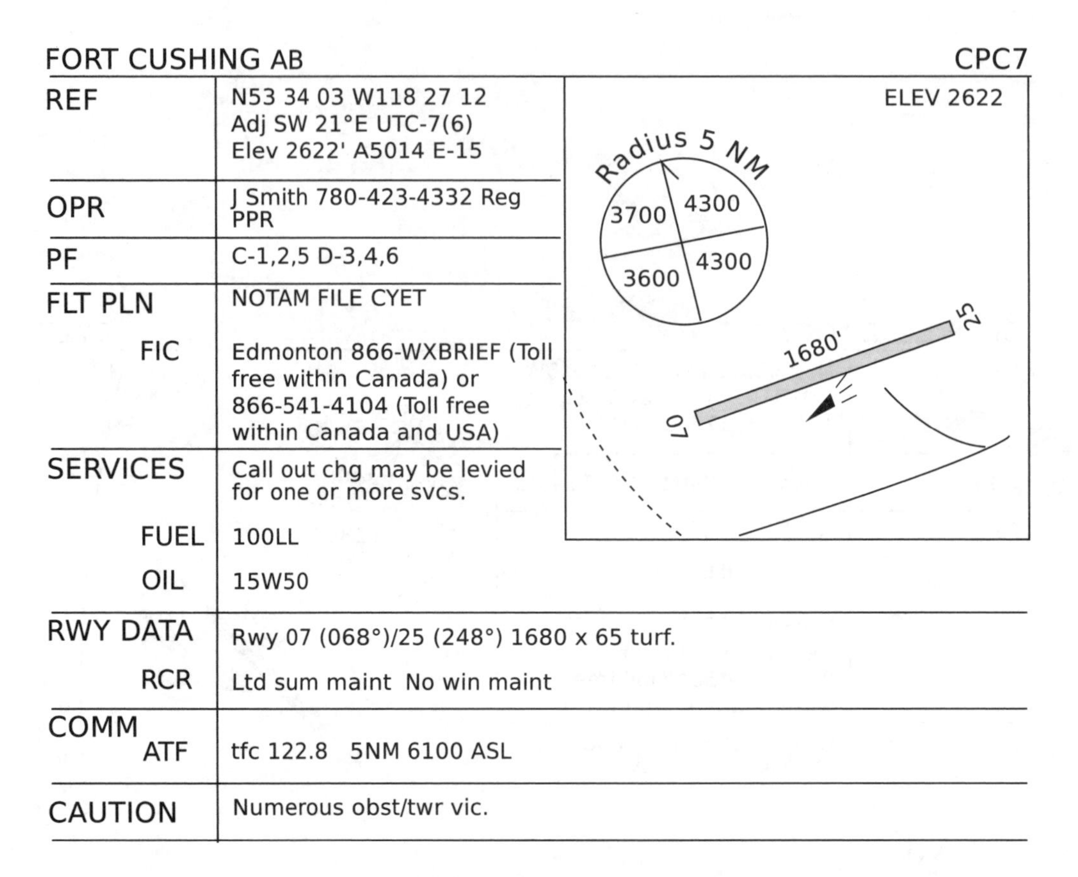

FORT CUSHING AB CPC7

REF	N53 34 03 W118 27 12 Adj SW 21°E UTC-7(6) Elev 2622' A5014 E-15
OPR	J Smith 780-423-4332 Reg PPR
PF	C-1,2,5 D-3,4,6
FLT PLN	NOTAM FILE CYET
FIC	Edmonton 866-WXBRIEF (Toll free within Canada) or 866-541-4104 (Toll free within Canada and USA)
SERVICES	Call out chg may be levied for one or more svcs.
FUEL	100LL
OIL	15W50
RWY DATA	Rwy 07 (068°)/25 (248°) 1680 x 65 turf.
RCR	Ltd sum maint No win maint
COMM ATF	tfc 122.8 5NM 6100 ASL
CAUTION	Numerous obst/twr vic.

Figure B.11: CFS Entry for Fort Cushing

Figure B.12: A Magnetic Compass

Figure B.13: A Barometric Altimeter

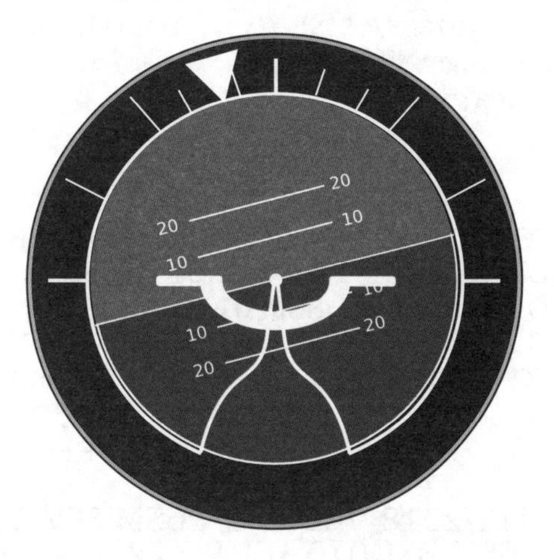

Figure B.14: An Attitude Indicator

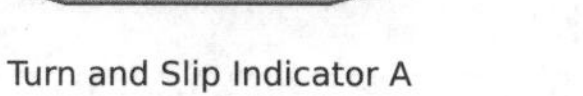

Turn and Slip Indicator B

Figure B.15: A Turn and Slip Indicator

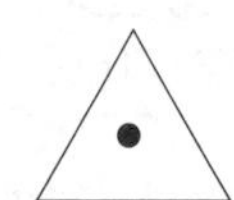

Figure B.16: Symbols from Weather Charts

```
METAR CYZZ 261600Z 08015KT 5SM BR FEW005 BKN020 22/20 A2946 RERA RMK
SF2CU5 SLP080=
SPECI CYZZ 261530Z 06016KT 4SM BR FEW008 BKN016 20/ RERA RMK SF2SC6=
METAR CYZZ 261500Z 08016KT 5SM -SHRA BR BKN004 OVC010TCU 19/19 A2946
RMK SF6TCU2 SLP080=
```

Figure B.17: METARs for Bear Lake Lookout

```
CYOW 152200Z 33024G29KT 15SM DRSN FEW025
BKN081 OVC150 M07/M11 A2972 RMK
SC2AC4AS2 DRSN HVY PRESRR SLP070
```

Figure B.18: METAR for Ottawa International

```
CZUL SIGMET K2 VALID 162325/170325 CWUL-
CZUL MONTREAL FIR SQLN TS OBS WTN 20NM
OF LINE /N4608 W07554/9 SE CYMW
/N4541 W07655/18 SE CYTA TOP FL340
MOV E 15KT NC
RMK GFACN33=
```

Figure B.19: Example SIGMET

```
METAR CYKF 191200Z AUTO 33006KT 9SM CLR 02/02 A3034 RMK SLP276=
SPECI CYKF 191129Z AUTO 34006KT 3 1/2SM 01/01 A3033=
SPECI CYKF 191115Z AUTO 36004KT 1 1/8SM 01/01 A3032 RMK VSBY VRBL 0.3V9.+=
SPECI CYKF 191106Z AUTO 36002KT 1 1/2SM 01/01 A3031 RMK VSBY VRBL 0.7V6.0=
METAR CYKF 191100Z AUTO 01002KT 1SM 01/01 A3031 RMK VSBY VRBL 0.3V9.+ SLP268=
```

Figure B.20: METAR for CYKF

```
TAF CYYZ 221130Z 2212/2318 VRB03KT P6SM FEW100
FM221400 VRB03KT P6SM BKN070 TEMPO 2214/2220 P6SM -SHRA BKN030
  PROB40 2214/2220 VRB10G20KT 2SM +TSRA BKN015CB
FM222000 36012KT P6SM BKN040 TEMPO 2221/2312 P6SM -SHRA BKN020
 BECMG 2222/2224 35007KT
FM231200 33007KT P6SM BKN020
FM231500 03014KT P6SM -SHRA BKN030
RMK NXT FCST BY 221500Z=
```

Figure B.21: TAF for CYYZ

```
TAF CYQX 191131Z 1912/2012 20005KT P6SM SCT008 BKN050
     TEMPO 1912/1914 4SM -SHRA BR BKN008 OVC050
   FM191400 28010KT P6SM SCT015 BKN025
     TEMPO 1914/1922 5SM -SHRA BR OVC015
   BECMG 1918/1920 35008KT
   FM192200 36008KT 3SM -RA BR BKN004 OVC012
     TEMPO 1922/2002 P6SM -RA SCT004 OVC012
     PROB30 1922/2002 2SM -RA BR BKN003
    FM200200 32012KT 2SM -DZ BR OVC004
     TEMPO 2002/2012 6SM -SHRA BR OVC012
     BECMG 2004/2006 34012G22KT
RMK NXT FCST BY 191800Z
```

Figure B.22: TAF for CYQX

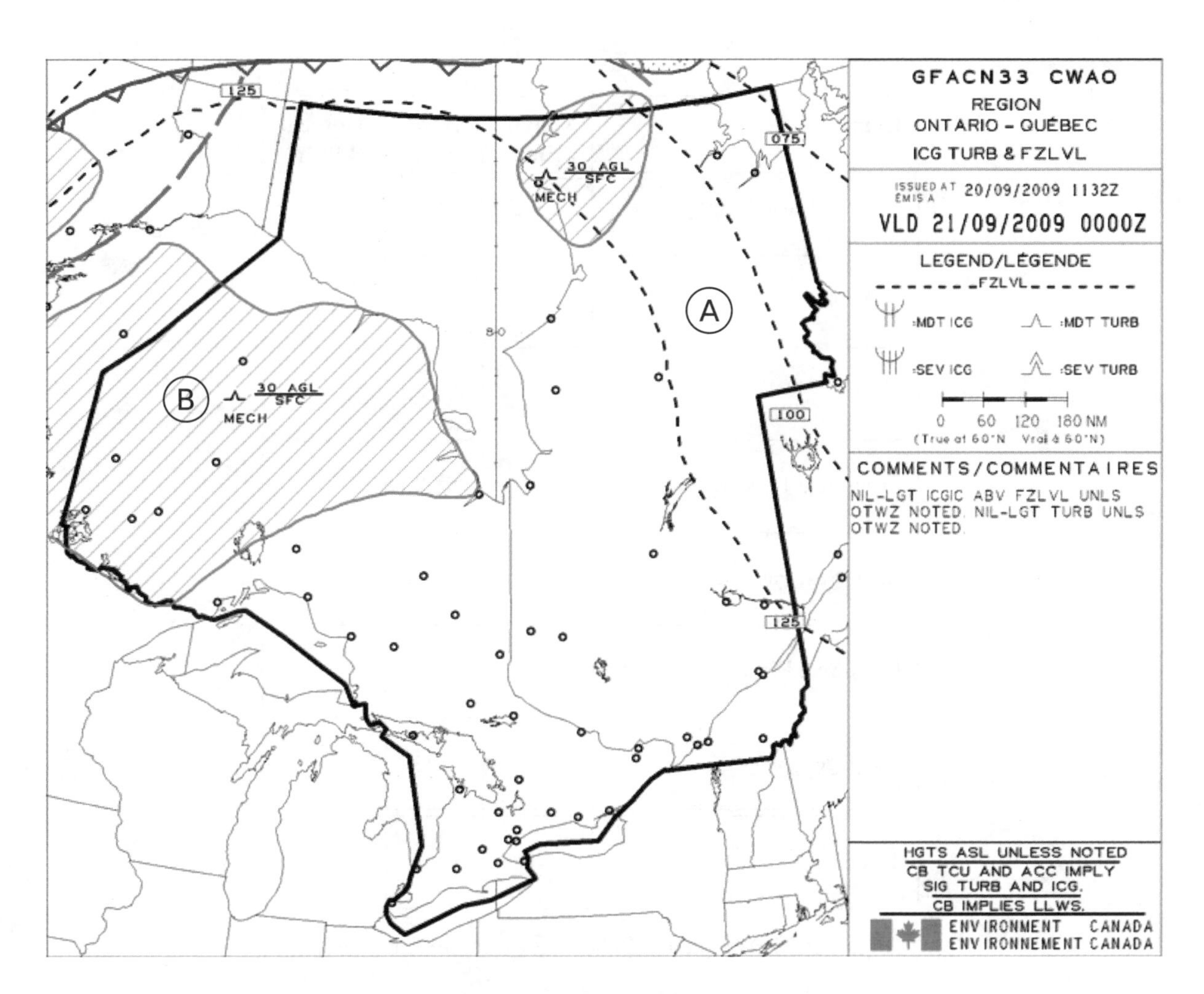

Figure B.23: GFA: Icing, Turbulence and Freezing Level

Item	Weight (lbs)	Arm (in)	Moment (klb-in)
Aircraft Basic Empty Weight	1,392	-55.78	
Useable Fuel		-47.19	
Pilot		-58.00	
Front-Seat Passenger		-58.00	
Back-Seat Passenger		-22.00	
Back-Seat Passenger		-22.00	
Baggage		0	
Totals			

Figure B.24: Weight and Balance for Experimental Aircraft

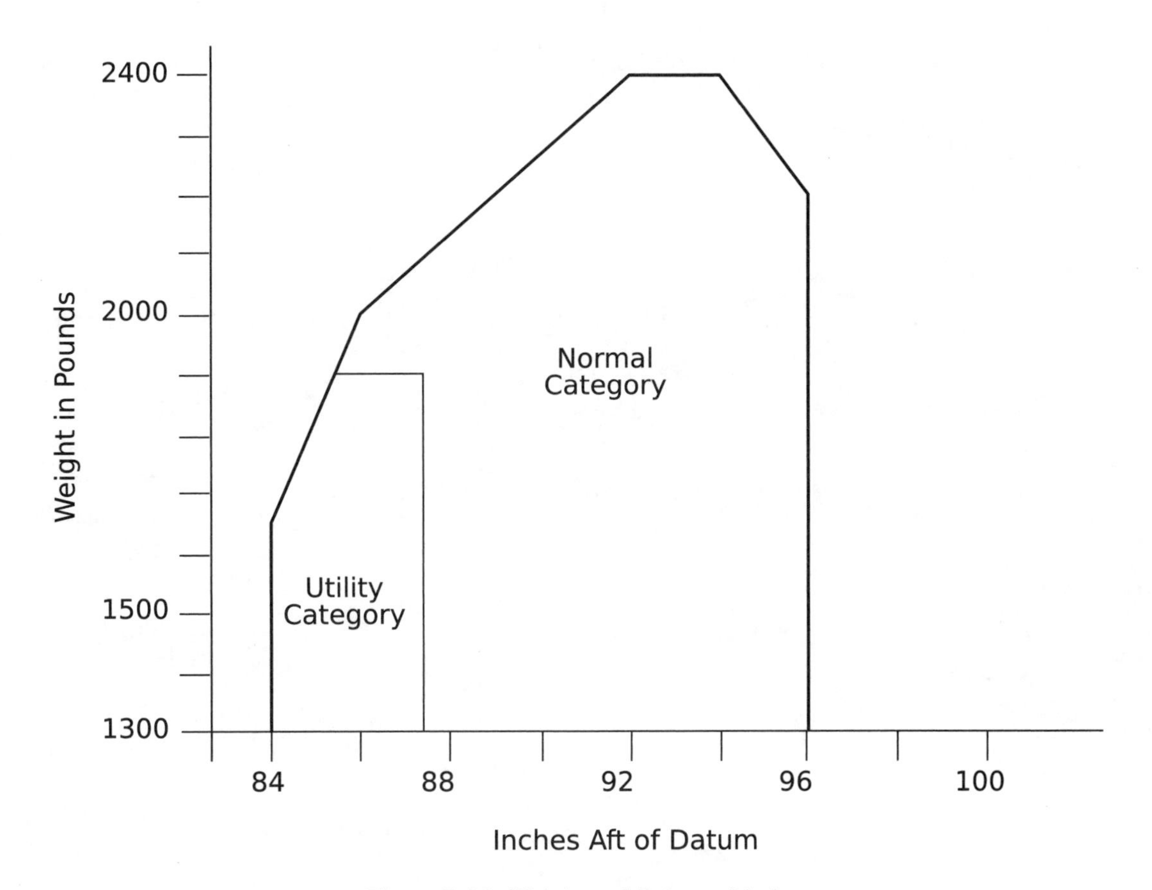

Figure B.25: Weight and Balance Limits

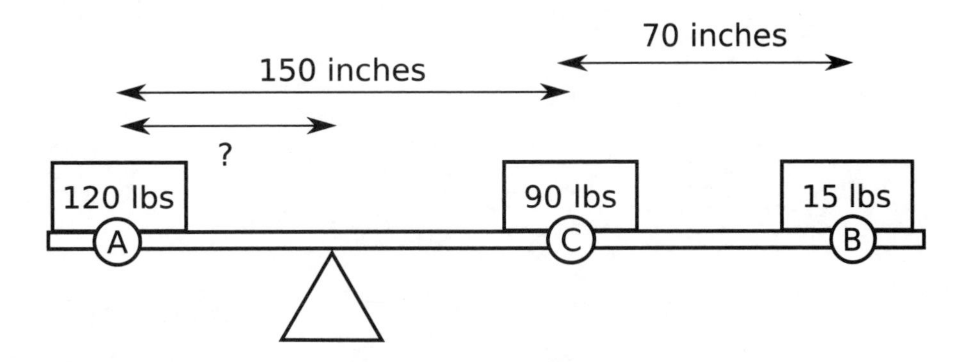

Figure B.26: Balance

Appendix C

Answers

Note that answers starting with E refer to examination questions.

1–1	2–4	3–4	4–1	5–2	6–3	7–1	8–1	9–4	10–4	11–1	12–1	13–1	14–1
15–1	16–3	17–2	18–4	19–1	20–1	21–1	22–3	23–4	24–3	25–2	26–1	27–3	28–1
29–4	30–2	31–1	32–2	33–2	34–2	35–4	36–1	37–2	38–4	39–3	40–4	41–1	42–1
43–3	44–1	45–4	46–3	47–3	48–3	49–2	50–1	51–4	52–2	53–3	54–1	55–4	56–3
57–4	58–2	59–1	60–3	61–4	62–2	63–4	64–4	65–2	66–4	67–3	68–4	69–1	70–4
71–4	72–1	73–3	74–2	75–2	76–2	77–3	78–1	79–1	80–4	81–3	82–1	83–1	84–3
85–4	86–2	87–3	88–4	89–2	90–2	91–4	92–2	93–1	94–3	95–3	96–3	97–1	98–4
99–4	100–3	101–2	102–4	103–2	104–2	105–1	106–4	107–4	108–1	109–1	110–3	111–1	112–3
113–1	114–3	115–3	116–2	117–2	118–3	119–4	120–1	121–2	122–2	123–2	124–4	125–1	126–2
127–2	128–1	129–4	130–2	131–1	132–1	133–2	134–1	135–3	136–4	137–4	138–4	139–1	140–3
141–3	142–2	143–2	144–2	145–2	146–1	147–4	148–1	149–3	150–2	151–4	152–4	153–1	154–4
155–4	156–4	157–2	158–2	159–1	160–4	161–3	162–1	163–1	164–2	165–1	166–2	167–3	168–1
169–1	170–3	171–1	172–3	173–2	174–4	175–1	176–1	177–1	178–4	179–3	180–2	181–2	182–4
183–3	184–2	185–2	186–3	187–4	188–1	189–4	190–4	191–1	192–1	193–3	194–1	195–2	196–2
197–3	198–1	199–1	200–2	201–1	202–3	203–4	204–3	205–2	206–1	207–1	208–1	209–1	210–2
211–3	212–4	213–3	214–4	215–4	216–4	217–2	218–1	219–1	220–3	221–3	222–3	223–2	224–1
225–4	226–2	227–1	228–1	229–1	230–4	231–1	232–1	233–1	234–3	235–4	236–1	237–4	238–4
239–4	240–2	241–3	242–1	243–1	244–3	245–2	246–2	247–3	248–2	249–1	250–2	251–4	252–4
253–4	254–2	255–2	256–1	257–2	258–1	259–3	260–3	261–4	262–4	263–4	264–4	265–4	266–3
267–3	268–1	269–1	270–2	271–1	272–4	273–4	274–1	275–3	276–2	277–2	278–3	279–3	280–3
281–2	282–4	283–2	284–3	285–4	286–4	287–2	288–4	289–1	290–3	291–4	292–1	293–3	294–2
295–3	296–4	297–2	298–2	299–1	300–1	301–1	302–2	303–1	304–3	305–1	306–1	307–4	308–2
309–4	310–4	311–1	312–1	313–4	314–1	315–3	316–4	317–4	318–3	319–4	320–4	321–2	322–1
323–1	324–3	325–2	326–4	327–4	328–1	329–1	330–4	331–1	332–4	333–1	334–2	335–3	336–4
337–3	338–3	339–1	340–3	341–2	342–3	343–1	344–1	345–3	346–2	347–4	348–3	349–4	350–4
351–2	352–4	353–3	354–2	355–4	356–2	357–2	358–2	359–3	360–1	361–4	362–1	363–2	364–1
365–2	366–2	367–4	368–2	369–4	370–4	371–2	372–1	373–2	374–2	375–3	376–1	377–3	378–3
379–4	380–4	381–2	382–3	383–3	384–1	385–2	386–2	387–3	388–2	389–4	390–1	391–1	392–4
393–3	394–2	395–2	396–4	397–4	398–4	399–1	400–4	401–2	402–4	403–3	404–3	405–3	406–4
407–3	408–3	409–4	410–1	411–1	412–2	413–1	414–1	415–4	416–3	417–1	418–2	419–2	420–2
421–3	422–4	423–1	424–1	425–3	426–3	427–4	428–3	429–4	430–3	431–2	432–4	433–1	434–3
435–2	436–1	437–1	438–3	439–1	440–3	441–1	442–1	443–3	444–2	445–4	446–1	447–1	448–3
449–3	450–3	451–3	452–4	453–3	454–1	455–1	456–4	457–1	458–3	459–3	460–1	461–1	462–2
463–2	464–3	465–3	466–2	E1–3	E2–3	E3–1	E4–1	E5–4	E6–4	E7–4	E8–2	E9–3	E10–3
E11–1	E12–3	E13–4	E14–3	E15–1	E16–1	E17–1	E18–2	E19–3	E20–1	E21–2	E22–4	E23–4	E24–3
E25–4	E26–2	E27–3	E28–4	E29–4	E30–3	E31–2	E32–4	E33–1	E34–3	E35–2	E36–3	E37–4	E38–3
E39–1	E40–1	E41–3	E42–1	E43–1	E44–3	E45–3	E46–3	E47–2	E48–4	E49–3	E50–4	E51–3	E52–2
E53–2	E54–1	E55–1	E56–2	E57–2	E58–4	E59–4	E60–3	E61–4	E62–2	E63–4	E64–4	E65–2	E66–1
E67–4	E68–4	E69–3	E70–2	E71–1	E72–4	E73–1	E74–3	E75–3	E76–1	E77–1	E78–4	E79–3	E80–4
E81–2	E82–1	E83–3	E84–3	E85–1	E86–1	E87–1	E88–2	E89–1	E90–3	E91–4	E92–2	E93–1	E94–4
E95–3	E96–4	E97–2	E98–4	E99–2	E100–3								

Index

References are to questions and not to pages